Josh,

I am grateful f

God gave me these words to inspire you everyday.

God Bless You!

Trevor A. Wendee

5-1-2019

DAILY GUIDANCE
FROM GOD

Providing Godly guidance & perspective
for your daily life circumstances.

TREVOR A. WINCHELL

WESTBOW
PRESS®
A DIVISION OF THOMAS NELSON
& ZONDERVAN

Scripture taken from the King James Version of the Bible.

Scripture taken from the New King James Version®. Copyright © 1982 by Thomas Nelson. Used by permission. All rights reserved.

THE HOLY BIBLE, NEW INTERNATIONAL VERSION®, NIV® Copyright © 1973, 1978, 1984, 2011 by Biblica, Inc.® Used by permission. All rights reserved worldwide.

Scripture quotations marked (NLT) are taken from the Holy Bible, New Living Translation, copyright © 1996, 2004, 2007 by Tyndale House Foundation. Used by permission of Tyndale House Publishers, Inc., Carol Stream, Illinois 60188. All rights reserved.

Scripture quotations are from the ESV® Bible (The Holy Bible, English Standard Version®), copyright © 2001 by Crossway, a publishing ministry of Good News Publishers. Used by permission. All rights reserved.

Scripture taken from The Message. Copyright © 1993, 1994, 1995, 1996, 2000, 2001, 2002. Used by permission of NavPress Publishing Group.

Scripture taken from The Voice™. Copyright © 2008 by Ecclesia Bible Society. Used by permission. All rights reserved.

WestBow Press books may be ordered through booksellers or by contacting:

WestBow Press
A Division of Thomas Nelson & Zondervan
1663 Liberty Drive
Bloomington, IN 47403
www.westbowpress.com
1 (866) 928-1240

ISBN: 978-1-9736-3901-5 (sc)
ISBN: 978-1-9736-3902-2 (hc)
ISBN: 978-1-9736-3900-8 (e)

Library of Congress Control Number: 2018910743

Print information available on the last page.

WestBow Press rev. date: 09/11/2018

DAILY GUIDANCE FROM GOD
By Trevor Winchell

**I give this book to you as a special gift to you from me.
My hope is this devotional book will inspire you to live your life
guided and inspired by God and His written Word every day.**

Presented to:

_____

By:

_____

Date:

_____

*And whatsoever ye do in word or deed,
do all in the name of the Lord Jesus,
giving thanks to God and the Father by him.*

Colossians 3:17 (KJV)

ABOUT THE BOOK

And you shall know the truth, and the truth shall make you free. John 8:32 (NKJV)

In my devotional writings, I might say things that a lot of people don't agree with, or I might say a lot of things that people don't like. But the fact of the matter is that every single word I write is given to me by God, not because people want to hear it but because people need to listen to it. The truth of God's word is undeniable in every way, and only the truth of God's word will set you free in the end. So those who want everything sugar-coated to their satisfaction according to their standards will keep them in denying the truth. As most of you know, I don't sugar coat anything, and I don't tell people what they "want" to hear, I tell people what they "need" to hear. Is it easy to tell people what they don't want to hear? Of course not, but when God commands me to write the words, He gives me I must obey Him regardless if people are going to like it or not. The truth and only the truth of God's words will set you free in the end.

The devotionals that I write are 70 percent scripture context, 30 percent practical context and 100 percent inspired by God. They are easy to relate to because a lot of people are often dealing with tough circumstances or going through difficult situations. It's usually difficult to interpret and understand the actual meaning of a particular bible verse. Each devotional that I write includes a bible verse and a prayer. The Bible verse directly correlates with the devotional so that people can relate to the bible verse and understand it. The prayer also refers directly to the devotional so that people can say the prayer and ask God for help.

I believe that Daily Guidance from God is a great tool that will help people better understand real-life issues they are facing and how God can help them. The devotional will help guide people positively and biblically to seek God. The purpose of Daily Guidance from God is to allow His guidance and direction to help people through their difficult circumstances and situations and to lead them down the correct path.

Bind them on your fingers; Write them on the tablet of your heart. Proverbs 7:3 (NKJV)

INTRODUCTION

When you allow God to be the center of your life amazing things will happen that you will not even be able to imagine. Everyone has good days and bad days, but if you look to God for guidance in every situation you face, He will help you and guide you to make the right choices and decisions. I invite you to use this devotional to start and end your day with the positive words of God. I promise that when you read this devotional when you wake up and before you go to bed, each of your days will be brighter and your attitude will be more positive.

Trevor A. Winchell

DEDICATIONS

I would like to dedicate this book to the following people:

My Mother:
Kathy F. Winchell

My Father:
Joseph Paul Winchell (1959-2016)

My Brothers:
Jason James Winchell (1980-2017)
Cory William Winchell

My Grandparents:
James Whalen (1919-1983)
Ruth Whalen (1919-2010)
William Winchell (1933-2010)
Barbara Winchell

I would also like to dedicate this book to all my children:
Zac Wilkerson, Breann Ward, Libby Winchell

To my Grandchildren:
Jayden Ward, Zain Wilkerson

To my Nieces:
Indee Winchell, Ajae Winchell

JANUARY

JANUARY 1

And after you have suffered a little while, the God of all grace, who has called you to his eternal glory in Christ, will himself restore, confirm, strengthen, and establish you. **1 Peter 5:10 (NKJV)**

Start the new year right by allowing God to lead you, encourage you, guide you and strengthen you in every area of your life. Every setback, disappointment, and roadblock in your life might seem discouraging, but it is ultimately a direct sign from God. He is directing you to allow His strength, courage, and guidance to help you through your daily struggles with more determination and perseverance than ever before. When you face trials and tribulations, you can either let them define you or you can allow God to use these circumstances to strengthen you. In every situation, you must seek God and allow Him to reveal His plan for your life. The choice is yours, you can either allow God to help you and benefit from His grace and enjoy His rich blessings or deny Him and continue to struggle on a daily basis. When you accept God into your life He will give you the strength to handle any situation you face. You may not be where you want to be yet, but you are exactly where God wants you to be according to His plan for your life.

LET'S PRAY: Dear Heavenly Father, my faith lies in You alone for You are the God of all flesh and there is nothing impossible for You. Lord, I know that I can do all things through You that gives me strength, so I come to You today asking for strength to overcome every single challenge I face today and those I will face in the near future. I know that nothing good is accomplished easily, so I do not ask that You take the struggle away. Instead, I ask that You give me the strength to get up each time I fall, dust myself and move on because I know that You are leading me to greatness and I will get there in Your time. In the name of Your Son Jesus Christ, we pray, Amen.

If the timing is right and it is God's will,
it will happen in God's time!
Have faith and be patient.

JANUARY 3

You ask and do not receive, because you ask amiss, that you may spend it on your pleasures. **James 4:3 (NKJV)**

Have you prayed to God for something you wanted or needed, and the prayer was never answered? Of course, you have, we have all prayed at times, and our prayers were never answered. Does that leave you wondering why there were not answered, or does that make you wonder if God heard your prayers? God hears every single one of our prayers, He answers them based on importance, and He answers them based on His will for you. God doesn't answer our prayers because He doesn't hear them, He sometimes doesn't answer our prayers because He knows what your intentions are and He knows what you need and what you don't need. He also knows if you will do good or not if He answers your prayer. And He will not answer our prayers if they do not align with His will for our lives and what we truly need. You can be assured that if you prayed to God and the prayer has not been answered either it was not what you truly needed, or you need to be more patient as God answers our prayers in His time, not ours. God also teaches us that if we moderate our wants and needs and we genuinely seek God himself; what we truly need will be done, but that in which we don't need shall be preserved from wicked contentions, from fraud and violence, and from doing what is wrong. If you pray to God for something that you know in your heart is not going to be used for the purpose you have asked and knowing that it is not right by God, you should be ashamed of yourself.

LET'S PRAY: Dear Heavenly Father, I ask that I may receive. May I not be consumed with my intentions, that my prayers may be answered. I know that man shall not live by my wants and needs, but by Your Word. I choose to serve You alone, and not be held captive by things of this world. Hear my prayers, and meet my humble needs. Lord, I know that Your ways are not the ways of man and that Your timing is not our timing. Give us the wisdom to understand this better. Job's prayer was not answered immediately, but when it was, it was perfect. Lord, I patiently wait for You, and I know that You will hear my cry. Jeremiah's prayer was answered ten days after he prayed, so I'm sure that my prayers will be answered at the right time. May Your will be done. Lord, may I be selfless with my prayers and requests to You. May I not be only concerned about myself alone, but also about others around me that are in need of Your help, and are too proud or ignorant to call upon You for help. Lord, as I pray for others, may You meet my needs simultaneously. Lord, may I be persistent in prayer like Abraham who repeatedly asked You to spare Sodom for the sake of the righteous. Lord, may I always realize that it is profitable to pray according to the Scriptures that my prayers will be in alignment with Your will and will have no selfish motive. Lord, as I endeavor to pray each day with the Scriptures, fill my heart with the love that comes with knowing Your will. In the name of your Son Jesus Christ, we pray. Amen.

Are your words, actions, opinions, and intentions making you part of the problem or part of the solution? Are your words, actions, opinions, and intentions spreading positive influence in the situation or spreading negative influence? If you are not sure, you must seek God for guidance and direction.

JANUARY 5

> And Mary said: "My soul magnifies the Lord, And my spirit has rejoiced in God my Savior. For He has regarded the lowly state of His maidservant; For behold, henceforth all generations will call me blessed. **Luke 1:46-48 (NKJV)**

Does your soul magnify the Lord? Does your spirit rejoice in Jesus Christ our Savior? Does your heart long to be filled with Joy in the Lord? If your soul does not magnify the Lord, if your spirit does not rejoice in Jesus Christ, and if your heart does not long to be filled with Joy in the Lord, you are not truly living your life for God. Have you ever felt that your worth to Jesus was much less than it actually is? Does your mind tell you one thing but you feel something different in your heart? As children of God, we are all very important to Him in every way. We are His masterpiece, His work of art, and every one of His children were created in His image. But as weary sinners, we sing the praises of God with an open mouth, unaccompanied by any affection of the heart, but we praise God from an inward feeling of the mind. What this means is that our words from our mouth claim to believe God and praise Him and strive to live for Him, but deep in our hearts we don't always have the feeling of joy towards God that we should for all He has done for us. This causes us to praise God from our thoughts but not from the feelings in our hearts. Those who pronounce his glory, not from the heart, but from the mind and the tongue alone, do nothing more than profane his holy name. This is why you must understand the importance of rejoicing and praising God from the heart instead of just from the thoughts in your mind and the words from your tongue.

LET'S PRAY: Dear Heavenly Father, I want my thanksgiving to be pleasing and my songs of praise to be acceptable in Your sight. As I continuously rejoice, singing songs of praise to Your Holy Name, continually bless me, holding nothing back from me. Lord, I come to You today, asking You to renew my mind, body, and soul. I ask You to renew me in strength and my faith in You. Lord, I ask You to lay Your hands of healing Your hands of hope and Your hands of mercy upon me. Make me whole in every aspect of my life. I rejoice when I'm lost because You have blessed me with the gift of life, and I know that You want me to be thankful in every circumstance. Lord, I ask You to make all things possible in my life because I believe in You. Please, hold my heart within Yours, and enfold it with Your love. Renew my mind, body, and soul with Your love, joy, and strength. Lord, I ask You to teach me, guide me, strengthen me and counsel me. I invite You to dwell in me as Your Word dwells in my heart, mind, and soul. Lord, may all that I do be done with You, under Your light, according to Your Will, in a way that pleases You. In the name of your Son Jesus Christ, we pray. Amen.

JANUARY 6

Stop and think for a minute if you did not have a job, a car, a house, food on the table, or healthy children. Then stop and think for a minute about all that you do have and that God is the reason for what you have. If you are not having a great day or today was kind of rough think about this statement and be grateful and give thanks to God for waking you up today and for the things you do have.

You have heard that it was said, 'An eye for an eye and a tooth for a tooth.' But I tell you not to resist an evil person. But whoever slaps you on your right cheek, turn the other to him also. **Matthew 5:38-39 (NKJV)**

Have you ever been persecuted, wronged, accused or judged by someone and the first thing you wanted to do was get revenge on them or retaliate to get even? When this happens, you need to stop and seek God so that you will not act out on your account but that you let God handle the situation. As we read in Matthew 5:38 God says: An eye for an eye and a tooth for a tooth. Now you must remember that this does not mean that you must get even with the person on your own, but to let God handle the situation and apply due punishment to this person on His terms. I'm sure you have heard the phrase, kill them with kindness? This is what God expects you to do when someone persecutes you or wrongs you in any way. Matthew 5:38 tells us: But I tell you not to resist an evil person. But whoever slaps you on your right cheek, turn the other to him also. This verse tells us not to resist an evil person and not to return or retaliate. There are two ways of resisting: First by warding off injuries through offensive conduct; meaning words or actions, the other, by retaliation, doing something to them to get even. The best interpreter of this passage that we can have is Paul, who inspires to "overcome evil by good" (Romans 12:21) rather than contend with evil-doers. You need to always remember to seek God and give the situation to Him when you face people who wrong you or try to persecute you. Getting even with someone or trying to retaliate to get even is not going to solve anything. Letting God handle people who persecute you or wrong you is the best way to resolve any issue because only God can give you peace through any situation.

LET'S PRAY: Dear Heavenly Father, I want to thank You for Your mercy upon Your children and for forgiving us of our sins. Lord, may I extend such love to those around me, especially those that have wronged me. May

I find it in my heart to completely forgive them and forget everything wrong they have done to me. You are the refuge of the oppressed; You are the protector of the persecuted, You are the stronghold of those who face trials. When Your Son came into the world, He taught us differently. Lord, may I never take revenge. May I always know that vengeance is Yours. Lord, forgive me for the times I nurtured revenge within me. Lord, may I use good to overcome evil. May I use Your Word to overcome my troubles. May I always come to You in time of my trouble, asking for deliverance that You may deliver me from any evil acts and from those who try to persecute me. Lord, I know that You will never allow me to be destroyed by those who persecute me. I know that every trial I face today, You shall transform to a triumph. I know that You will never make me a victim of troubles, but a victor. I know that You will fight my battle for me and hold my peace. In the name of your Son Jesus Christ, we pray. Amen.

JANUARY 8

Please recite this with me today.
Devil, you are not going to win in my life today,
you are not going to control my words, my
thoughts, or my actions today. I will not allow
you to creep in and fill my mind with negative
thoughts today that will cause me to become weak
and vulnerable. I will always seek God to help
me push out all negativity and allow Him to fill
my mind with positive thoughts that will bring
me peace, tranquility, and serenity. And devil you
are not going to dictate my decisions and deceive
my thoughts today because I am covered in the
BLOOD of JESUS CHRIST, and God has me
fully covered in His grace at all times. Amen.

For though we live in the world, we do not wage war as the world does. The weapons we fight with are not the weapons of the world. On the contrary, they have divine power to demolish strongholds. We demolish arguments and every pretension that sets itself up against the knowledge of God, and we take captive every thought to make it obedient to Christ. **2 Corinthians 10:3-5 (NKJV)**

God won't always make your journey easy, but He will make it worth it. If you don't struggle now and then, you will never grow. God will often use your struggles to not only test you but to help you grow mentally, physically, spiritually. God is not concerned with what has happened or what you've done if you have asked Him to forgive you. What matters the most to God is that you always trust in Him and His plan for your life. You must accept the situations and circumstances that God puts in your life, to learn from them, and then move on. Letting go is hard but often a step forward. Sometimes you must walk away from what you thought you wanted for God to show you what you truly need.

LET'S PRAY: Dear Heavenly Father, we trust in Your sovereign power, Your relentless mercy, Your unlimited grace, and Your divine will. We know that there is a perfect reason for everything that happens in our lives. We may never understand your whole plan, but we know that altogether it is good, just and wise. Grant us the courage, patience and strength Lord to endure the challenges and trials that come in our lives. Fill us with your peace. Help us learn valuable lessons from our current conditions and teach us to never repeat the same mistakes. Let your ultimate and perfect peace reign in the end. In the name of Your Son Jesus Christ, we pray, Amen.

JANUARY 10

Life is precious, each day is a gift, and everyone who is in your life or crosses your path is a blessing. We all have to live life and serve our purpose according to God before we pass on and go to heaven.

Tell someone you love them today.

JANUARY 11

> Seek the Lord while he may be found; call on him while he is near. Let the wicked forsake their ways and the unrighteous their thoughts. Let them turn to the Lord, and he will have mercy on them, and to our God, for he will freely pardon. "For my thoughts are not your thoughts, neither are your ways my ways," declares the Lord. **Isaiah 55:6-8 (NKJV)**

All positive thoughts come from God, and all negative thoughts come from evil. Allowing positive thoughts into your mind will bring you peace and comfort from God. if you allow negative thoughts into your mind, it will only bring you fear and cause you to worry. The devil will continuously try to creep in and fill your mind with negative thoughts that will cause you to become weak and vulnerable. Always seek God to help you push out all negativity and allow Him to fill your mind with positive thoughts that will bring you peace, tranquility, and serenity.

LET'S PRAY: Dear Heavenly Father, I ask today that you will guide my thoughts and only allow me to think positive throughout this day. Lord, help me to overcome any evil thoughts and give me the strength to push out any negativity that the devil will try to use to cloud my mind. Lord, I want to focus entirely on you so that my mind will be clear and free from interruption from the evil one. Finally, Lord, I ask that every thought in my mind will come from you so that I can think properly and perceive what you are directing me to do according to your will for me. In the name of Your Son Jesus Christ, we pray, Amen.

A daily prayer for you

Dear Heavenly Father, thank you for waking me up and giving me the gift of this beautiful day and allowing me to enjoy all that you have created. Lord, thank You for this life and thank You for all the opportunities, gifts, and blessings You have granted me. Thank You for all the opportunities to learn and grow in Your word. Lord, please forgive me of all my sins and cleanse my heart, mind, body, and soul of all unrighteousness. I ask that You lead me, guide me, direct me, strengthen me, and protect me through this day. In the name of Your Son Jesus Christ, I pray, Amen.

JANUARY 13

In the same way, let your good deeds shine out for all to see, so that everyone will praise your heavenly Father.
Matthew 5:16 (NKJV)

God wants you to be the first person that comes to people's minds when they think of someone who is honest, fair, respectful, caring and lives their life with integrity. God wants you to start noticing what you like about the people in your life and tell them. God wants you to have an appreciation for how amazing the people in your life are because it will lead to good places that will allow you to be productive, fulfilling, and peaceful. God places people in your life not only to serve a purpose but to help you fully appreciate and respect them. All of God's people are His children, and He has a reason for every single person He places in your path.

LET'S PRAY: Dear Heavenly Father, may Your love and peace bring us together in difficult times. Help us to set aside our differences and personal feelings and focus instead on rebuilding Your Kingdom. May we learn to bring comfort to one another so that we can rise in any situation we face. May those who are in power be inspired to make sacrifices and extend their blessings to the needy. Bring out the goodness in each one of us and unite us as one Godly family. In the name of Your Son Jesus Christ, we pray, Amen.

When you feel down, irritated, frustrated or stressed, don't react to this feeling and never take it out on the people you love or anyone who is around you. The best medicine to cure these type of feelings, lift you up and make you feel better, and redirect your feelings from negative to positive is to give whatever you are feeling to God by seeking Him. He will saturate your heart, mind, body, and soul with His positivity and He will fill your inner being up with His goodness, but you must reach out to Him and let Him know what you're feeling. Each day you are given on this earth is a gift stay blessed, unstressed and full of God's love.

JANUARY 15

> Trust in the Lord with all your heart; do not depend on your own understanding. Seek his will in all you do, and he will show you which path to take. **Proverbs 3:5-6 (NKJV)**

God will make things happen in your life that you will not always understand, you're not supposed to understand everything He does and why He does it. You just need to have faith and accept that it's part of His plan for your life and allow it to happen in His time. When you try to force things that are not meant to happen in your life, it will only lead you down a path of heartache and disappointment. For God to put the right people in your life and make the right things happen, you need to trust him wholeheartedly and surrender every aspect of your life to Him. God has prepared, planned, and facilitated a life better than you could ever imagine, He has ordained a life full of blessing, opportunity, and prosperity for you specifically. Are you going to take the high road and allow God's abundant and exuberant plan to work in your life, or are you going to live your life according to your own mediocre and meandering plan?

LET'S PRAY: Dear Heavenly Father, the Giver of all things good, the Lord that provides, the Lord that never forsakes His people. Lord, I know that You can do exceedingly abundant works in my life. Lord, I know that there is no limit to the greatness You can unleash in my life. Lord, according to the power that works in me, direct my path that I may do the right things, be at the right place, and make the right decisions according to your plan for my life. Lord, guide me at all times to do what's right, that I may not destroy the good plans and future You have for me. In the name of Your Son Jesus Christ, we pray, Amen.

JANUARY 16

The devil will continuously try to creep into your mind and turn your positive thoughts, words, and actions into negative ones that will only leave you feeling vulnerable, weak and worried. When this happens you have two options, you can either allow him to succeed in using his deceptive ways to define what you think, what you say, and what you do, or you can seek God completely by allowing His grace, strength, mercy, and power to overcome these evil actions from the devil. You must remember that if you choose to allow the devil to get the best of you; it will have an enormous impact on the outcome of your day and how you think and feel. So today, seek God wholeheartedly so that you can enjoy the gift of this day that will overflow with positive thoughts, words, and actions.

But blessed is the one who trusts in the Lord, whose confidence is in him. They will be like a tree planted by the water that sends out its roots by the stream. It does not fear when heat comes; its leaves are always green. It has no worries in a year of drought and never fails to bear fruit."
Jeremiah 17:7-8 (NKJV)

God wants you to stop worrying about what could go wrong, and have faith that He will make all the right things happen in your life in His time and according to His plan for you. God wants you to be thankful for all the gifts and blessings that He has already placed in your life. God wants you to be grateful for nights that He turned into mornings, friends that He turned into family, and the opportunities that He turned into realities. God wants you to focus on Him every day and rely on the positive thoughts that only He can place in your mind. When you rely on the positive thoughts from God, your day will be filled with happiness and joy just as God intended it to be.

LET'S PRAY: Dear Heavenly Father, I pray to You with confidence and boldness because I know that You are the One True Living God and there is nothing I should worry about because You are in control. Lord, take control of my life into Your able Hands, I commit all my ways. Direct my steps, and lead me. I worry no more because I know that my worries are now Yours. I know that worrying never solves anything but keeps a man busy doing nothing and achieving nothing. Lord, no matter the situation I find myself in, I will always come to You in prayer, giving thanks to You for all that You have given me, and trust in You completely for all that I may need. I will rejoice because I know that all Your plans for me will be fulfilled in my life. In the name of Your Son Jesus Christ, we pray, Amen.

God put it on my heart to ask
you these five questions.

1. Were all your actions pleasing to God today?

2. Did your actions inspire someone
to seek God today?

3. Did you follow what God
commanded you to do today?

4. Did your actions fulfill God's will today?

5. And if you are unable to answer yes to
all these questions today, will you be able to
answer yes to all these questions tomorrow?

JANUARY 19

Seek the Lord and his strength; seek his presence continually. **1 Chronicles 16:11 (ESV)**

Instead of making life-changing decisions on your own, God wants you to seek Him continually so that He can guide your life according to His plan. When you try to make decisions that will change your life without seeking God, you will be interfering with His plan and disrupt any potential blessings He has prepared for you. God knows the entire plan for your life, and He knows what you need and what direction you need to be heading in order for His plan for you to unfold precisely how He has designed it. When you try to make changes in your life without consulting God and seeking Him for guidance, you will be wasting precious time trying to figure things out on your own. God wants your life to be enjoyable and filled with meaning and purpose. To bring glory to God, you must allow His plan to prosper in your life at all times. When you find yourself struggling to make the right choices and decisions, that is a sign that you need to seek God and allow Him to guide your life on a daily basis.

LET'S PRAY: Dear Heavenly Father, today I ask for you to give me the strength to seek You in all choices and decisions I make. Lord, I never want to make a decision without Your guidance that may interfere with the blessings that you have carefully prepared for me. Lord, You know the entire plan for my life, I need to learn to seek you wholeheartedly before making decisions on my own. Lord, I ask that You help me and guide me to live my life with meaning and purpose according to Your plan. Lord when I am struggling, may I be assured that You will lift me up with Your helping hands of hope and direct the path of my journey according to Your plan for my life. In the name of Your Son Jesus Christ, we pray, Amen.

JANUARY 20

Each day how often is God on your mind and how often do you think about Him?

A - All the time!
B - Often (once an hour)
C - Off and on throughout the day.
D - Only once a day
E - Not very often
F - Not at all

Take a moment to think about what your choice is today and think about ways you can do better tomorrow.

But now that you have been set free from sin and have become slaves of God, the benefit you reap leads to holiness, and the result is eternal life. For the wages of sin is death, but the gift of God is eternal life in Christ Jesus our Lord. **Romans 6:22-24 (NKJV)**

As we all understand the wage of sin is death, we also understand the gift of God is eternal life through Christ Jesus our Lord. In the last seven days, how many sins have you committed? Then ask yourself in the past 30 days how many of those same sins have you committed? The devil will play tricks on Christians by trying to convince us that any sins we commit are not forgiven by God, even though He promises that we are forgiven. You have one of two choices, you can keep committing sins over and over, or you can repent and believe in our Lord Jesus Christ and be forgiving of all your sins.

We must understand that today is a day of salvation. Jesus said, "Come to Me, all who are weary and heavy-laden, and I will give you rest. Take my yoke upon you and learn from me, for I am gentle and humble in heart, and I will forgive you of all your sins." But you must repent and therefore be converted, so that times of refreshing and cleansing may come from the presence of the Lord. I urge you to come to Christ while you still have the chance! If you are still sinning over and over, it is time for you to make a choice.

LET'S PRAY: Dear Heavenly Father, I confess my love for You. I love You because You loved me first, and You even loved me even though I have committed sins. Lord, I ask that You forgive me of my sins. Purify my heart, and envelop it with Your love. Lord, bless me beyond measures and without bounds. I want to be with You after my life here is over. Lord, forgive me for the times I intentionally or unintentionally allowed the enemy to control me and use me for their evil purposes. Lord, Bless me with wisdom and understanding to walk uprightly and the grace to rise above all sin, and all things that continuously try to draw me away from You. In the name of Your Son Jesus Christ, we pray, Amen.

Where God guides, He provides if it's God's will He will fulfill, live according to God's ways you'll have better days, do what God commands be assured you're in the palm of His hands.

Lying lips are an abomination to the Lord, but those who act faithfully are his delight. **Proverbs 12:22 (ESV)**

God wants you to understand that being honest and truthful with everyone in your life is very important. The word of God was founded on truth and honesty, and God expects you to be truthful and honest in every situation you face. When you are dishonest it is not only hurting the people in your life it is very displeasing to God. When you are unable to be truthful and honest about something it means you are doing something that you know is not right or pleasing to God. Your primary purpose in life should be to please God in everything you do, and when you're not honest it is not only disrespectful it is impertinent to God. When you are dishonest, and you think you are getting away with something, always remember that God knows all and He will use what He knows to judge you to determine if your heart is pure, honest and sincere. Your life will be easier when you are not only honest with yourself and with others but more importantly with God.

LET'S PRAY: Dear Heavenly Father, I ask that You guide me away from all dishonesty and untruthfulness. Lord, keep my heart pure, honest, sincere and free from all unrighteousness. Lord, I know that Your word was founded on truth and honesty, and I want to please You by being truthful and honest in every situation I face. Lord, I ask You to guide me towards always being honest because I never want to disrespect you or show lack appreciation for all you have done for me. Lord, I know that one day I will stand before You on judgment day where I will be judged for all the actions I have done and all the words I have said. Lord, when I stand before You, I want to have a good record with You that is filled with honesty, truth, and delight. Lord, I want You to be able to look at my entire life and see that I had the desire in my heart always to bring You glory. In Jesus name, we pray, Amen.

Some things in life are not worth the difficulties and the struggles. These things are not worth the challenges and the struggles because they are often not a part of God's plan for your life. That is when you need to have a heart to heart talk with God through prayer and supplication for guidance and direction of God's will in your life.

JANUARY 25

> For if you forgive other people when they sin against you, your heavenly Father will also forgive you. But if you do not forgive others their sins, your Father will not forgive your sins. **Matthew 6:14-15 (NKJV)**

God forgives us of our sins daily, and He expects us to forgive others when they wrong us. Forgiveness is recognizing the reality that what has happened has already happened and that there's no point in allowing it to dominate the rest of your life. When you forgive others, it shows God that you are worthy of His forgiveness, thankful for His grace and grateful for His salvation. Ultimately, forgiveness refreshingly cleans the slate in God's sight and enables you to step forward into the light of His glorious ways.

LET'S PRAY: Dear Heavenly Father, I come to You today, asking for forgiveness. With total sincerity, I ask for forgiveness, promising to turn away from my sinful ways. Lord, may sin and every form of unrighteousness be a thing of the old. May they pass away, and may Your righteousness be my portion from now on. Lord, I ask that You allow me to forgive others as You have forgiven me. Lord, grant me the grace to walk along the path of righteousness without slipping away that my prayers may bring You joy. In the name of Your Son Jesus Christ, we pray, Amen.

It takes an effort to show your actions. Your actions will always speak louder much louder than your words. Your words mean nothing without the actions to back them up. All positive thoughts that are put into your mind come directly from God. Seek God to guide your actions before you act, seek God to guide your words before you speak, and seek God to guide your thoughts before you think.

JANUARY 27

The Lord makes firm the steps of the one who delights in him; though he may stumble, he will not fall, for the Lord upholds him with his hand. **Psalm 37:23-24 (NKJV)**

One of the biggest reasons why you might feel that you're failing is due to self-doubt, negative self-talk and the lack of guidance from God in your daily life. This happens when you allow your thoughts and actions to be overshadowed by your plans instead of God's plans. You don't ever fail; you only stumble when you choose to refuse God's help. When you try to follow your plans and live your life without guidance from God, you will become weak and vulnerable. This is what makes you stumble, and that is when the devil will creep in and attack you and saturate your mind with negativity and doubt. The only way to overcome all negative thoughts and destructive actions is to seek God and allow Him to replenish your mind with positive thoughts. This will lead to positive actions that will change the trajectory of your life and help you succeed in whatever you do.

LET'S PRAY: Dear Heavenly Father, I want to thank You for the many amazing plans that You have for me. I know that You have wonderful plans to prosper me and protect me. I know that You have no evil thoughts toward any man. Lord, as long as I live, I will always seek You when I am stumbling because I know that I will find You as long as I seek You with all my heart. Lord, I know that You are always with me, and I am forever grateful for Your love, guidance, and faithfulness that endures forever. In the name of Your Son Jesus Christ, we pray, Amen.

JANUARY 28

Focus on God instead of focusing on your worries and concerns in this world, and you will be amazed at how your problems quickly become microscopic.

JANUARY 29

However, as it is written: "What no eye has seen, what no ear has heard, and what no human mind has conceived" the things God has prepared for those who love him. **1 Corinthians 2:9 (NKJV)**

No matter how difficult, challenging, and chaotic the past has been, the future is a new, clean, fresh, slate that has been prepared for you specifically by God. You are not the person you were yesterday, last week, last month or even last year. Your past habits do not define you. Your past failures do not define you. You are not defined by how others have at one time treated you. You are the person that God has created you to be today. He wants you to be happy, peaceful and completely free. God can pull you out of any situation that is not a part of His plan according to His will. He can show you a glimpse of what lies ahead, but you have to be willing to let go of what you're hanging on to. The path He has established is right in front of you, but you must have faith and allow Him to guide your steps. Once you take that leap of faith, you will never have to look back so that you can focus on God and where He is leading you.

LET'S PRAY: Dear Heavenly Father, I know today is the day I have been waiting for. The time for my transformation and my restoration begins today. I know that You have started working in my favor. Lord, I know that You will wipe every tear from my eyes, and this brings me great joy already. Now is the time You will restore all that I have lost, and transform my life according to your will. Lord, I know that You are making things happen in Your time, and I am still, trusting in You for I know that You are God. In the name of Your Son Jesus Christ, we pray, Amen.

JANUARY 30

Your worst days are never so bad that you are beyond the Reach of God's grace & your best days are never so good that you are beyond the Need of God's grace.

JANUARY 31

The Lord is my strength and my shield; My heart trusted in Him, and I am helped; Therefore my heart greatly rejoices, And with my song I will praise Him. **Psalm 28:7 (NKJV)**

When you believe in God and have faith, you know that He is always in your heart and the strength He gives you on the inside is greater than any challenges you will ever face. When you find yourself in a difficult situation, you must always have faith and realize that God's strength is inside your heart and you need to rely on Him to get you through. That is what having faith is all about, knowing that God will make way for you to get through a difficult situation even though you can't see any possible way.

LET'S PRAY: Dear Heavenly Father, thank you for guiding me and directing me down the path you have established for me. Lord, I know that without your strength and guidance I would be lost and I would not be the person I am today. Lord, please continue to give me strength, courage, and guidance today and every day for the rest of my life here on earth. Lord, thank you for always leading me through every difficult situation that I have faced in my life. Lord, without your unconditional love and everlasting grace, I would not be able to face the challenges of life and be able to overcome them. In the name of Your Son Jesus Christ, we pray, Amen

FEBRUARY

FEBRUARY 1

Therefore, I urge you, brothers and sisters, in view of God's mercy, to offer your bodies as a living sacrifice, holy and pleasing to God—this is your true and proper worship. 2 Do not conform to the pattern of this world, but be transformed by the renewing of your mind. Then you will be able to test and approve what God's will is— his good, pleasing and perfect will. **Romans 12:1-2**

The best part of your life will start on the day you decide to accept Jesus Christ into your heart and dedicate your entire life to God. When you lean and rely solely on God, and allow Him to take full control of your life, He will reveal His amazing plan for you. Accepting Jesus Christ into your heart will give you the ability to believe with all your heart that you will do what you were made to do according to God's plan. It may be tough at times, but if you refuse to follow the path God has prepared for you it is both unpleasing to God, and going against His will for you. Following God's plan for your life will allow Him to bring you more peace, happiness, joy, and prosperity than you could ever imagine.

LET'S PRAY: Dear Heavenly Father, I give You thanks for the gift of this day and the gift of this life. I give You thanks for finding me worthy to see another beautiful day that You have created. Lord, starting today, may Your plans for me prevail, and may You allow me to lean and rely solely on Your will. Lord, I am happy, thankful, and grateful for everything You have done for me. May I always remember that Your plan for me is of good and not harm, and to give me a future filled with blessings. In the name of Your Son Jesus Christ, we pray, Amen.

Are you having a bad day?
Read your Bible

Are you feeling depressed?
Read your Bible

Are you feeling hopeless?
Read your Bible

Are you feeling stressed?
Read your Bible

Are you feeling angry?
Read your Bible

Are you feeling irritated?
Read your Bible

Are you feeling emotionally drained?
Read your Bible

Are you feeling mentally drained?
Read your Bible

Are you feeling physically drained?
Read your Bible

Are you feeling financially strained?
Read your Bible

As you can see reading your Bible will help you with everything you face in life. It will change your thoughts, it will change your outlook, it will change your feelings, and it will change your perspective.

FEBRUARY 3

Consider it pure joy, my brothers and sisters, whenever you face trials of many kinds, because you know that the testing of your faith produces perseverance. Let perseverance finish its work so that you may be mature and complete, not lacking anything. **James 1:2-4**

The obstacles you face in life are never enough to stop you. What prevents you is when you don't rely entirely on your faith and believe that God can help you get past any obstacle you face. The problem is not that you have too much of this or too little of that, because God will give you exactly what you need. The problem is that you're waiting for perfect conditions that don't exist. Nothing in this life is perfect but God. Everything that happens in life takes place according to God's perfect plan in this imperfect world. Never make excuses for why you can't accomplish something or get things done. You must focus on God, and He will guide you and show you all the reasons why you must make it happen. There will always be challenges, but when you seek God, He will reveal how you can get past them and grow beyond them.

LET'S PRAY: Dear Heavenly Father, full of grace and steadfastness, lead me to remember that Your power is greater than any obstacles or challenges I will ever face. Lord, I look to You for You are the Author and Finisher of my faith. Lord, I will remain sincere and truthful to You, I will trust in You and rely completely on You. Lord, I believe that your greatness will transform every obstacle into a blessing. In the name of Your Son Jesus Christ, we pray, Amen

FEBRUARY 4

Beware of false prophets, who come to you in sheep's clothing, but inwardly they are ravenous wolves. Matthew 7:15

Be very careful who you associate with, there are wolves in sheep's clothing everywhere you turn. The devil will use these people to fool you, deceive you, hurt you, and commit evil acts against you.

FEBRUARY 5

> If we confess our sins, He is faithful and just to forgive us our sins and to cleanse us from all unrighteousness. **1 John 1:9 (NKJV)**

We are all human, and we have all done things that we think are unforgivable by God. And deep down, we all yearn for forgiveness from Him. Remember, God will forgive you of all your sins, you need to ask Him to forgive you wholeheartedly with truth and meaning. The word "forgive" means to clean the slate, remove a debt that was owed, or to pardon a person for their actions. When a person commits a sin against us, and they seek forgiveness from us, we don't grant them forgiveness because they deserve it. We offer them forgiveness because God forgives us through love, mercy, and grace. The Bible tells us that we are all in need of forgiveness from God. We have all committed many different types of sin. No person in this world has never sinned, who has done nothing wrong and is right all the time. 1 John 1:8 says, "If we claim to be without sin, we deceive ourselves, and the truth is not in us. Sinning against another person harms them, but, ultimately, all sins are committed against God. We must then seek forgiveness from God to restore our relationship with Him.

LET'S PRAY: Dear Heavenly Father, I want to thank You for sending Your Son my Savior Jesus Christ not only because He died on the cross for our sins, but because You showed us what love, mercy, and grace truly means. Lord, I ask You to keep me along the path of righteousness. I ask You to keep me from sinning. Lord, I want to dwell in Your righteousness for it comes with blessings, healing, protection, and strength. Lord, I ask You to please clean my heart of all sin, and fill it entirely with Your peace that surpasses all understanding, and all measures. In the name of Your Son Jesus Christ, we pray, Amen.

FEBRUARY 6

Sometimes we try too hard on our own only to feel like we are spinning our wheels and not getting ahead or accomplishing anything. This often happens when we try to live our lives according to our plan instead of God's plan. The only thing you can do when you feel like this is to stop living your life according to your plan and your agenda and start living your life according to God's plan. If you choose to continue living your life your way you are only going to waste precious time and wear yourself out which will cause you to become weak, stressed, frustrated, and vulnerable to the devil. Are you feeling weak, stressed, frustrated, and vulnerable today as a result of living your life according to your plan?

FEBRUARY 7

For those who live according to the flesh set their minds on the things of the flesh, but those who live according to the Spirit set their minds on the things of the Spirit.
Romans 8:5

When everything seems to be going wrong, it means that it is time to stop and refocus on God and what His plan is for your life. God will often allow things to go wrong in your life so that you will be forced to grow closer to Him and rely on Him wholeheartedly and depend on His strength and guidance. Life may leave you feeling discouraged and alone but you are never alone with God, and He will never abandon you. You must allow God to guide you in every aspect of your life. When you try to control circumstances that are out of your control, it will leave you feeling empty on the inside. Once you understand that God's plan for your life is the only plan you need to follow, you will be able to enjoy every aspect of your life and appreciate the unlimited benefits of living a life for God.

LET'S PRAY: Dear Heavenly Father, Thank You for guiding me down the path You have set forth in my life. I ask that you will draw me close when I am not entirely focused on you. Lord, make me worthy of Your many blessings, forgive me of my sins, surround me with Your protection, soaked in Your provision, and enfolded in Your strength. Lord, thank You for Your generosity, faithfulness, and kindness. Lord, I am happy, thankful, and grateful for everything You have done for me. In the name of Your Son Jesus Christ, we pray, Amen.

You can spend your day accomplishing great positive things that are good for the Lord, or you can spend your day doing not so great negative things of the world. What are you going to choose to do today?

FEBRUARY 9

For I know the plans I have for you," declares the Lord, "plans to prosper you and not to harm you, plans to give you hope and a future. **Jeremiah 29:11**

Even before you were born, God already had the plan for your life set in motion. Before you were even born, God already had every second, every minute, every hour, and every day of your life predetermined and planned according to His will and purpose for your life. He already knows every exact detail about your entire life from the very beginning to the very end. He knows every circumstance you will face and every situation that will take place in your life. He knows every single person who will enter into your life and exactly how long they will remain there. He knows every job you will have and what your career will be. There is nothing that he does not already know about you and your life and everything in it. When things seem to be very difficult in your life, there is a reason for it. When things seem to be going very easy in your life, there is a reason for that too. There is a reason for everything that He does; He knows what is best for us even though it may not be what we want, He will always give us exactly what we need. We have to trust His plan for our life because ultimately that is the way it was meant to be.

LET'S PRAY: Dear Heavenly Father, I am very thankful for Your many blessings, Your Unconditional love, and Your marvelous plan for my life. Lord, without You my life would not exist, and I would not be able to enjoy the blessing of this day. Lord, I want to follow the plan You have for my life in every way, and I want Your will to be done in my life. Lord, You know what I need and who I need in my life according to Your plan. Lord, I ask that You will fill my heart with Your love and fill my mind with Your thoughts and guide me along the path you have established for me. In the name of Your Son Jesus Christ, we pray, Amen.

Each day is what you make of it. Every day you wake up is a gift from God. Regardless of the difficulties and struggles, you face you must be grateful for the gift of each day. And always remember it's not the difficulties and struggles you face that defines you, what defines you is how you react, learn, and grow from them.

FEBRUARY 11

If you openly declare that Jesus is Lord and believe in your heart that God raised him from the dead, you will be saved. **Romans 10:9**

When you accept Jesus Christ as your Lord and Savior, it has to come from your heart genuinely and authentically. God knows the difference if you say it with words or if you honestly mean it from your heart with true feelings. This situation is between you and God; you're the only one who will be affected if you are dishonest with God. Either you have accepted Jesus Christ as your Lord and Savior, or you haven't, there is no halfway, in between or partial salvation. You can't expect to reap the rewards of being saved and the gift of eternal life in heaven, and being forgiven of your sins and their consequences if you have not wholeheartedly accepted Him into your heart.

LET'S PRAY: Dear Heavenly Father, I thank you for sacrificing your Son Jesus Christ and raising Him from the dead so that I can be forgiven of my sins and have eternal life in heaven. Lord, I am thankful for your understanding, your unconditional love, and the protection only you can provide. I appreciate all the blessings you have placed in my life, and I ask that you guide me each day so that I can live with meaning and purpose according to your will for my life. In the name of Your Son Jesus Christ, we pray, Amen

No matter if you believe in God or not, He created you, and He has control of your life. He decides how many days you live and if you wake up to see another day. God is the Ultimate Supreme Court and He the is the judge of judges. And regardless of the laws of this land His word and His ruling will stand forever.

FEBRUARY 13

Fear not, for I am with you; be not dismayed, for I am your God; I will strengthen you, I will help you, I will uphold you with my righteous right hand. **Isaiah 41:10**

In your moments of silence, what important things do you think about? How far you've come in your life, or how far you have to go to reach the goals you have set for yourself? Do you think about how much you've improved your strengths or do you think about how much you have decreased your weaknesses? Your quiet moments should always consist of a good conversation with God. After all, He is the one who has brought you to where you are today, and He can also bring you from where you are today to where you need to be tomorrow. As we all know, God is the one who gives us our strength, and He can also help us to overcome our weaknesses. When you have faith in God, and you allow Him to control every aspect of your life, He can bring you to places you thought were never possible and He can give you the strength that you never thought you had.

LET'S PRAY: Dear Heavenly Father, I ask you to lift me up today and give me strength when I am weak. Lord, I ask that you will draw me close to you in my quiet moments so that I can be in close communication with you every day. Lord, I want to seek you and allow your love and grace to flow through me so that you can guide me to where I need to be in this life. Lord, I need you to be the center of my life so that I can overcome the weakness I encounter when I don't rely entirely on you. In the name of Your Son Jesus Christ, we pray, Amen.

This day and this devotional is dedicated to my father Joseph P. Winchell

February 13, 1959 - January 7, 2016

One thing I have noticed over the years is the amount of children (no matter their age) not going to church because their parents do not force the issue. When I was growing up, and even in my teen years it was automatic we went to church every Sunday even if we complained that we didn't want to go our parents never gave in and we still had to go unless we were legitimately sick. Some of this might have to do with the fact that my great grandpa and my grandpa were pastors of a church.

When children see their parents going to church, and they are strict with them about attending church every week, it will eventually make a huge difference in their life especially as they get older. We all know that with each passing day our world is becoming a more and more evil place so instilling in our children's minds that going to church every Sunday and seeking God and needing Him in the forefront of our mind is an essential part of our daily lives. So do your children a favor that they will thank you for later in life, make sure that they are going to church every Sunday and don't give up just because it's the easy thing to do.

Do not be anxious about anything, but in everything by prayer and supplication with thanksgiving let your requests be made known to God. And the peace of God, which surpasses all understanding, will guard your hearts and your minds in Christ Jesus. **Philippians 4:6-7**

When life gets stressful, and you feel like you're losing your emotional balance seek God. When you feel yourself being overtaken with anxiety and you can't seem to grasp the situation supplicate God. When you start to worry about things you can't control, and you feel like you're sinking invite God to help you relax and re-focus your mind on Him. In every situation, you face it is important to put God in the center of it so that He can guide you and lead the way for you. When you seek God instead of going on your understanding, you will find that you will have fewer trials and tribulations in your life. Allow God to take your hand so that he can direct you down the path that He has established for you.

LET'S PRAY: Dear Heavenly Father, I seek you today to help me keep you in the center of my life and in every situation I face. Lord, help me to overcome stressful thoughts that lead to unnecessary anxiety and allow me to remove pointless thoughts that cause me to worry. Lord, please give me strength and courage to control my feelings and emotions when I feel weak and vulnerable. Last Lord, I ask that every thought in my mind and every feeling in my heart is directly from you. In the name of Your Son Jesus Christ, we pray, Amen.

Stand fast therefore in the liberty by which
Christ has made us free, and do not be entangled
again with a yoke of bondage. Galatians 5:1

People who are living their lives without God at
the forefront of their lives are living in denial of the
truth. These people are missing out on the freedom
from bondage to sin that only God can provide. For
those who are living like this, all you have to do to
be freed from the bondage of sin is confess to God
that you are broken and that you need Him every
single day of your life. If you know somebody, who
is living like this speak to them in love speak to
them in truth and speak to them in understanding.

For where two or three are gathered together in my name, there am I in the midst of them. **Matthew 18:20**

Prayer is how we communicate with God to ask Him for help in every aspect of our lives. Prayer itself is powerful but praying when two or three are gathered together in God's name is extremely powerful. Praying with those who you love or care about is very important, and God wants you to pray with these special people in your life.

It is important to stay in continued prayer with God so that He can hear your prayers and answer them in His time and if they are His will for you. We often get discouraged if we pray over and over and our prayers don't seem to be answered. God's timing and His will are what will determine if and when your prayers get answered. Sometimes we pray for what we want rather than what we need. At times we know that we are in a situation that is not part of God's plan for us. Deep down in our hearts, we know this is not God's plan for us. We will put off doing what we know God wants us to do, and instead, we pray for Him to show us an easy way out.

God will not always show us the easiest way out of a difficult situation. In fact, there is a reason why He does not answer all of our prayers. He may want you to take an honest leap of faith, or He may want you to trust Him in a particular situation fully. He does this to see how big our faith is in Him and how much trust we have in Him. Whenever you pray about a situation and your prayer does not get answered, this might be a sign that it is time to do what you feel God is telling you in your heart. Remember, God will not honor you as long as you are not honoring Him.

LET'S PRAY: Dear Heavenly Father, I cry out today and pour my heart out like water before You. I ask that you will guide me and give me the strength to handle the difficult situations I am facing. Lord, keep me from getting discouraged or backing down from what you're telling me in my heart. Allow me to approach the situation knowing that I have you there with me to guide me through without faltering or becoming weak. Lord, I know that you have amazing plans for my life that are beyond my imagination. Lord, I ask today that you will give me the courage to speak my mind honestly and truthfully regarding my current situation. In the name of Your Son Jesus Christ, we pray, Amen

FEBRUARY 18

Always go out of your way to help others by doing things for them that are difficult for them to do. Place higher importance on the needs of others than your own needs. Make the happiness of others a priority over your happiness. Think about how others will feel before you speak. Think about how others will feel before you act. It's not about you. It's not about your wants. It's not about your needs. It's not about your opinions. Always have the mindset of putting others first in everything you do. Selfishness is not a good character trait to have. Thinking about yourself first will not get you very far in life.

Do nothing out of selfish ambition or vain conceit. Rather, in humility value others above yourselves, not looking to your own interests but each of you to the interests of the others. Philippians 2:3-4

FEBRUARY 19

I will instruct you and teach you in the way you should go;
I will counsel you with my loving eye on you. **Psalm 32:8**

When you seek God, your transformation and growth can be remarkably rewarding, but only when the process of change is based on honesty and truth. When you don't allow God to guide you, being authentic in all areas of your life and with everyone in your life will be very difficult. When you don't have God at the center of your life, any attempt at transforming it eventually leads to anger and frustration because God needs to be the one to lead you. Whenever you feel the need to become angry or frustrated, seek God immediately, and He will soften your heart and allow you to remain calm in every circumstance.

LET'S PRAY: Dear Heavenly Father, I ask you to lead me in every step I take and every decision I make. I ask that you will allow me to be honest and truthful in every situation. I pray today Lord that you will allow me to be authentic in all areas of my life and with everyone in my life. Lord, I promise you today that I will place you in the center of my life so that you can lead the transformation in my life and allow me to surrender to you and your ways fully. In the name of Your Son Jesus Christ, we pray, Amen

FEBRUARY 20

True love for your children and the commitment and dedication to their happiness is shown in your actions, not by your words. Always remember that God is watching at all times and He expects you to take care of your children. He also expects you to teach them right from wrong and the importance of moral, beliefs and goals. God expects you to treat your Children like He has treated His children.

FEBRUARY 21

But if we hope for what we do not yet have, we wait for it patiently. **Romans 8:25**

When you trust God He will give you the ability to be patient. This might be difficult for you, but nothing is difficult for God. Being patient means that you are allowing God's plan to work in your life in His time. You will feel pain when you lose patience, but peace will take the place of your pain when you allow His will to overcome your will. Only God can give you true patience because He knows what is best for you and what He has planned for you. If you get impatient and feel the need to make a decision on your plan stop immediately. You will know when it is part of God's plan because it will feel right and everything will go smoothly. Always follow the intuition that God gives you because He will never lead you down the wrong path.

LET'S PRAY: Dear Heavenly Father, I pray that you will give me the patience I need to be able to wait for good things to happen in my life in your time. Lord, I need you in my life every day, and I want your will to be done in my life. Lord, I often become impatient because I want things to happen now instead of waiting for them to happen on your timetable. Lord, whenever I try to force things to happen according to my plan and not yours, please allow me to stop and think about what I truly need. Lord thank you for always looking out for my best interests even when I don't understand your plan for me. In the name of Your Son Jesus Christ, we pray, Amen.

THE TEN ATTRIBUTES OF TRUE LOVE

In any healthy relationship, God must come first and be the center of the relationship because God is love and all love comes from God. There must be trust, honesty, respect, appreciation, understanding, communication, commitment, dedication, and sacrifice. If your relationship does not have all ten of these attributes, it is not a healthy relationship, and it is not true love plain and simple. So if your relationship does not currently have all of these attributes, you must both work together on acquiring all of these attributes before your relationship will be true love, healthy, and be fulfilling for both people. Pray about it, and God will guide you, direct you, and strengthen you. Couples who pray together, stay together.

> In him we were also chosen, having been predestined according to the plan of him who works out everything in conformity with the purpose of his will. **Ephesians 1:11**

Not all the puzzle pieces of life will seem to fit together on our timetable, but in God's time, He will reveal precisely how all the pieces fit together, perfectly. Be thankful for what God didn't allow to work out so that He could make room for what will work out according to His plan. What He allows to work out in your life will be generous compared to what He did not allow to work out. You must always remember that God knows what He is doing even if it takes longer than you would like. When you are patient, God will show you how the most amazing pieces of an extraordinary puzzle fit together.

LET'S PRAY: Dear Heavenly Father, I offer You my thanksgiving for what You have done for me. I come before You with songs of praise for this is Your will. I know that You will reveal how the pieces of the puzzle fit, and I want to also thank You for showing me one piece at a time, in your time. Father, from today, I promise to never lean on my understanding and timetable, but on Yours. I promise to use all that I do to glorify You. In the name of Your Son Jesus Christ, we pray, Amen.

Telling someone the truth is not disrespectful, telling someone the truth is being honest, sincere, and shows that you are communicating openly. Others may not always want or like to hear the truth, but God expects us to speak the truth in every situation we face.

FEBRUARY 25

Have I not commanded you? Be strong and courageous.
Do not be afraid; do not be discouraged, for the Lord your
God will be with you wherever you go. **Joshua 1:9**

However bad a situation may seem, God is in control of it, and He will change it for the better. As a Christian that is one of the many benefits, you can count on. It may not happen right away, or on your timetable, it will happen according to God's timing. You must embrace the Holy Spirit and realize that God makes things change for a reason. It won't always be easy or obvious at first, but it will be worth it. With some patience and perseverance, it will always work out perfectly according to God's plan. We must realize that our world is ever changing, that is by design according to God's plan. If nothing ever changed there would be no sunrise the next morning, and we would not be able to enjoy the gift of another day.

LET'S PRAY: Dear Heavenly Father, even as the day gets tough, I will not lose heart. I will trust in You for everything that I need. I will bear in mind that You're with me and that You're Almighty God. Lord, renew me in strength day-by-day, hour-by-hour, over and over again, that I will fulfill my purpose on earth, and motivate others to do the same. Lord, no matter what comes my way tomorrow and in the near future, I fear not because I know You are with me at all times, and that You go ahead of me to make my way harm-free and blessed. In the name of Your Son Jesus Christ, we pray, Amen.

FEBRUARY 26

It's incredibly joyous to know the Lord and to fellowship with Him. It is excruciating when you get out of fellowship with Him. The problem is when you have known the joy of the Lord, and then you get away from it you know what you're missing. For those who have never come to Christ, they don't know what they are missing because they have never experienced the full joy of Christ. So they will remain happy within all their pain and misery. But a person who is a Christian and has gotten out of fellowship with the Lord, they know what they are missing and the joy they had when they were in close fellowship with the Lord. So this is why it is so essential to stay in close fellowship with the Lord in the good times and the bad times. The Lord will make you feel great when times are good, and He will lift you up and make you feel better when you are down.

FEBRUARY 27

Then the Lord reached out his hand and touched my mouth and said to me, "I have put my words in your mouth. **Jeremiah 1:9**

God wants you to seek Him before you speak and He wants to guide your words when you communicate with your spouse or significant other. Excellent communication is the cornerstone of a great relationship as long as you allow God to guide your words. If you have resentment, you must seek God then talk it out rather than letting the resentment grow. We must remember that resentment stems from the love of worldly things rather than having faith in God and His plan. If you are having feelings of jealousy or insecurity, you must first seek God and allow Him to guide your words. Once you have received guidance from God, you will be able to communicate openly and honestly, which will help you come to a positive and effective resolution. God does not want you to hold your partner to a strict set of requirements or expectations. He wants you to love them for who He created them to be, and He wants you to be kind, caring and understanding. Whenever problems arise, you must remember to seek God, and He will guide your words and help you communicate effectively with your partner so that you can work things out.

LET'S PRAY: Dear Heavenly Father, I want my communication to be free from covetousness. I want my words to be free from the curse, my thoughts to be free of evil, and my actions to be free from unrighteousness. Lord, may all that I say be pleasing in Your light. May all communication between my partner and I be pleasing in Your sight. Lord, I commit my relationships, communication, activities, thoughts, and desires into Your holy care. May the communication in my relationship be free from discontentment, covetousness, and jealousy. Lord, may my relationships draw me closer to You. May all my communications be positive, honest and sincere. Lord, I will seek Your guidance before I speak. I seek to bring glory to You with all that I say and do. I want my relationship to bring glory to your name. Lord, may I always realize that jealousy is of the devil and not of You. Lord, bless me with guidance, faith to always seek you, the patience to always wait on You, and the perseverance to always pray without ceasing. In the name of Your Son Jesus Christ, we pray, Amen

Everyone in this world needs prayer regardless
if you realize it or not. Some people might need
prayer more than others, but we all need prayer. No
matter what you are facing in life, prayer is essential
in talking to God about what you are facing so
that He can help you through it. It's necessary
to include prayer as a significant part of your
daily routine; prayer should also be an important
part of your life. Prayer is how we communicate
with God and to have a good relationship
with Him you need to pray to Him often.

MARCH

MARCH 1

Have I not commanded you? Be strong and courageous. Do not be afraid; do not be discouraged, for the Lord your God will be with you wherever you go. **Joshua 1:9**

God does not want you to ever give up, and He will never give up on you, so don't ever give up on Him. This is the life God has given you, appreciate it and allow Him to shape it and mold it into what He has planned for you. Strength from God will not only give you the ability to hold on and keep going, but it will give you the ability to see your life from God's perspective. It is never too late for God to get you back on the path he has chosen for you. You must keep seeking God every second of every minute of every hour of every single day. He will use every experience in your life as a way for you to learn, adapt and grow according to His will for your life. You may not be all the way back on the path He has established for you, but you are closer than you were yesterday.

LET'S PRAY: Dear Heavenly Father, Lord, I want to thank You for the many amazing plans that You have for me. Lord, I want to use this moment to let you know how much I appreciate You and to give You thanks for Your love, faithfulness, and blessings. Lord, I honor You, and I honor Your Name. Lord, may I be obedient to You at all times. Lord, Give me the grace and strength to always keep Your commandments. Lord, give me the strength to stay faithful to You, and may I bring You glory with all that I do. Lord, I ask you to guide me at all times to do what's right. Lord, I ask You to bless me with a God-focused understanding that I may see things in a more divine perspective. Lord, today I seek You diligently, I shall find You, as I knock on the gates of heaven in prayers, and You shall open it and shower me with Your many blessings. Lord Jesus, today, I do these things, which You may withhold not Your blessings from me. In the name of Your Son Jesus Christ, we pray, Amen.

Or do you not know that your body is the temple of the Holy Spirit who is in you, whom you have from God, and you are not your own? 20 For you were bought at a price; therefore glorify God in your body and in your spirit, which are God's. 1 Corinthians 6:19-20 (NKJV)

For those who are addicted to something that is harmful to your body. Always remember that your body is a temple of God and the Holy Spirit resides within it. If you are struggling today to break an addiction stop and think what you and your body mean to God. Stop and think about what Jesus went through and what His body endured while He was on the cross shedding His blood for our sins. Jesus paid the ultimate price for us not because He needed to but because He wanted to. So the next time you feel the devil urging you to fall for his scheme and pull you into whatever addiction you are struggling with, stop and seek God wholeheartedly and remind yourself the price that Jesus paid for you. It may not completely stop you from your addiction, but I will put you in the right mindset and help lead you to a path that will lead you away from your addiction.

MARCH 3

It is the one and only Spirit who distributes all these gifts. He alone decides which gift each person should have. **1 Corinthians 12:11**

God wants you to stop being hard on yourself for everything you think you aren't, and start being thankful for everything He has made you to be. There is a reason for all of the gifts, talents, and abilities God has given you. He wants you to make good use of them to glorify His name. Behind you, God's infinite power is driving you to be the person He intended you to be. Before you, God's endless possibility is leading you and making a path for you to follow. God's boundless opportunity is all around you, opening doors and creating a way for you to prosper so that you will have a fulfilling life according to His plan. When you look down on yourself instead of looking up to God, you are interfering with His plans for your life.

LET'S PRAY: Dear Heavenly Father, as I lean on Your understanding, and delight in Your Word, may I prosper on earth according to your will. I know that man is naturally insatiable, but I ask You to bless me with a contented, grateful, and thankful heart. May I never be covetous with my words, actions, or thoughts. May I rather be generous, humble, and kind. May I never do anything without You. May I always put You first in all that I do that I may come first in all that I do. In the name of Your Son Jesus Christ, we pray, Amen.

Everyone who does evil hates the light, and will not come into the light for fear that their deeds will be exposed. But whoever lives by the truth comes into the light, so that it may be seen plainly that what they have done has been done in the sight of God. John 3:20-21

Those who commit evil acts are in the darkness, and they hate the light for the light will expose them. Those who commit evil acts are foolish and reject correction.

MARCH 5

I will instruct you and teach you in the way you should go;
I will counsel you with my loving eye on you. **Psalm 32:8**

God has made things happen in your past so that you could learn lessons, gain wisdom and become stronger spiritually from them. Everything God has made happen in your life up to this day so that He can prepare you for your future and everything He has in store for you. He has your future already planned out, every single second, minute and day and it will be amazing. The people with the greatest wisdom are the ones who have been through the most. God allows His strongest and toughest servants and disciples (soldiers) to face the toughest and most difficult situations and circumstances (battles). When you think you have gone through a lot of tough times, there is a reason for it. Stay strong in your faith, remain patient and know that even though times may seem too difficult to handle, God will never give you more than He knows you can handle. Living your life for God means learning and growing from everything he is teaching you.

LET'S PRAY: Dear Heavenly Father, I am not worried about the future because I know that You're already there working in my favor. Lord, I do not worry about what tomorrow may bring because I am certain that You will take care of my today and my tomorrow just as You have taken care of my past. Lord, I know that You care for me and that is why I cast all my worries, concerns, and anxieties on You because I know that You will help me get through every day. Lord, I ask You to fill me with hope, courage, confidence, and boldness to look into the future because I know that You're there and You have prepared an awesome future for me. In the name of Your Son Jesus Christ, we pray, Amen.

MARCH 6

The best way to live. Don't stress and worry about what you can't control, seek God at all times, focus your thoughts, words, and actions on what God is leading you to do. Open your heart and be receptive to God's will for your life. And talk to God often through prayer and supplication.

MARCH 7

> Peace I leave with you; my peace I give you. I do not give to you as the world gives. Do not let your hearts be troubled and do not be afraid. **John 14:27**

How different would your life be if you stopped worrying and started allowing God to guide your life? Let today be the day you free yourself from worthless worry and stress and realize the vast possibilities of God's greatness and allow His plan to take effective action in your life. Make a stand today, stop allowing stress and worry to take control of your life. Give all your troubles to God and let him handle them and guide your life according to His plan. God has you in the palm of His hand, and He will handle everything. When you give it all to God and stop worrying about the things that only God can control, you will be able to experience God's perfect peace and enjoy the amazing life He has planned for you.

LET'S PRAY: Dear Heavenly Father, I know today is the day I have been waiting for. The time for my transformation and my restoration begins today. Lord, I know that You have started working in my favor. Now is the time You will restore all that I have lost, and transform my life from zero to hero. Lord, I know that You are opening new doors in my life in Your time, and I am still, and always will be trusting in You for I know that You are God. In the name of Your Son Jesus Christ, we pray, Amen.

MARCH 8

At times, we all need someone to talk to about what we are facing and what we are feeling. Always remember that God is always near and He is always listening, and He is willing and able to help you through whatever it is that you are facing. All you need to do is seek Him and tell Him how you feel. He will give you strength, courage, and guidance so that you can handle whatever struggles or difficulties you are facing today. And remember you will never travel down a path of uncertainty alone, God will be right beside you every step of the way.

> But in your hearts honor Christ the Lord as holy, always being prepared to make a defense to anyone who asks you for a reason for the hope that is in you; yet do it with gentleness and respect. **1 Peter 3:15**

God expects you to treat everyone with respect and appreciation. He expects you to have a positive outlook towards everyone you meet. God expects you to encourage them, inspire them, compliment them, lend them a helping hand and make them smile. God created Love and kindness for a reason, and it is contagious for a reason. God will bless you when you help others find happiness and success. God will see all of your good deeds, and He will give you the desires of your heart for being kind and caring to others. There is no better feeling than treating someone with respect and knowing that you inspired them enough to make them smile.

LET'S PRAY: Dear Heavenly Father, enable me to be able to live with everybody with peace, love, and understanding. May I treat everybody with love, politeness, respect, appreciation, and kindness. Lord, renew my love for everybody, renew my patience in You, renew my delight for Your Word, Lord, help me to treat everybody around me, and everybody that I meet with love and respect. I want to speak politely and with kindness. I want to speak with humility and compassion. I want to relate with everybody that I meet with love. Lord, may I never speak rudely or proud. May I never breed contempt with anybody. May I never forget that all of Your children are of great value in Your sight, and You love all Your children equally, and I should love everybody just the same. In the name of Your Son Jesus Christ, we pray, Amen.

Talking to God through prayer should be a part of your daily routine. You should talk to God through prayer every single day not just when you are hurting or going through a difficult situation. When you talk to God on a daily basis, not only will your days be better, but you will feel better, and He will guide and direct every step you take through the day.

LET'S PRAY: Dear Heavenly Father, I pray that all who read will this will feel your unconditional love, the comfort of your peace, the warmth of your joy and is blessed with peace and wisdom. In Jesus Name we pray, Amen.

> Consider it pure joy, my brothers and sisters, whenever you face trials of many kinds, because you know that the testing of your faith produces perseverance. Let perseverance finish its work so that you may be mature and complete, not lacking anything. **James 1:2-4**

God won't always make your journey easy, But He will make it worth it. If God made your life easy without any trials and tribulations, you would never grow or learn any lessons. To never struggle is to never grow. To never face difficult situations or circumstances is to never experience God's grace. Allow God to teach you lessons and allow Him to guide you to make the right choices and decisions in every situation you face. God expects you to accept the circumstances, acknowledge the situations, learn from them and always remember what they taught you. God loves you unconditionally, and He only wants the best for you. The trials you face are His way of preparing you for the incredible journey He has planned for your life.

LET'S PRAY: Dear Heavenly Father, Your Word is a lamp to my feet, guiding me in my journey along the path of righteousness. Lord, today, I thank You for all the good things You have done for me. I thank You for all the trials I endured because they strengthened my faith in You. Lord, I thank You for all the sufferings too because, with it, I learned to be humble. Lord, I thank You for everything I have faced because everything happens for a reason. Lord, may I never cease to say Thank You to You each day I wake to see another beautiful day that You have given me. Lord, I know that You give Your toughest battles to Your greatest soldiers, so I consider the trials I face as a message from You that I am one of Your trusted soldiers, and it is an honor to me. Lord, I know that Your presence will always go before me, and make a way. Bless me with wisdom to make wise choices and decisions, and the strength to overcome every obstacle that I may face. In the name of Your Son Jesus Christ, we pray, Amen.

MARCH 12

Stop and ask yourself these questions today. Are you really wholeheartedly happy? Are you living your life the way God intended it to be, or are you just getting by? It's important that you take this question very serious because you only get one life here on earth and God's purpose for your life is set in stone. To be completely 100% happy with your life, you need to live according to God's plan for your life. If you live your life according to your plan, you will never be happy because you will always be focused on what you want instead of what you need. When you follow God's plan for your life, he will provide you with what you need, and the things you want won't be your primary focus. If you are not happy with the way your life is going, then you need to start living your life according to God's plan. True happiness is not having the most money, the biggest house, the biggest boat, are the nicest car. True happiness is following God's will for your life and knowing that He will always guide you, protect you, and strengthen you and provide you with all the needs and necessities of life.

MARCH 13

He said to them, "Go into all the world and preach the gospel to all creation. **Mark 16:15**

The best part of inspiring others and leading them to live for God is being able to see them grow spiritually and watching the positive changes God can make in their life. God wants you to share your personal stories about Him, He wants you to teach others what you've learned along the way from Him, He wants you to talk about all your failures and achievements, and He wants you to ask people questions about their progress regarding their walk with God. By sharing your stories and experiences about God, you can help people avoid the mistakes you've made in the past. This will inspire them to allow God to help them down the path He has prepared for them. When you spread the word of God and share the good news, life will be transformed.

LET'S PRAY: Dear Heavenly Father, thank You for making me realize the power of Your word. Lord, we know that during prayer, when two or three are gathered together in Your Name, you are always within their midst. Lord, as I endeavor to spread Your word to those who are hopeless and need you, bring us together in Your love. As we share Your Word, open our understanding that we may get the deepest meanings of what You are speaking to us about. Lord, as we come together in prayer, declaring progress, healing, and protection over our lives, may it be done for us all by the Father in heaven who created us all, and through You, all good things come. In the name of Your Son Jesus Christ, we pray, Amen.

It is very important to realize that every difficult situation, every heartache, and every tragedy happens for a reason, we may not know the reason but God does. And just because we think something is really bad does not mean that God intended it to be that way, that is just how we perceive it as humans. God's ultimate plan for your life is already set in stone, and there is nothing you or anyone can do to change what is meant to be according to God's plan. So the next time when you face a difficult situation, a heartache, or a tragedy instead of thinking about how bad it is, stop and think about the reason why God made it happen in the first place. There is a reason for everything that happens, and if you trust God and believe in Him wholeheartedly, you will understand that He has the final say and a reason for everything single thing that happens.

MARCH 15

For we are his workmanship, created in Christ Jesus for good works, which God prepared beforehand, that we should walk in them. **Ephesians 2:10**

As we all know every day is a gift from God. But with each day brings choices: to allow God's plan for your life to take place or your plans, to practice stress or to practice peace. If you choose your plan instead of God's plan and you chose to be stressed instead of at peace, you'll find plenty of reasons to be unhappy and not at peace. But if you choose to trust God and allow Him to bring you peace your life will be a lot less stressful. It is very easy to find ourselves feeling unhappy or stressed, but when you focus on God and have faith, He will motivate you to to be active and fulfilled. Everything you achieve comes from trusting God and following His plan. The choice is up to you.

LET'S PRAY: Dear Heavenly Father, I give You thanks for the gift of this day and the gift of this life. I give You thanks for finding me worthy to see another beautiful day that You have created. Lord, I give You all the honor and praise for Your abundant mercy and grace upon my life. I thank You for everything I have been through. Lord, I give you thanks for Your love and faithfulness that endures forever. Lord, I ask You to bless me with peace of mind, body, soul, and spirit. Leave Your peace in my heart, and may Your peace heal me completely and remove everything within me that causes stress, pain, sorrow, and grief. In the name of Your Son Jesus Christ, we pray, Amen.

MARCH 16

Some people might as why we serve God? Our answer to them is this. We serve God because we are His children and He is our heavenly Father. He loves us, He cares for us, and He Guides us down the path He has established for our lives. We serve God because we love others. We serve God because we want to bring hope to the hopeless. We serve God because we want to spread His word to as many people as we can. And we serve God because we want to introduce as many people to God as we can.

MARCH 17

The Lord is my strength and my defense he has become my salvation. He is my God, and I will praise him, my father's God, and I will exalt him. **Exodus 15:2**

God is powerful, and He will give you the ability to accomplish any task you put your mind to when you seek Him. You are a beautiful child of the most high God, and He will give you strength and guidance as you follow the path He has prepared for you. You won't be disheveled by the obstacles or hurdles that are placed in your path when you put your faith in God. When you allow God to be in the forefront of your mind, you will be unstoppable, and He will allow your mistakes to educate you not hurt you. When you seek God and allow Him to use your experiences to teach you lessons, you will realize that you can fall down, get up, and move forward.

LET'S PRAY: Dear Heavenly Father, Strengthen my faith in You that no obstacle will be able to stop me from doing Your will. Lord, I come to You, asking You to bless me with the strength to overcome any hurdle, wisdom to make wise decisions, and understanding to do the right things when I face difficult times. Lord, transform my weakness to strength, my struggling to thriving. Lord, I commit all my ways, direct my path, establish the works of my hands, and make Your strength perfect in my weakness. Lord, I seek You today with all my heart, mind, that I may find strength and comfort in You. Lord, reveal to me and lead me to where You want me to be. Lord, show me what I need to do, and strengthen me to do your will. In the name of Your Son Jesus Christ, we pray, Amen.

Whenever you feel the devil creeping into your mind to tempt you to do something negative or something that is not pleasing to God pick up your Bible hold it in your hand and start praying. The best way to deter the devil's plan is to slap him with the power of God's word. You can also communicate directly with God through prayer, and that will also stop the devil right in his tracks. When we allow the devil to creep into our minds and take control of our thoughts and actions it makes us feel like we are tied down and unable to break free from the schemes of the devil because we allow them to weigh us down.

So I challenge you today to stand up and stop the devil in his tracks by pulling your bible out and reading the following verse.

Put on the full armor of God, so that you can take your stand against the devil's schemes. Ephesians 6:11

MARCH 19

God, whom I serve in my spirit in preaching the gospel of his Son, is my witness how constantly I remember you in my prayers at all times; and I pray that now at last by God's will the way may be opened for me to come to you. I long to see you so that I may impart to you some spiritual gift to make you strong. **Romans 1:9-11**

God does not want you to force things to happen. By doing this you are not only interrupting His plan, but you will also drive yourself crazy trying to force something that only God can make happen. You have to let go and let what's meant to be according to God's will for you. Loving God and appreciating everything He has done for you means having faith in Him and trusting His plan not yours. It means learning from the experiences and situations that God places in your life. You have to stop worrying, wondering, and doubting every step of the way and allow God to lead you in the right direction. You might not always understand His reasons, but you must live consciously in the moment, and enjoy your life as it unfolds struggles and all. You might not end up exactly where you wanted to be, but you will end up precisely where you need to be according to God's plan.

LET'S PRAY: Dear Heavenly Father, I ask You to send Your angels of peace to me that they may go with me, and ahead of me when I go out. May Your angels of peace stay by my side. May they protect me, guide me, teach me, counsel me, and prosper me through You. Lord, I ask You to bless me with peace of mind and calm my troubled heart with Your love that surpasses all understanding. Lord, my heart is like a turbulent sea; always troubled and afraid. I am constantly worrying about what I can't control. I know that without You I cannot do anything that's why I ask You to bless me with strength in my weakness, and clarity of mind to find the purpose of my life. I ask You to bless me with wisdom that I may figure out the path You have laid out for me. Lord, I trust completely in You. I trust entirely in Your love. I know that nothing, no one, and no power can separate me from Your love, and I thank You for such amazing unconditional love. Lord, just as the sun rises every day, I ask You to bring my life a sense of purpose through Your light of blessing. In the name of Your Son Jesus Christ, we pray, Amen.

Do you ever feel irritated by what is allowed to go on in our world today? Like what is allowed in schools, on tv, in commercials, in music, and in public places. Do you think God is pleased with what is going on our or world today?

All the negativity, drama, gossip, fake people, lack of integrity, lack of honesty, false motives and agendas. We desperately need to pray for our leaders, for each other for our country, and for our world.

The world we are living in today is so very far from what God intended it to be. Man has altered the purpose of life and the reason we wake up every day has been skewed by man and the place we should all strive to go after this life has been made less important than it is by man.

With each generation what it is right and what is important seems to slip away a little more and more. Our children and grandchildren are not learning the importance of morals, beliefs, and values like they should be. Our children and grandchildren are not being taught the importance of the word of God and what it means to live for Christ and what the reward for doing God's will is.

We all need to pray for our children, our grandchildren, parents, our grandparents, our family, our pastors, our church leaders, our Sunday school teachers, our teachers, our principals, our bosses, company owners, our CEO's, our president, and everyone else.

MARCH 21

Live as people who are free, not using your freedom as a cover-up for evil, but living as servants of God. **1 Peter 2:16**

Of all the things that can be stolen from you – your possessions, dignity, your solitude, your peace, your hope, your money, your words, your rights, what no one can ever take from you is your freedom to love God and believe in Him wholeheartedly. God wants you to be able to love Him and believe in Him without restriction. This also means He wants you to have faith in Him and trust in Him at all times. Peace and freedom begin when you give all your fear and resentment to God so He can handle it. Just because something happened to you today or recently that was not pleasant does not mean you should take it out on the world. God wants you to forgive others just as He has forgiven you.

LET'S PRAY: Dear Heavenly Father, I set my eyes on You because You are the Author and the Finisher of my faith. I know that my faith, my freedom to love You and believe in You can never be taken away. Lord, I offer my words, actions, and thoughts to You, may they glorify You all the time. Lord, may I love my enemies and not hate them, may I pray for those who persecute me, and treat those who hate me with love, may I forgive those who have stolen from me. May I never pay evil with evil, but good with evil. In the name of Your Son Jesus Christ, we pray, Amen.

Today use the acts of the devil to help strengthen you in resisting his evil ways by seeking God and His will for your day. We all know that as Christians the devil will tempt us any way he can and in every way he can to get us to fail in order to fall for his evil schemes. So it's not a surprise that we can expect to be taunted by the devil in many different ways throughout our day and we have to be mindful that the devil never stops he works 24/7 in order to get Christians to fall away from God and commit evil and sinful Acts. So we must remember this every time the devil tries to tempt us or persuade us to do something that we know is not right. We have, and we need to seek God in order to refrain from falling for the evil acts of the devil so that we can bring glory to God.

MARCH 23

The Lord has done it this very day; let us rejoice today and be glad. **Psalm 118:24**

God wants you to begin each day with love, grace, and gratitude. When you arise in the morning, always give thanks to God for the gift of another day and make sure you live it to the fullest and make the most of it. Be sure to think of what an incredible privilege it is to be alive, to breathe, to see, to hear, to think, to love, to be able to experience all the beauty of what makes up this day. Happiness is the emotional state of well-being defined by positive or pleasant emotions from God; joy is simply the feeling of appreciating and enjoying all of God's amazing creation. God has granted you another day for a reason, and he has plans for you to not only accomplish something, He has more work for you to do. Each morning when you wake up, always remember that if you see another day, it means your journey is not over yet and that God has more in store for you.

LET'S PRAY: Dear Heavenly Father, in the morning, I shall wake up to a beautiful day. You have made and give thanks to You for letting me see another day. In the morning, I shall offer a prayer of thanksgiving to You blessing Your Name for giving me the gift of life. I am grateful for the gift of this day and the gift of life You have blessed me with. I am grateful for all the things You have blessed me with. Lord, You are the God of love, grace, gratitude and every good and perfect gift comes from You. Lord, thank You for blessing mankind with the gift of knowing what Your will for us all is through Jesus Christ Your Son. Lord, thank You for giving us all the gift of life that we may all experience Your love in a special way on this beautiful day that You have made. In the name of Your Son Jesus Christ, we pray, Amen.

MARCH 24

Do you want to let go of what is holding you back from receiving the blessings that God has prepared for you? Do you want to live your life according to the purpose in which God has created you to serve? And do you want to receive the gift of eternal salvation for living your life for God according to His will?

MARCH 25

Always giving thanks to God the Father for everything, in the name of our Lord Jesus Christ. **Ephesians 5:20**

You are not perfect; you are human, You must smile every chance you get; not because life has been easy, perfect, or exactly as you had anticipated, but because you choose to be happy and grateful for all the good things God has given you. You must thank God every day and be grateful for all the problems that He has helped you through in your life. You must realize that life is not perfect, people are not perfect, and you are not perfect, but God is perfect, and His plan for your life is perfectly planned out. God does not reward you for trying to be perfect; He rewards you for being patient, obedient and sincere. Patience comes from God; obedience comes from God and sincerity comes from God. You must seek God, and He will teach you how to be patient in His timing, obedient in His love and sincere in His word.

LET'S PRAY: Dear Heavenly Father, I want to praise Your Name. Today, I want to give You thanks for everything that You have done for me. Today, I want to appreciate You. Today, I want to be grateful for everything that I am, and everything that I have been through. Lord, my soul delights in Your presence because, in You, there is a fullness of joy. Lord, thank You for all the many benefits You have bestowed upon me, including the gift of life. In the name of Your Son Jesus Christ, we pray, Amen.

Are you feeling weak, tired, and defeated today? Don't ever lose hope in God's Grace and His word. God's grace is sufficient, and His word is the truth, and it is sovereign. The written Word of God is sovereign and offers us many rewards. When you read God's word, you will feel cleansed, revived, renewed, restored and refreshed in His presence and His Word.

MARCH 27

And the God of all grace, who called you to his eternal glory in Christ, after you have suffered a little while, will himself restore you and make you strong, firm and steadfast. **1 Peter 5:10**

God does not give you trials and tribulations to transform you into someone you're not. He wants to use the trials and tribulations to strengthen you, transform you and allow you to grow and prosper into the person He made you to be. Everything He does for you will benefit your life according to His plan. As a child of God, He will never give you more then He has already enabled and equipped you to handle. You must always remember that what might seem like something inadequate in the flesh, God is using it for good in your life. Our faith in God is revealed when we walk directly into the light of His salvation by faith instead of trying to see in the darkness of defeat.

LET'S PRAY: Dear Heavenly Father, I face several trials. Every difficult situation I face always seems to happen all at one time. I have a lot of pressure on me right now. I can't seem to meet all my responsibilities. Nevertheless, I rejoice because I know that even before I come to You in prayer, You know my every need and You are simply waiting for me to acknowledge that You are God and You have the power to rectify all my situations. Lord, I acknowledge that You are God and there is nothing impossible for You to accomplish in my life. I know that I am much more precious than gold and silver. I know that though I am tried with fire, I will strength by praising, honoring, and glorifying Your Holy Name. Lord, today, I give You all the praise, honor, and glory. Come into my life and take absolute control over it. In the name of Your Son Jesus Christ, we pray, Amen.

How many of you no longer have the chains of the devil holding you hostage in the darkness of deception? How many of you no longer have the chains of the devil holding you hostage in the darkness of defeat? And how many of you no longer have the chains of the devil holding you hostage in the darkness of Denial? The devil is Devious, Disobedient, Dangerous, Delusional, Desperate, Dishonest, Deceitful, Doomed in Darkness, in Denial and Defeated. The devil is a Dictator, a Deceptor, a Deceiver, a Destroyer, a Debauchery, and a Disgrace. Are all of your chains of the devil gone because of God's Amazing Grace?

For if you forgive other people when they sin against you, your heavenly Father will also forgive you. But if you do not forgive others their sins, your Father will not forgive your sins. **Matthew 6:14-15**

We must learn to forgive others because God always has and always will forgive us. Forgiveness allows us to see everyone in our lives as a teacher. God is our ultimate teacher, but He places people in our lives to teach us and help us grow. Family members, spouses, friends, bosses, etc. everyone is brought into our lives to teach us more about ourselves. We must always be thankful to God and realize that He has placed every person in our life for a specific reason. He made them a part of our journey to teach us valuable lessons that will ultimately help us to educate others and help them grow. God uses this same philosophy applies to our failed relationships too. Once you truly learn the lessons and the reasons behind a failed relationship you will understand why God allowed that person to come into your life. You will understand the situation and know that God puts people in your life and He places you in certain relationships for a reason.

LET'S PRAY: Dear Heavenly Father, I ask You to forgive me for all my faults. I come to you today Lord asking for you to forgive me of all the sins I have committed and all my thoughts, words, and actions that were not of You. I ask You to help me forgive others so that I will be forgiven. I ask You to forgive me especially for all the good things I failed to do. Lord, make me worthy of Your Mercy, Grace and many blessings. Forgive me of my sins, and find me worthy to be surrounded with Your protection, soaked in Your provision, and enfolded in Your strength. Lord, thank You for Your generosity, faithfulness, and kindness. In the name of Your Son Jesus Christ, we pray, Amen.

You know that the devil is controlling someone when they want to achieve something, but they don't want to do the hard work to achieve what they want. And then they cause trouble and start rumors about people who are doing the hard work to achieve what they want so they can be successful. Make sure you are part of the solution and not part of the problem. Always seek God and pray for those who are being controlled by the devil. They are not only fighting a battle with the devil, but they are also fighting a battle with themselves. We need to show love to these people, and we need to pray for these people.

This is the day the Lord has made. We will rejoice and be glad in it. **Psalm 118:24**

There is no question that our life here on earth is short compared to our eternal life in heaven. Even though each day is a precious gift from God, we often go about our day forgetting how fortunate we are to have the gift of each new day. We get so involved in our busy lives that it causes us to worry about pointless deadlines, stressful meetings and daunting tasks that seem to be far beyond our means. This will only cause you to lose focus on what God has prepared for you and His plan for your life. Folks, the gift of life is the most precious gift you could ever receive, and without it you have nothing. When we wake up each day we need to thank God for every second, every minute, every hour and every day He has given us here on earth. We bring glory to God by living each day according to His plan and allowing Him to be in the center of our lives every moment throughout our day.

LET'S PRAY: Dear Heavenly Father, thank you for the precious gift of this day. I give You praise for Your abundant mercy and grace upon me. I thank You for everything I have been through. Lord, I ask You to bless me with peace of mind, body, soul, and spirit. Thank You for giving mankind a chance to inherit Your kingdom. Lord, I want to make it to heaven after my time here on earth is over. I ask You to bless me with the strength to continue doing what's right according to your plan. Lord, Bless me with the grace never to draw away from You. In the name of Your Son Jesus Christ, we pray, Amen.

APRIL

APRIL 1

This is the day the Lord has made. We will rejoice and be glad in it. **Psalm 118:24**

There is no question that our life here on earth is short compared to our eternal life in heaven. Even though each day is a precious gift from God, we often go about our day forgetting how fortunate we are to have the gift of each new day. We get so involved in our busy lives that it causes us to worry about pointless deadlines, stressful meetings and daunting tasks that seem to be far beyond our means. This will only cause you to lose focus on what God has prepared for you and His plan for your life. Folks, the gift of life is the most precious gift you could ever receive, and without it you have nothing. When we wake up each day we need to thank God for every second, every minute, every hour and every day He has given us here on earth. We bring glory to God by living each day according to His plan and allowing Him to be in the center of our lives every moment throughout our day.

LET'S PRAY: Dear Heavenly Father, thank you for the precious gift of this day. I give You praise for Your abundant mercy and grace upon me. I thank You for everything I have been through. Lord, I ask You to bless me with peace of mind, body, soul, and spirit. Thank You for giving mankind a chance to inherit Your kingdom. Lord, I want to make it to heaven after my time here on earth is over. I ask You to bless me with the strength to continue doing what's right according to your plan. Lord, Bless me with the grace never to draw away from You. In the name of Your Son Jesus Christ, we pray, Amen.

Stop and think about what you say to people and how you say it. Stop and think about how you react to what someone says to you. In the flesh, it's very easy to say something that is hurtful or mean to someone. But in the spirit, our words should always be positive, kind, and pure. This is the result of seeking God before you say something to someone rather than just speaking your mind on your own will. Always remember that once you say something you can't ever take it back, so make sure you are speaking out of love.

APRIL 3

For I, the Lord your God, will hold your right hand,
Saying to you, 'Fear not, I will help you. **Isaiah 41:13**

All your days will be better when you remain positive in every situation. Positive thinking is the ability to allow God's strength to help you overcome negativity when it creeps in and still maintain enough hope to remain positive. The situations you face in life cannot be tailor-made, but when you give God control of your life and every situation, you face He can tailor-make the actions to fit those situations. You must view your life through the eyes of Jesus and know that every situation is facilitated by Him. In any situation, you face, instead of asking yourself, "What was I thinking?" you need to take a deep breath and think about what you can learn from the situation and ask God to guide your thoughts and actions towards a positive outcome. There is a reason for every situation you face. God wants you to look at every situation with a positive mindset regardless of how bad the situation might seem. A positive mindset towards a difficult situation is God's way of teaching you perseverance and steadfastness.

LET'S PRAY: Dear Heavenly Father, I admit that I am weak, and I need You, and You're a strong God. I admit that I can do nothing without You, and You're the God of all flesh, and there is nothing too hard for You. Lord, You are mightier than all. You are holy above all, and through You, I can remain positive and hopeful. Lord, may Your peace, which surpasses all understanding, come into my home and bring us together in unity. May Your peace bring Your love and blessings into my home. May Your peace keep our hearts and minds free from trouble through Christ Jesus, in whose Name I pray. Amen.

APRIL 4

We must never walk by sight; we must always walk by faith. For we are blinded by darkness in the flesh, but our faith will show us the light of our Lord, and He will lead us.

APRIL 5

Rejoice always, pray continually, give thanks in all circumstances; for this is God's will for you in Christ Jesus. **1 Thessalonians 5:16-18**

Today, God wants you to stop and think about how grateful you should be that you woke up to live another day. God wants you to stop and think about all the amazing things He has placed in your life and all the difficulties and struggles He has brought you through. God wants you to stop taking life for granted and start being thankful for your life and appreciate all the people in it. There will come a day when you go to bed, and you won't wake up to see your family and friends, and there will come a day when you take your last breath. God wants you to remember that life is a precious gift from Him and that it will end when He wants it to end according to His will for your life. From this moment forward, appreciate your family, your friends and all the things God has placed in your life. You will never know when it's your time to go home to be with the Lord, so live your life graciously and show God that you are grateful for all He has done for you.

LET'S PRAY: Dear Heavenly Father, I am grateful for the gift of this day and the life You have blessed me with. I am blessed and grateful for all the special people You have placed in my path. Lord, when I come to You in prayer asking for what I need, may I never forget the importance of giving thanks to You in every situation. Lord, may I never forget that the devil will always try to plant ungratefulness in the hearts of humans to prevent them from giving thanks to You for the things You have blessed them with. May I resist the foul spirit of ungratefulness by constant prayers. Lord, as I continue to pray every day, keep listening to me every day, answering my prayers, and delivering me from all my troubles. Lord, I want to thank You for the many amazing plans that You have for me. Lord, for as long as I live, I will always seek You because I know that I will find You for as long as I seek You with all my heart. Lord, I know that You are always with me, and I am forever grateful for Your faithfulness that endures forever. In the name of Your Son Jesus Christ, we pray, Amen.

APRIL 6

Our sincerity, our commitment and our dedication to God is not measured by our words but rather by our actions. Our faith and trust in God is not proven by what we say it is proven by what we do.

APRIL 7

For my thoughts are not your thoughts, neither are your ways my ways," declares the Lord. "As the heavens are higher than the earth, so are my ways higher than your ways and my thoughts than your thoughts. **Isaiah 55:8-9**

God wants you to let go of the things you can't control. You constantly think and worry about these things because your mind is focused on them instead of being focused on God. Positive things will happen in your life when you put faith in God and allow Him to distance you from anyone or anything that is negative. God has allowed things to happen in your life that has changed your perspective, taught you lessons, and forced your spirit to grow. God shows you, unconditional love, every single day because He wants only the best for you. Instead of stressing out and worrying about things you can't control, trust God wholeheartedly and allow Him to show you peace, joy, and happiness.

LET'S PRAY: Dear Heavenly Father, today, I put forth my worries before You, I ask You to take control right now. I go on my knees, praying that You turn Your face to me and listen to my voice in prayer. Lord, I pray to You with confidence and boldness because I know that You are the One True Living God and there is nothing I should worry about because You are now in control. Lord, take control of my life, into Your able Hands, I commit all my ways. Direct my steps, and lead me. I acknowledge You in all my ways, establish the works of my hands, and keep me safe from evil and negative people. Lord, please help me from becoming anxious about the things I can't control. May I be assured that You are in control and that there is nothing that I may need that You cannot possibly give. Lord, You are the God of all mercy and grace, and every blessing and gift comes from you. In the name of Your Son Jesus Christ, we pray, Amen.

SPIRITUAL INTEGRITY

Is a characteristic of "love, trust, respect, honesty, responsibility, humbleness, and adherence to a pattern of good works that bear spiritual fruit which is exhibited by a person's' actions and deeds."

APRIL 9

I will instruct you and teach you in the way you should go,
I will counsel you with my loving eye on you. **Psalm 32:8**

You will always end up exactly where you're meant to be according to God's plan for your life. God will make the most tragic and stressful situations teach you some of the most important lessons that you will ever learn. Remember, when things seem like they are falling apart in your life, God is making things fall into place. When you step back and look at all the things that took place in your life, you will realize that all the times you thought that you were being rejected from what seemed to be an excellent opportunity because things were not going as you had planned, God had better things already in store for you according to His plan for your life. You can't control everything, only God can. You need to relax, trust God and have faith that He will make everything work out. Sometimes the things you can't change will end up changing you and helping you grow according to God's plans.

LET'S PRAY: Dear Heavenly Father, May I always rely on You for everything and put You first in everything. Lord, teach, instruct, counsel, and guide me every day, and in everything. Help me to keep my eyes, and my mind focused on Your will and Your Word. No matter how black the storm may be, I know that You are always with me, and each time I pray, You are always there to listen, and come to my aid because I believe and trust in You with all my heart. Lord, I seek You today knowing that You will instruct me and I will learn valuable lessons from what you are teaching me. Lord, as I read Your word today from the Scriptures, may it dwell and sink deep in my heart that it may transform me from worldly to Godly. Lord, may I always be reminded that it is better to be humble for following your plan than to be prideful for the pleasures of sin that brings destruction. Lord, counsel me and I will take correction, teach me and I will learn, and instruct me and I will obey. In the name of Your Son Jesus Christ, we pray, Amen.

I WILL PRAY FOR YOU!

Use this as a daily guide if someone is negative, disrespectful, unappreciative, or dishonest.

If you have something positive to say, tell me about it because I want to hear it. If you have something negative to say, I will pray for you.

If you treat me with respect I will treat you with respect; if you disrespect me, I will pray for you.

If you show appreciation for the things I do for you, I will show appreciation for the things you do for me, if you show lack of appreciation for what I do, I will pray for you.

If you are honest with me, I will be honest with you, but if you are dishonest with me, I will pray for you.

If you live your life for Jesus we can be friends, if you don't believe in Jesus, I would love to become your friend so that I can introduce you to Him, but if you refuse to get to know Him, I will pray for you. Amen

It is best to remain positive and respectful whenever you face someone who is negative, disrespectful, unappreciative, or dishonest. Your integrity and your character will be shown by how you react to a negative situation. God gives us plenty of opportunities to learn from our mistakes, but He also gives us many opportunities to grow from the way people treat you.

Praise the Lord! Give thanks to the Lord, for he is good!
His faithful love endures forever. **Psalm 106:1**

When we least expect it, God will place the most amazing opportunities and people in our lives out of nowhere. We can't always understand why, but we must trust in Him and be thankful for all the gifts He has given us. I know you might want to second guess things or wonder why something happened the way it did. But you must have faith in every situation, the more faith you have in God, the more gifts you will receive from Him. To show God that you are truly thankful, you must believe in Him through tough times. You must believe in His capacity to succeed. You must believe that every relationship He puts you in is worth the effort. You must believe in God wholeheartedly, especially when you must choose between two good paths, your path or the path God has established for you. Believe that God will astonish you over and over with His greatness, but you must remain obedient to Him.

LET'S PRAY: Dear Heavenly Father, God of all blessings, you are the source of everything I need. You gave me the gift of this beautiful life with love, strength, courage, and hope. Lord, Lord, I want to thank You for Your love, mercy, grace, forgiveness, and faithfulness. I want to thank You for Your mercies that endures forever. I want to thank you for all the days you have woke me up and allow me to experience the gift of another day. I thank you for all the blessings and most importantly the gift of life. Lord, I ask today that you will help me to take time every day to spend in Your presence; praying and giving thanks to You for everything You have done for me. Last Lord, I want to thank You for allowing us to speak to you directly through the gift of prayer. Thank You for giving us the opportunity to talk to you about any time of the day or night. In the name of Your Son Jesus Christ, we pray, Amen.

When you find yourself in the middle of a situation that is escalating and seems impossible to resolve seek God and pray about the situation. God will give you guidance and direction that will help you find comfort and peace in any situation you face. After you seek God and pray, pick up your Bible and read some scripture or a devotional. It will put your mind at ease, and you will feel better once your mindset is focused on God and not on the difficulties at hand. Always try to remember that God's grace is enough when you face the struggles and challenges of life. It's not the situation or circumstance that defines you; it's the way you choose to handle it that defines you. You can choose to let the struggles and difficulties get the best of you by going about it on your terms, or you can turn your struggles and difficulties into opportunities to learn and grow by seeking God and going about it His way.

And the God of all grace, who called you to his eternal glory in Christ, after you have suffered a little while, will himself restore you and make you strong, firm and steadfast. **1 Peter 5:10**

If your day started off with some difficult situations or if you're struggling in any way at all today, you must remember that you are not alone. God is always in control, and He is aware of the difficulties and struggles you are facing, and He will guide you through them all. When you are facing a difficult situation or if you are struggling with someone or something, you must never give up but seek God wholeheartedly to give you strength, guidance, and direction. When you give it all to God He will give you patience and peace so that you will be able to think more clearly and stay focused on Him so that He can guide your path. When you give the steering wheel of your problems to God and allow Him to sit in the driver's seat, He will show you the best way to resolve all your difficulties and struggles.

LET'S PRAY: Dear Heavenly Father, today I know that you are able to see my affliction, my pain, my struggle, my suffering, and my tears, and I know you will have mercy on me. Lord, I know that You have prepared greatness ahead of me. I know that You will take me away from this point of struggle to Your dwelling place of blessing. Lord, I come to you before Your throne of mercy and grace asking that you will remove and deliver me from the difficult people and difficult situations I am facing in my life. Lord, Whatever Your Will for me is, let it be done in my life. Lord, I admit that I am weak, but Your strength is made perfect in my weakness. I admit that it's difficult, but I know that You will always see me through. Lord, my faith lies in You alone for You are the God of all flesh and there is nothing impossible for You. Lord, I ask that You give me the strength and courage to get up each time I fall, dust myself and move on because I know that You are leading me to greatness and I will get there in Your time. In the name of Your Son Jesus Christ, we pray, Amen.

There are a lot of people today who say well my life has been good and I have everything I need why do I need God? One important aspect that they don't realize is that God has been there all along and if it were not for God they would not have a single thing. Things might seem to be going great for them now, but one day they will need God more than they ever thought they needed Him. So for those of you who have had a good life and you seem to have everything you need, don't forget the most important need in your life, God! It's people like this that we need to reach out to and witness and minister to them.

APRIL 15

The Lord makes firm the steps of the one who delights in him; though he may stumble, he will not fall, for the Lord upholds him with his hand. **Psalm 37:23-24**

It might be difficult to understand, but God is making everything in your life come together perfectly, even though it looks as if some things in your life are falling apart. You must trust in God and know that He is revealing the perfect plan that He has created for your life in His time. Happiness is allowing yourself to be perfectly ok with what God has prepared for you, rather than wishing and worrying about what is not part of God's plan for you. When you do not stay focused on God and His plan for your life, you will not be able to see the light of His salvation. It's important that you not only understand but appreciate that God does everything according to His plans for you because only He knows what is best for you. The more you show God patience and appreciation for what He has done, the more He will bless you.

LET'S PRAY: Dear Heavenly Father, I want to thank You for the many amazing plans that You have for me. Lord, I am grateful for the bright future that You have prepared for me. Grant me the patience to wait as You lead me to it and reveal it to me in Your time. Lord, shine Your mighty light upon me and dispel any form of lack in me. May Your light surround me and bless me with abundance. Lord, I want nothing to interfere with the future You have prepared for me, so I ask You to completely set me free from my past that I may walk into the future with nothing holding me back. Lord, I ask You to fill me with joy and peace. By the power of Your Spirit may I be filled with hope. In the name of Your Son Jesus Christ, we pray, Amen.

It's my mission to help strengthen your day to day walk with God by praying with you and offering you words of inspiration, encouragement, and motivation. The Body of Christ is meant to grow together, work together and learn together. Daily Guidance from God is an avenue of encouragement and exhortation in your life. I want to inspire you, motivate you, guide you, and help you strengthen your walk with God every day anyway I can. I want you to know that I am always here for you and I want you to understand that you are never alone because God is always near.

Be completely humble and gentle; be patient, bearing with one another in love. 3 Make every effort to keep the unity of the Spirit through the bond of peace. **Ephesians 4:2-3**

In life because of our human nature, we will often make the relationships we have with people much harder than they have to be. God does not want your relationships to be difficult; He wants them to be pleasant, enjoyable, and meaningful. A Godly relationship will always be founded on honesty, trust, respect, and appreciation. A healthy relationship that is of God should always help your growth not hinder it. The difficulties start when God is no longer the center of the relationship. When you start to text more rather than talking face to face, your conversations will become impersonal, your feelings will become subliminal, and your words and emotions won't be seen as authentic. As a result, your trust and honesty will become waned, and it will cause insecurities and jealousy to become a way of living. Being hurt and left wondering will start to become natural and running away from life and hiding behind your phone will become the solution. God does not want running away to become the solution. He wants you to focus on Him, and he will direct you into the right relationships that will not only be healthy, but they will help you grow.

LET'S PRAY: Dear Heavenly Father, I need Your grace in my heart, my life, and in all my relationships. Lord, I know that every relationship that is Godly will help me, strengthen me and help me grow. Lord, I ask for you to fill my heart with your grace and guide me in every relationship in my life. No matter if it is a romantic relationship, a friendly relationship or a work relationship, I know you will use it to your benefit to build Your Kingdom. Lord, may Your peace, which surpasses all understanding, come into my life and in all my relationships to bring all believers together in unity. In the name of Your Son Jesus Christ, we pray, Amen.

God put it on my heart to ask you
these five questions today.

1. Are all your actions pleasing to God today?

2. Are your actions inspiring
someone to seek God today?

3. Are you following what God
commanded you to do today?

4. Are your actions fulfilling God's will today?

5. And if you are unable to answer yes to
all these questions today, will you be able to
answer yes to all these questions tomorrow?

Whoever pursues righteousness and kindness will find life, righteousness, and honor. **Proverbs 21:21**

God wants you to smile at people who look like they are having a rough day and He wants you to be kind to them. A smile, love, kindness, and respect are investments that will never fail. When you smile at someone and treat them with love, kindness, and respect, it will change the course of their day in a positive and encouraging way. When a person comes into the presence of God, there will always be an opportunity for a smile, love, kindness, and respect. God wants you to give to others, even if it's just a smile, not because you have too much, but because you understand there are so many others who feel like they have nothing at all. There are so many people out there who are sad and down because they have not experienced the presence of God in their life and what He can do for them. So today, smile at someone who seems down or sad, offer to share the word of God with them so that they will have a chance to see the light of God's salvation instead of only seeing the darkness of defeat.

LET'S PRAY: Dear Heavenly Father, I want to be kind, humble, polite, cheerful, grateful, and righteous. Lord, I want to please You in any way possible, and in every way. Lord, I know that You reward the kindness of every man. Lord, I ask you today to bless me with kindness, patience, gentleness, righteousness, and selflessness. Lord, help me make wise decisions especially when my choices directly or indirectly affect the lives of others. Lord, may I treat everybody with love, politeness, respect, tolerance, and kindness. May I never forget that all those who endeavor to be at peace with everybody have their prayers never hindered. Lord, renew my love for everybody, renew my patience in You, renew my delight for Your Word, and renew my willingness to share the light of your salvation. In the name of Your Son Jesus Christ, we pray, Amen.

APRIL 20

We don't know, see, or understand the purpose God has for the difficulties we face in this life. But I can promise you that God has a purpose for everything we face, and He knows what He is doing, and we must trust, obey and rely on Him at all times.

Oh, taste and see that the Lord is good; Blessed is the man who trusts in Him! Oh, fear the Lord, you His saints! There is no want to those who fear Him. **Psalm 34:8-9 (NKJV)**

The happiest and most successful people are kind, caring and always looking for ways to help others. These people are happy and successful because they have been blessed by God's grace for putting Him first and living their life according to His plan. They know that God's plan for their life is ultimately better than following their plan. The unhappiest and most unsuccessful people are still asking, "What's in it for me? How can I benefit? and how come I don't get any good breaks?" This is because they have been living life according to their plan and putting God and His plan for their life on the back burner. These types of people are lost, and they are traveling down the wrong path that will end up leading them to a dead end. As genuine, wholehearted Christians, we must reach out to these people and offer them a way to see the light of God's salvation. They may resist at first and want to remain living their life in the darkness. Don't give up on them, keep trying to show them the greatness of God's light even if it takes you several attempts. Ultimately, your greatest successes in life will not be measured by how much you have accomplished, but by how many people you have helped see the light of God and introduced them to His righteous ways.

LET'S PRAY: Dear Heavenly Father, I ask You to make perfect Your strength in my weakness. I ask You to bless me with confidence and courage. I ask You to uproot any source of fear and dismay within me. Lord, I ask You to be with me at all times, blessing me in my lack, keeping me safe from danger, strengthening me to do all that You created me to do, and using me as an instrument of blessing to all those around me. I ask You to reward my faith, courage, confidence, and trust in You with abundant and unlimited blessings. In the name of Your Son Jesus Christ, we pray, Amen.

Don't sweat the small stuff and never let
the opinions of others stop you from doing
God's work. Respect those who respect you,
remove those who don't and pray for them.
Appreciate those who appreciate you, remove
those who don't and pray for them. Trust those
who have earned your trust, remove those
who cannot be trusted and pray for them.

Trust in the Lord with all your heart and lean not on your own understanding. In all your ways submit to him, and he will make your paths straight. **Proverbs 3:5-6**

Take a deep breath; it is going to be alright because God is in control. Everything might not be fixed today, but eventually, God will make all your paths straight in His time. There will be times when it seems like everything that could possibly go wrong is going wrong, but you must trust God and have faith in Him at all times. You might feel like you will be stuck in this rut forever, but you won't because God has amazing plans for you. The important thing is that you continue to seek God and rely on Him to give you strength to get past these difficult times. The sun might go behind the clouds at times, and you may get stuck in the middle of a huge thunderstorm now and then, but eventually, the sun will come out and shine brighter than ever before. Sometimes it's just a matter of us staying focused on God so that we can remain positive in order to see the sunshine break through the clouds again.

LET'S PRAY: Dear Heavenly Father, as I lean on Your understanding and acknowledge You in all that I do, I ask that You make my paths straight, blessed, and established. Lord, may I never forget that in Your time You will bless me with what I need to get past these difficult times I am facing. Lord, Your grace is a constant reminder every day that I must stay completely focused on You at all times to receive any blessings. Lord, may I always be reminded that You that is in me is greater than he that is in the world, and that You have overcome my troubles, and delivered me from them all. Lord, I know You are using these brief trials I face today to prepare me for an everlasting weight of glory beyond all measure and understanding. Lord, may I never walk by sight but only by faith in You so that I will not focus on what I can see but only what I can't see. May I never look at my problems that are temporal but focus on You who is eternal. In the name of Your Son Jesus Christ, we pray, Amen.

Old ways never open new doors. No man can open a door that God has shut, and no man can close a door God has opened. If God opens a door, it's for a reason according to His will. You must walk through the door God has opened without hesitation. Trust God he knows what He is doing, and He knows what is best for us. God is good all the time!

One who has unreliable friends soon comes to ruin, but there is a friend who sticks closer than a brother. **Proverbs 18:24**

When God places a true friend in your life, you will have four things in common: a strong love for the Lord, a soft, caring heart, a mind that is filled with positive thoughts and a soul that is always accepting and never judging. A strong love for the Lord is what initiates the connection between two people; a soft, caring heart is what maintains the connection. A positive mind will keep your thoughts and soul always accepting and never judging, and this is what will keep the friendship in tune with the Holy Spirit. If all these attributes are present in your friendships, you will know that these types of friendships are for real and of God. A friendship that has all these attributes will not only help both of you grow stronger in God. They will also stand the test of time; this type of friendship will also remain strong even with prolonged absence without wavering or faltering. God places these special people in your life for a reason, so appreciate them, respect them and enjoy the time you spend with them.

LET'S PRAY: Dear Heavenly Father, I seek you today and ask you only to allow true friends in my life who have You at the center of their life. Please allow only friends in my life that have a soft, caring heart, a mind that is filled with positive thoughts and a soul that is always accepting and never judging. Lord, please allow these types of friends to flow into my life and help me to create friendships that are in tune with the Holy Spirit. Last Lord, please allow the type of friendships that are for real and of God, and a friendship that has all these attributes will not only help both of you grow stronger in God, they will also stand the test of time, this type of friendship will also remain strong even with prolonged absence without wavering or faltering. Thank you for placing these types of people in my path. In the name of Your Son Jesus Christ, we pray, Amen.

APRIL 26

So often, people go to church on Sunday, and
they listen and hear what the pastor has to say,
but when they leave Church and walk out into the
world, they don't apply a single thing they learned
from their pastor. This results in them allowing
themselves to be defeated by worry, stress, and all
the difficulties of life without applying the Word
of God from the message that they listened to
from their pastor on Sunday. So instead of just
listening and hearing what your pastor says on
Sunday, apply it to your everyday life, and you
will notice how much of the stress, worry, and
difficult situations seem to vanish from your life.

And whatever you do, whether in word or deed, do it all in the name of the Lord Jesus, giving thanks to God the Father through him. **Colossians 3:17**

When God is not in the forefront of your mind, you will wake up stressed and worried about things only God can control. If you allow the busyness of phones ringing, emails and texts dinging, you will spend the whole day reacting to what you can't control, instead of letting God take control. You must take your hands off the steering wheel and put God in the driver's seat of your life. Take the first hour of your day and communicate with God trusting Him and allow Him to guide the rest of your day. Getting into a trusted routine like this can be extremely effective in helping you feel relaxed and at peace throughout the day. Instead of waking up worrying about things you can't control, get into the habit of seeking God fully. This will help reduce worry, anxiety, and stress, and therefore you will be more peaceful and mindful of God's presence.

LET'S PRAY: Dear Heavenly Father, I am still, and I know that You are God. I know that You know me better than I know myself, and before I was born, I was in Your Holy care. Through the valleys and the hills, I will be still and know that You are God. In the morning, evening, and night, I will be still and know that You are God. Even when I'm in a tunnel and fail to see the light, I will be still and know that You are God. Even when I'm troubled on every side and confused, I will be still and know that You are God and my Lord. I will always be still and know that You are God of all flesh and there is nothing impossible for You to do for me. In the name of Your Son Jesus Christ, we pray, Amen.

It's very easy to worry about what we can't control in the flesh, but in the spirit, we have nothing to worry about because God is in control of everything. It's very important to know and understand the difference.

As for the one who is weak in faith, welcome him, but not to quarrel over opinions. **Romans 14:1**

People will always think what they want to think. No matter what you say or do. Your words, thoughts or actions won't matter once they have formed their opinions. What is important to remember is that God's judgment is the only one that matters. If you are doing right in the sight of God, the opinions of others will not matter. When you're making important choices or big decisions always remember to seek God, He will always lead you to make the right choices or decisions that are in line with His plan for you. God has created you to serve a specific purpose in this life and what He thinks of you is what is important. Stay faithful to God and never be ashamed of what He is leading you to do in your heart.

LET'S PRAY: Dear Heavenly Father, help me not to let the opinions of others affect my life. May I make the right choices at all times, and the right decisions in everything that I do in my life to please You and glorify Your name. Lord, I need more wisdom that I may make wiser choices. I ask You to send forth Your Spirit to lead, teach, protect, strengthen, comfort, and bless me. Lord, I want my actions to bring You glory. I want my thoughts to be in agreement, alignment, and in accordance with Your Word and Will. Lord, forgive me for the times that my actions, words, or thoughts failed to glorify You. May I constantly find strength in You. Be my source of inspiration, my guidance, and my understanding. In the name of Your Son Jesus Christ, we pray, Amen.

Our true "heart" is not the physical organ in our chest that pumps the blood to all our organs. Our true "heart" is the spiritual core of our life; it is an organ of kindness, wisdom, knowledge, commitment, dedication, understanding, respect, honesty, and true feelings.

A spiritual heart is one that has grown to be patterned after the heart of God the Father, and Jesus Christ, in every aspect of one's relationships with God and man, because it is inspired, motivated, and powered by the leading and directing of God's Holy Spirit that was made available in a powerful way on the Day of Pentecost.

MAY

MAY 1

Whatever is good and perfect is a gift coming down to us from God our Father, who created all the lights in the heavens. He never changes or casts a shifting shadow.
James 1:17 (NLT)

Be thankful that you were not only able to wake up to the gift of another day but that you are able to see all God has created with your eyes, listen to all the sounds that God has created with your ears and smell all the scents that God has created with your nose. Your sight, your hearing and your sense of smell are all amazing gifts from God. Stop and think for one minute if you woke up today and you were unable to see, hear, or smell. Think about how much that would change your life and how you would go about your day. So many times, we take these special gifts for granted, and we don't ever stop to think about how precious these gifts truly are. If God did not grant you with one of these gifts, He wants you to appreciate the gifts he did give you. If you are unable to see or hear, God does not look at it as a disability; He looks at it as the ability for you to use the gifts you do have more efficiently. Today, God wants you to be grateful for not only the gift of this day but the gift of being able to see everything in this day, hear everything in this day and smell everything this day. God created this day, and He wants you to be able to fully enjoy it and experience all that this day has to offer.

LET'S PRAY: Dear Heavenly Father, I want to thank you for blessing me with the gift of this day. Lord, I am grateful to be able to experience every opportunity that this day has to offer. Lord, thank you for allowing me to see all You have created with my eyes. Lord, thank you for allowing me to hear all the sounds You have created with my ears, and Lord, I want to thank You for allowing me to smell all the scents You have created with my nose. Lord, I promise to never take The special gifts that you have given me for granted. Lord, thank you for the life You have given me and thank You for this beautiful day. In Jesus name, we pray, Amen.

God is our refuge and strength, an ever-present help in trouble. Therefore we will not fear, though the earth give way and the mountains fall into the heart of the sea, though its waters roar and foam and the mountains quake with their surging. Psalm 46:1-3 (NIV)

Despite the trials, tribulations, and unfortunate circumstances we all face in our daily lives we must still be grateful for what God has done for us. He knows about every single difficult situation and circumstance we face, He knows when we face them, and He knows why we face them. Always remember that everything that happens in your life happens for a reason, you may not know why, you may not like it, you may not understand it, or you may not agree with it. Every single day God makes good things come out of bad situations even if we don't know it or realize it. So, when you face a difficult situation instead of allowing yourself to get down, stop and realize that God is sovereign, He is almighty, and He is always working in your favor to bring light out of every dark situation. When you allow God to lead you through the tough situations in your life, you will not only come out of them stronger, but you will grow in your faith, and you will learn to trust in Him and know that His will and His purpose for everything you face is what is most important. So, in the challenging and dark times, look up to God so He can shine His light on you and show you His love, mercy, grace, and comfort.

But seek first the kingdom of God and His righteousness, and all these things shall be added to you. **Matthew 6:33 (NKJV)**

As children of God, we all have something to offer in building His Kingdom. He has given all of us special gifts, talents, and abilities for His purpose. God will use these special gifts, talents, and abilities in us to build His Kingdom in different ways according to our purpose. Whether you know it or not we are all in full-time ministry for God. You don't need to have a degree, a license or be ordained to be in full-time ministry and build up His Kingdom. The goal and purpose for all Christians should be to build and grow the kingdom of God on earth and help the lost and hopeless find God and find hope. He wants believers to seek unbelievers, He wants the faithful to seek the unfaithful, and He wants those who are hopeful to seek those who are hopeless. That is what building God's kingdom is all about. The kingdom of God exists everywhere and anywhere that Christians are gathered and worshipping together. As we come together as a united body of Christ pure in heart, and obeying all of God's commands, we can serve others with love, commitment, and dedication.

LET'S PRAY: Dear Heavenly Father, thank you for the precious gift of life and allowing mankind a chance to inherit Your kingdom. Lord, as I walk along the path of righteousness by doing what's right at all times, I ask that You bless me with Your grace that I may be able to stay along this path throughout my life. Lord, as I do that which You brought me to earth to do, may my heart never be troubled for I know that You've overcome the world. Lord, I ask that you guide me to bring Your word of truth to unbelievers, Your evident faithfulness to the unfaithful and Your light of hope to the hopeless. In the name of Your Son Jesus Christ, we pray, Amen.

Sometimes in life, you need to step back and pray about the situations you're facing and listen to God and what His will is for your life. God will answer in His time when you stop relying on what you want and what you think you need. You can't force something that you have no control of, and you can control something that you have no power over. God is in control of everything, and His Will shall be done over everything, and over everyone here on earth.

> And the God of all grace, who called you to his eternal glory in Christ, after you have suffered a little while, will himself restore you and make you strong, firm and steadfast. **1 Peter 5:10**

God does not allow you to live your life without any challenges and disruptions. Just as He does not allow you to go through life without losing someone you love, something you thought you needed, or something you thought was meant to be. God places trials and tribulations in your life to make you stronger and to prepare you for future opportunities that He has prepared for your life. Embrace these opportunities. Enter new relationships and new situations, knowing that God is with you and He is guiding you along the way. These new opportunities and relationships might feel like unfamiliar territory to you, but to God no territory is unfamiliar, and He has your future all planned out. Be ready for a blessing from God, be ready for His grace, and be ready to experience His will for your life.

LET'S PRAY: Dear Heavenly Father, I know that You are for me. I know that You always stand by my side, watching over me, protecting me, guiding me, teaching me, counseling me, fighting for me, going before me and making a way for me when there is none. Lord, even in trying moments when everything seems to be falling apart and going wrong all at one time, I will not lose hope because You will be my guiding light; reminding me that You are still with me, and everything will be alright. I need You in my life, working for my good, making a way for me, and creating opportunities around me. I need You, Lord, because I cannot do anything without You. Lord, I offer my life; myself, as a living sacrifice to You, use me as an instrument to bring Your glory. In the name of Your Son Jesus Christ, we pray, Amen.

When you are feeling down, weak, defeated, and unsure of what the future holds remember these two things. God is in control of everything, and His Will shall be done over everything, and over everyone here on earth.

> But grow in the grace and knowledge of our Lord and
> Savior Jesus Christ. To him be glory both now and forever.
> **2 Peter 3:18**

Everything God allows you to go through is meant to help you grow
spiritually. Even though it may seem like a waste of time in the flesh, it ends
up being one of the best things God ever put you through. Don't judge
this day before it unfolds; it is a gift from God so enjoy it and appreciate
it. Amazing things can and do happen when you have faith in God and
follow His plan. Each new day is a gift from God, each day you must find
at least one of these things: a sincere laugh, an act of kindness, a realization,
or a lesson that will lead you closer to God. If you follow His plan, He can
give you hope, peace, and prosperity.

LET'S PRAY: Dear Heavenly Father, I give You all the praise for who
I am, I glorify You for all that I have been through, I thank You for my
whole being; I ask You to use me to Your glory. I ask You to use me as an
instrument of greatness. I know that You want me to grow and prosper in
all that I do. I know that it delights You to see me grow in every aspect of
my life. Lord, bless me with Your wisdom, knowledge, and understanding
to make the right choices and decisions. I ask You to bless me with Your
favor and mercy that I may be completely established, both physically and
spiritually. Lord, as I hope in You, may Your mercy come upon me, remain
upon me, and bless me in all my endeavors. In the name of Your Son Jesus
Christ, we pray, Amen.

MAY 8

How strong you are in your faith will directly determine how you will handle difficult situations and circumstances in your life. When your faith is not strong, and you face difficult situations and circumstances it will be harder for you to overcome them and you will struggle. But when your faith is strong you know and understand that God is always with you and He will always help you through every situation and circumstance you face. The important words here are, trust, and have faith in God at all times. For those of you who are not strong in your faith right now, you must seek God so that He can help strengthen you so that you learn and grow from every difficult situation and circumstance you face in your life.

This is how love is made complete among us so that we
will have confidence on the day of judgment: In this world
we are like Jesus. There is no fear in love. But perfect love
drives out fear, because fear has to do with punishment.
The one who fears is not made perfect in love. We love
because he first loved us. **1 John 4:17-19**

God wants you to love yourself just the way you are, and He wants you
to accept who you are completely, just the way He created to you be. God
only wants you to make changes in your life as you see fit, not because you
think anyone else wants you to make changes, but because you feel in your
heart that God is telling you it's the right thing to do. These changes might
be a new job, a different relationship, or a different church, but you must
seek God, and He will guide you in the right direction. You should never
need to rely on anyone to be happy or to validate your self-worth because
God is all you need. God has created you to love Him first because He
is love and all love comes from Him. You will please God when you seek
Him and receive His love so that He can show you how to love yourself
enough to respect yourself and accept who He made you to be and realize
that He placed you on this earth for a reason.

LET'S PRAY: Dear Heavenly Father, Lord, I ask that You use Your love
to seal Your Word to my heart that Your Word may remain hidden in my
heart and may influence everything that I do, and every word that comes
out from my mouth. Lord, fill me completely with Your Holy Spirit. Fill
my heart with Your peace. Deposit Your love in my heart that everything
I do is out of Your love. Lord, speak directly to my heart, give me strength,
guidance, and direction for I am listening. I ask You to bless me with
Your wisdom. Lord, speak Your Word of promises to me for they liberate
me, strengthen me, bless me, restore me, and renew me. Lord, today, I
seek Your guidance. I ask to walk in Your light. I seek to bring glory to
You with all that I do. I seek to glorify You with my whole being. Reveal

to me all that I should do, and all that I shouldn't do. Advise me. Teach me. Speak to me, and I will listen. Call on me, and I will answer. Lord, I want to live a purposeful life, and I know that a life that is not focused on You is purposeless and fruitless. In the name of Your Son Jesus Christ, we pray, Amen.

Instead of being frustrated, irritated, and annoyed with your alarm clock and the fact that you had to wake up early today for work, church, or some other reason, be happy and grateful that God woke you up today and gave you the gift of another beautiful day. We often look at early mornings and alarm clocks as difficult and as a struggle. But instead, we need to look at them as an opportunity to start a fresh new day, to do something great or to accomplish a great task. When you wake up and start your day in a positive way your entire day will be filled with positive thoughts and actions. Remember, God woke you up today for a reason, so therefore He has a purpose for you to serve today.

MAY 11

So in everything, do to others what you would have them do to you, for this sums up the Law and the Prophets.
Matthew 7:12

God does not expect us to be perfect, but He does expect us to be honest and strive to make good choices and decisions. A mistake is an accident. Being dishonest and lying are not mistakes. They are intentional choices that are not of God. To live your life according to God's plan, you must stop hiding behind the words "mistake" and "sorry" and start living in the light of God's salvation. When you are honest with people, God will see it, and He will reward you for your honesty. As we all know God knows all and He sees all. So, ask yourself, is it worth it to be dishonest or lie to someone when you know that God will punish you for it? Your life will be much more enjoyable, and God will grant you many more gifts and blessings when you are honest.

LET'S PRAY: Dear Heavenly Father, I know that no one is perfect but you. I want to please You in everything that I do. I want to be honest and make good choices and decisions. I want to glorify You with all that I do. I want my words, actions, and thoughts to bring glory to Your Holy and mighty Name. Lord, may I never drawback in faith. May I never drawback in doing what's right. May I never drawback in serving You. May I never drawback in glorifying You in all that I do. Lord, may I live by faith and not by sight, and may You always find pleasure in me. In the name of Your Son Jesus Christ, we pray, Amen.

Be Blessed and always remember these words no matter where you are in life! "God's Will and Purpose" for your life will never take you to a place where the "Grace and Mercy of God" will not protect you.

I the Lord search the heart and examine the mind, to reward each person according to their conduct, according to what their deeds deserve. **Jeremiah 17:10**

God knows your heart, your intentions, your reasons and your thoughts. He knows your actions, your good deeds, and your kind acts and your needs. Don't ever worry about the opinions of others or what they think of you, your life, your choices, or decisions. The only opinion that matters is God's because He knows you better than anyone because He is our creator. God knows you from the inside out, and He knows every detail of your life. People will form opinions based on what they hear and what they see, but these opinions are meaningless and empty. Stay focused on God and the plans He has for your life and know that only His opinion of you is the only one that matters in the end.

LET'S PRAY: Dear Heavenly Father, I want to please You with the words I say, the actions I make, and the very thoughts of my mind. I want to please You with the desires of my heart, the content of my character, and the way I treat people around me. I want my everyday life to be an example of what a true Christian should be like. I want my daily life to glorify You. Lord, as I come forward to You today, making the desires of my heart known to You, I ask that You find delight in rewarding me for the diligent work of my hand. In the name of Your Son Jesus Christ, we pray, Amen.

MAY 14

**The Lord is my strength and my shield;
My heart trusted in Him, and I am helped;
Therefore my heart greatly rejoices, And with
my song I will praise Him. Psalm 28:7**

When you believe in God and have faith, you know that He is always in your heart and the strength He gives you on the inside is greater than any challenges you will ever face. When you find yourself in a difficult situation, you must always have faith and realize that God's strength is inside your heart and you need to rely on Him to get you through. That is what having faith is all about, knowing that God will make a way for you to get through a difficult situation even though you can't see any possible way.

And whatever you do, in word or deed, do everything in the name of the Lord Jesus, giving thanks to God the Father through him. **Colossians 3:17**

By putting the needs of others before your own needs, you will bring Glory to God. There are several ways that you can bring Glory to God when you do nice things for others you will not only bring Glory to God, you will feel better mentally and emotionally. Helping others can be in many different forms, it can be a random act of kindness, a polite gesture, or something as simple as holding the door for someone or letting someone go ahead of you in the line at the store. Regardless of how big or small, the deed is when you help someone, God will always see it, and He will recognize your efforts to help others. God will not only recognize the good deeds you do to help others, But He will also reward you for your efforts. It is important to help others not to be rewarded by God but more importantly to bring Glory to God.

LET'S PRAY: Dear Heavenly Father, I want to bring glory to You in every way that I can. Lord I will always put the needs of others before my own needs. Lord, I ask that You keep my heart filled with courtesy, kindness, and compassion. Lord, I know that You see every good deed that I do even when others may not notice. Lord, I want to do all things that are pleasing to You. Lord, I want to make a difference in as many lives as I can. Lord, I ask that You give me the courage to be able to help others when they need help. Lord, there are so many people in this world that do not know You, I ask that You guide me to find the people who need You the most. Lord, make me your worthy servant, lead me to places where people are hopeless and need hope. Lord, lead me to places where your work needs to be done. And Lord, lead me to places where your word needs to be heard loud and clear. In Jesus name, we pray, Amen.

I often have people ask me how to know what God's will is for their life? Here is the most profound and simple way I can explain how to find out what God's will is for your life.

Do you want to know what God's will for your life is and what your purpose is according to God? Just put yourself in a place where you are uncomfortable, inexperienced, vulnerable, and in a place where it seems impossible for you to succeed and speak to God and tell Him that you are willing to do whatever it is He wants you to do. God will not only show you what your purpose is, But He will also give you the strength, guidance, direction, and wisdom to fulfill His will for your life. God will reveal His will for your life once you are willing to do His will based on the true motives in your heart. And in the midst of God showing you what your purpose and what His will is He will give you many opportunities to learn and grow from these experiences.

MAY 17

This is what the Lord says your Redeemer, the Holy One of Israel: "I am the Lord your God, who teaches you what is best for you, who directs you in the way you should go. **Isaiah 48:17**

Just before you take your first step on the righteous journey that God is leading you on, people around you, even those who deeply care for you, will try to give you advice that might steer you from your Godly path. It's not because they have evil intentions. It's because they don't understand the big picture and what God is leading you to do, the plans He has for you, and the purpose He has for you on this earth. They don't understand that, but to you, the reward is living every aspect of your life for God so that you can receive the blessings He has for you. In order to receive these blessings, you must trust Him and have faith in Him and allow Him to direct the path of your life.

LET'S PRAY: Dear Heavenly Father, Lord, I commit my ways into Your able Hands. Straighten, establish, and bless my path. Lord, may I never cease to say thanks to You for all that I have already, and make my request known to You for all that I need. Lord, keep my feet from slipping away from the path of righteousness. Keep my feet rooted in Your Word. May Your Word be a lamp to my feet, leading me along the path of righteousness that blesses every man who walks uprightly with all good and perfect gifts. Lord, according to the power that works in me, direct my path that I may do the right things at the right time, be at the right place at the right time, and make the right decisions at the right time. Lord, guide me at all times to do what's right, that I may not destroy the good plans and future You have for me. In the name of Your Son Jesus Christ, we pray, Amen.

The fear of the Lord is the beginning of wisdom; all those who practice it have a good understanding. His praise endures forever. Psalm 111:10

God has the power to turn your wounds and worries into wisdom; you must allow Him to guide you. As a believer, you must accept what has happened and use it as learning lessons from God and learn and grow from them so that you can move forward and allow Him to open new doors and new opportunities in your life. God is always working in your life, and He knows everything you've experienced, and He will use tough situations to give you strength and guidance to deal with everything you have yet to experience. Once you allow God to take control of your life and you realize that His plan is the only way, only then will you be set free from difficult circumstances and unpleasant situations.

MAY 19

This is the day the Lord has made. We will rejoice and be glad in it. **Psalm 118:24 (NLT)**

So often you see God taking your family and friends home to rest in heaven without having a chance to say goodbye. You repeatedly take life for granted without even realizing how amazing this life is and how much you should appreciate every single day. God wants you to understand that every day He grants you in this life is a special blessing and the time He gives you on this earth is a precious gift that you must spend wisely. Every day when you wake up, you need to not only thank God for the gift of another day you need to be thankful and appreciate all the people in your life who received the gift of another day with you. Instead of worrying and stressing about things that won't even matter tomorrow because they are pointless, enjoy this day that God has made and appreciate the fact that you are still alive and able to experience all of God's great creations. Your days here on earth are numbered, and God knows the plan for your life, and He knows exactly when your last day will come. So, enjoy every aspect of this day and appreciate everything you experience and every person you spend time with today because you might not have the gift of waking up to another day tomorrow.

LET'S PRAY: Dear Heavenly Father, I promise that I will appreciate every day that You grant me and I will show You how grateful I am for the gift of each day by spending my time wisely and bringing glory to You in everything I do. Lord, every day when I wake up the first thing I will do is thank You for the gift of a new day. Lord, thank you for all the amazing people you have placed in my life, I know there is a reason for every person that You place in my life. Lord, I know that You bring your children home with you for a reason in Your time and according to Your marvelous plan. Lord, when You bring people home, it may be unexpected to us, but it is never unexpected to You because You know when it's time to bring Your children home. Lord, I know that I often take people in my life for granted, so I ask You today to give me strength and courage to make sure I spend time with those who matter most. Lord, when I woke up this morning, I did not know what was in store for this day, but you knew everything that would take place today because this is a day that You have made. In Jesus name, we pray, Amen.

As most of us think of GPS as a helpful way to direct us to places we want to go. I think of GPS as a different way of helping direct and Guide us down the path that we need to go according to God's plan. GPS - God Provided Service.

Give thanks in all circumstances; for this is God's will for you in Christ Jesus. **1 Thessalonians 5:18**

Even when you feel like you are struggling, you must remember that God is in control and He wants you to realize that you have so much to be grateful for. Stop and think for a minute, what if you woke up today with only the things you were blessed with yesterday? We often forget that happiness doesn't come because of God giving us something we don't have, but of appreciating everything that He has already given us. Stress will consume your life when you worry more about things on your own rather than being grateful what God has provided for you. Happiness will thrive in your life when you are grateful for what God has given you rather than worrying about things you have no control of. You can bring Glory to God for all He has given you by showing Him that you are thankful for everything He has done in your life.

LET'S PRAY: Dear Heavenly Father, I want to thank You for yet another day and for giving me the gift of life. Many were alive yesterday but didn't see today, and I want to thank You for finding me worthy to be part of today. I know that Your will doesn't take Your children to a place where Your grace will not protect them. Lord, from today, I promise to never lean on my understanding, but on Yours. I promise to use all that I do to glorify You. Lord, may I wake up each day stronger and more courageous. May I never worry about what the future holds for me because I know You are already there for me. In the name of Your Son Jesus Christ, we pray, Amen.

True love is not loving someone for the material possessions that they have or how much money they have. True love is a feeling; it can't be bought it can't only be felt and received. True love is not expressed in words but by actions. True love is loving someone for who they are not for what they have. True love is sacrificing your own needs for someone else. True love is loving someone in the good times and the bad times. God is love, and all love comes from God. In order to experience true love, God must be at the center of your marriage or relationship.

> However, I consider my life worth nothing to me; my only aim is to finish the race and complete the task the Lord Jesus has given me—the task of testifying to the good news of God's grace. **Acts 20:24**

Living the good life is when you allow every aspect of your life to be guided by the word of God. You can live the good life only when you allow Him to direct the path of your life in every way and every moment of every day. The good life that God has prepared and planned for you consists of the gifts that He gives to you daily. The simple pleasures in life that God has provided that make you happy, the compassionate deeds you perform to glorify His name, the personal goals you strive to achieve to honor Him, and the relationships He has created for you to enjoy. Being sincerely and truly thankful for all God has done in your life and having faith in Him and trusting Him is the best way to show Him appreciation for the blessings He has given you.

LET'S PRAY: Dear Heavenly Father, I want to share Your word with everyone. I want to tell them about Your love for them all. I want to make them aware that they have the keys to heaven and authority over the devil and his minions. I want to tell them that with You nothing is impossible and without You, they can do nothing. I want to tell them that Your strength is made perfect in their weakness and You give rest to those who are heavy laden. Lord, thank You for appointing me one of Your prophets. As I endeavor to spread the gospel wherever I go, guide my tongue, and bless me with the wisdom to speak. Lord, trust and I commit myself and my life into Your able Hands. Use me as an instrument to propagate Your good news to every corner of the earth. Lord, I believe in the gospel for it is good news that makes known Your love for us all. I take heed to Your Word for they are promises made to those who walk along the path of righteousness, and will be fulfilled in our lives. In the name of Your Son Jesus Christ, we pray, Amen.

MAY 24

The best medicine for your pain is the word of God. Get a dose today by opening your Bible. It will bring you comfort you when you are hurting.

And whatever you do, whether in word or deed, do it all in the name of the Lord Jesus, giving thanks to God the Father through him. **Colossians 3:17**

God has allowed you to have a whole lot to be grateful for. So, at the end of the day before you close your eyes, make sure you give thanks to Him for all the amazing things you have experienced, all the struggles you have triumphed through, and all the difficulties you have overcome. Your life is not perfect, your journey is not perfect, but God's plan for you is perfect, so smile and be happy with the life He has blessed you with. God created you to be one of a kind, that means your fingerprints and DNA are truly one of a kind. The gifts, talents, and abilities that God has given you are what makes you different from everyone else. God wants you to embrace your individuality, uniqueness, and originality. Self-worth comes from God because we are made in His image, the very image of God. We are fearfully and wonderfully made in God's image, and to Him, we are worthy of everything He has created us to be. So today, appreciate what it feels like to be you because you are amazing just the way God created you.

LET'S PRAY: Dear Heavenly Father, I am grateful for the gift of life You have blessed me with. I am grateful for all the things You have blessed me with. Lord, may I never forget the importance of giving thanks to You in every situation I face. Lord, I want to thank You for the many amazing plans that You have for my life. Lord, thank you for blessing me with courage in the time of struggle, thank you for blessing me with strength in time of difficulties, thank you for blessing me with wisdom in time of trouble. Lord, I know that You will never let any trial I face destroy me. I know that every trial I face You will transform into a triumph. Lord, I know that You will never make me a victim of troubles, but a victor. Lord, I know that You will fight all my battles for me and hold my peace. Lord, as I continue to pray every day, thank you for listening to me every day, answering my prayers, and delivering me from all my troubles. In the name of Your Son Jesus Christ, we pray, Amen.

God's not looking for a few of His children to do a lot; He's looking for all of His children to do something! As a child of God, He expects you to do your part. God has created you with unique skills, abilities, and gifts. Not only does God expect you to use these unique skills, abilities, and gifts to build His kingdom, He expects you to use them wholeheartedly and wisely to help others who are lost and hopeless.

> For my thoughts are not your thoughts, neither are your ways my ways, declares the Lord. "As the heavens are higher than the earth, so are my ways higher than your ways and my thoughts than your thoughts. **Isaiah 55:8-9**

God's Perspective is everything. When faced with long check-out lines, traffic jams, or waiting an hour past your appointment time, you have two choices. You can either get frustrated and enraged, or you can relax and view it as God's way of giving you a break from rushing through your busy day. Be sure to spend that time communicating with Him instead of worrying about keeping up with your busy schedule. Getting frustrated and enraged will only create stress and raise your blood pressure. God's way will raise your consciousness of His timing and His ways, and it will bring you peace and patience. You must always remember to look at everything in your life through God's Perspective instead of your own.

LET'S PRAY: Dear Heavenly Father, from this moment, I promise not to lean on my understanding but Yours. I ask You to bless me with a God-focused understanding that I may see things in Your divine perspective. I ask for the patience that I may wait on You with a good attitude. Lord, faith is seeing things through Your Heavenly perspective which is without limits and knows no bound. Lord, may I never have a fixed or planned time to pray. I will always realize that praying is the only means to communicate with You. May I enjoy the time when I am able to talk to You. Lord, may I always be reminded that prayer is a means of communication between You and I and that I often want to give thanks to You with all that You have blessed me with that You may be motivated to bless me with more. In the name of Your Son Jesus Christ, we pray, Amen.

You must trust in God, His timing and His plan even when others have given you reasons not to trust them. When you trust God, He will put the right people in your life who will always be honest with you so that you will never have a reason to worry. As long as you seek God and trust Him in every situation, He will remove those who are not trustworthy, and He will give you peace.

Trust in the Lord with all your heart and lean not on your own understanding; in all your ways submit to him, and he will make your paths straight. **Proverbs 3:5**

When you feel something that God places in your heart, you feel it for a reason because it's real to you, so you must act on it without hesitation. Always remember that nothing anyone says has the power to invalidate the feelings God has placed in your heart. No one else lives in your body, or sees life through your eyes, and no one else has lived through the exact experiences that God has placed in your life. Therefore, no one else has the right to dictate or judge how you feel based on what God has placed in your heart. What you feel in your heart is important because those feelings come from God. Don't ever let anyone lead you to believe anything other than what God has placed in your heart.

LET'S PRAY: Dear Heavenly Father, I want to please You with the desires of my heart, the content of my character, and the way I treat people around me. Lord, purify my heart and my thoughts towards others and myself. May I never be double-minded but seek Your Will in everything that I do. Lord, may I never judge that I may not be judged. May I never condemn that I may not be condemned. Lord, I believe in You. I believe without a doubt that You are able to do all that I ask for in prayer. Lord, I know that with You everything and anything is possible. I know that in all things You work for the good of all those who believe in You and have been called according to Your purpose. Lord, I invite You to dwell in me as Your Word dwells in my heart. Lord, may all that I do be done with You, under Your light, according to Your Will, in a way that pleases You. In the name of Your Son Jesus Christ, we pray, Amen.

**Judge not, and you shall not be judged.
Condemn not, and you shall not be condemned.
Forgive, and you will be forgiven. Luke 6:37**

Do not allow those who try to judge you and condemn you for your works and your actions to build God's Kingdom and Glorify His name. When someone judges you based on your opinion or your beliefs just because it does not align with their opinion or their beliefs it only shows their lack of integrity, truthfulness, and honor. You cannot bring glory to God or His Kingdom by judging, or dishonoring others, these types of actions are very displeasing to God. Anyone who is Christian knows that it is not our place to judge others, especially when someone judges another person's faith or if they are a Christian or not. All we can do when someone judges us in this way is to do what God would expect us to do, pray for them and pray often.

> He answered, Love the Lord your God with all your heart and with all your soul and with all your strength and with all your mind; and, Love your neighbor as yourself.
> **Luke 10:27**

As Christians we love God for the feelings He puts in our heart and the thoughts that he places in our mind because we can't see Him. We should use this as an example when we love a person. Stop and think for a minute of you were blind and you fell in love with someone. You would ultimately fall in love with that person for the things that matter the most. You would not fall in love with them for how beautiful or handsome they are; you would fall in love with them for their heart, mind, and soul. It is important to fall in love with someone for what's on the inside because a person's heart, mind, and soul Will never change. Just as God's love for us will never change because He has unconditional love for all of us.

LET'S PRAY: Dear Heavenly Father, I seek you today and ask that you will always be the source of every feeling in my heart and every thought in my mind. Lord, I ask that you guide me not to judge people but to accept people for what is in their heart and soul. I pray that you will always keep me sincere and genuine and allow my feelings to come from my heart. And last Lord, I ask that you always allow my thoughts and feelings to not be pretentious according to your ways. In the name of Your Son Jesus Christ, we pray, Amen.

JUNE

JUNE 1

Just imagine for a minute how much of an impact we would make if we all did one nice random act of kindness for someone else each day. We can make such a huge difference just by doing something minimal for someone who might be having a difficult day. As Christians, it is our responsibility daily to allow others to see God and His word through us. You will make a significant impact by sharing a random bible verse, offering to pray for someone, or even tell someone that God loves them. You can be the light of God's salvation for someone who is walking in the darkness today.

JUNE 2

Yet God has made everything beautiful for its own time. He has planted eternity in the human heart, but even so, people cannot see the whole scope of God's work from beginning to end. **Ecclesiastes 3:11**

Although God does not create all relationships to last forever, He does create them for a reason. In God's sight, there are no failed relationships, because He places every person and every relationship in your life for a reason. It might be to teach you a lesson or to help you grow, but you must understand there is a purpose for every person He places in our path. The lessons you learn from each person or relationship will prepare you for what God has planned for you in the future. It is very important that you allow God to place the right people in your life according to His plan. God will often use people and relationships to build you up and make you stronger so that you will be able to handle the plans He has for you.

LET'S PRAY: Dear Heavenly Father, I ask that You fulfill my purpose on earth with Your great counsel. Establish me. Place people in my life who will counsel me to do what You have destined me to do. Lord, I want to see myself the way You see me, which is with a purpose. Lord, You have made everyone and everything beautiful in their time, and that includes me too. Lord, I know that I will be established in my time. Lord, renew me day-by-day, hour-by-hour, over and over again, that I will fulfill my purpose on earth, and motivate others to do the same. In the name of Your Son Jesus Christ, we pray, Amen.

JUNE 3

For too often people today only want God and the Bible in their lives when times get difficult. People today only want God and the Bible in their lives when it does not inconvenience them. And people today only want God and the Bible in their lives when it does not interrupt their plans for each day. Men and women, you must understand that God and the Bible must always come first above the difficulties you face. God and the Bible must always come first above your busy schedules and agendas. And God and the Bible must always come first above your plans and whatever else you do each day. God should be the first person you talk to after you wake up and the last person you talk to before you go to sleep. And the Bible should be the first thing you read after you wake up and the last thing you read before you go to bed. Is it too much to ask for you to take some time each day to talk to God and read His written word, after all, He has done for you? In a time when we need God in our lives more than ever before, He is the last person, and His written word is the last thing you should be neglecting in your daily life.

JUNE 4

Rejoice always, pray continually, give thanks in all circumstances; for this is God's will for you in Christ Jesus. **1 Thessalonians 5:16-18**

Your circumstances do not determine the path you take in life. The path you are meant to take is determined by God's plan for you. The situations you face in life are simply tests from God to make you grow and get you headed in the right direction. God does not want these situations to define you; instead He wants to use these situations to refine and mold your life according to His plan. We often struggle and create more problems in our life simply because we are not putting complete faith in God and following His plan for us. We often get impatient and become disappointed with the circumstances we face. We look at the situations he places in our lives as roadblocks instead of building blocks that will help us grow and prosper. God wants the best for all of His children, and He will reveal His greatness in everything he gives us. We need to be understanding and patient and realize that every circumstance and situation we face is for a reason according to His plan, not ours.

LET'S PRAY: Dear Heavenly Father, I ask You to draw nearer to me as I draw nearer to You every day with everything that I do. Lord, I call on You today that You may turn Your face to me and reveal Your greatness to me. Lord, may I always realize that You will raise me from the current situation I am in into greatness. I know that every day comes with its challenges, and I know that every challenge I face today has a message from You. Father, I ask that You fill me with Your joy no matter the circumstance of the day. May I rejoice in Your Sovereign way at all times. In the name of Your Son Jesus Christ, we pray, Amen.

JUNE 5

Often people don't rely on their faith nearly as much as they should. They don't trust in God and have hope in His promises and His will. Instead, they struggle day in and day out with the fact that life is difficult and every situation they face is impossible to overcome. All this does is cause stress, worry, anxiety, and fear. People who don't rely on their faith in God and have hope in His promises and His will have a negative mindset as a result following their ways instead of God's way. If you are struggling today, if you are facing a difficult situation today, or if you are stressed, worried, or fearful you must stop what you are doing and seek God immediately. Open your Bible, start praying, and put your faith, trust and hope in Him and His promises and you will see amazing things happen in your life.

JUNE 6

> Peace I leave with you; my peace I give you. I do not give to you as the world gives. Do not let your hearts be troubled and do not be afraid. **John 14:27**

God never wants us to feel miserable or stressed. If you are feeling this way, it means that you are not allowing God to handle your worries and your burdens. If you are feeling miserable or stressed, it's a sign that you have developed an unhealthy attachment to things you have no control over. So, stop trying to control these things and allow God to control every aspect of your life. You were never really in control of them anyway, but God was because He controls everything. Positive change will happen in your life only when you allow God to control the things in your life that you can't control. Surrender all things to God, and you will be able to experience peace and tranquility.

LET'S PRAY: Dear Heavenly Father, I know that You have given Your children the power to speak to their troubles. I know that You have given us the key to heaven to unlock the doors of blessing around us. I know that You have bestowed upon us the strength and authority to overcome all acts of the devil. Lord, today, I ask that You forgive me for the times I failed to realize this. Lord, with faith, I claim this same authority. Today, I speak to my mountains of trouble that they may be removed from around me and be cast back into the dark abyss where they come from. Lord, my heart is not troubled or in doubt because I believe that every Word that proceeds from Your righteous mouth are promises and that they will all be fulfilled in my life. In the name of Your Son Jesus Christ, we pray, Amen.

God will never call you to do something that He has not already enabled and equipped you to do. God calls you to serve according to the gifts He has given you. Do you know what your gifts are? Do you know what the nine gifts of the spirit are and where to find them? You can find the nine gifts of the spirit in these three sections of the bible. Ephesians 4:7-16, Romans 12:6-8, and 1 Corinthians 12:8-10. Many of you already know what your Gifts of the spirit are and you are already using them to serve God and build His kingdom. But there are those of you who possess the gifts of the spirit, but you are not using those gifts to serve God and build His kingdom. Ask yourself today, am I using the gifts that God has given me and equipped me with to serve Him and build His kingdom?

> Do not conform to the pattern of this world, but be transformed by the renewing of your mind. Then you will be able to test and approve what God's will is—his good, pleasing and perfect will. **Romans 12:2**

You can't expect to live a long, fulfilling, enjoyable life if you refuse to accept God's will daily. God already has the plan for your life set in motion. It is up to you if you're going to allow God into your heart and allow Him to show you the right path to take. When you follow the path that God leads you down, not only will you faceless trials and tribulations, you will also receive His rich blessings of favor. In God's sight, trials and tribulations are His way of making us humble, teaching us a lesson and showing us discipline when we don't follow the right path according to His will.

LET'S PRAY: Dear Heavenly Father, I admit that I am weak, I admit that I can do nothing without You, You're the God of all flesh, and there is nothing too hard for You. I admit that I do not have the strength of my own to get through any trials and tribulations I might face, so I come to You in prayer because I know that You will answer me and deliver me. I know that You will never bring me this far to abandon me. I know that You will bring me through if I allow Your will to set place in my life. Lord, I ask You to bless me with the strength I need to go through this day. I do not worry about the next day. Your Word says that we should not worry about tomorrow because today has enough troubles of its own. So, I ask that You give me the strength that I need to go through the day. In the name of Your Son Jesus Christ, we pray, Amen.

Today, choose to look above any negativity in your life. Instead, choose to react positively towards any negative words, actions or situations. You may not be able to control what is said to you and what is done to you, but you can control how you react to it. You must always remember to react positively and take the high road in any negative situation that you face. Stay focused on God, and He will guide you through the negative circumstances and help you see only positive outcomes.

JUNE 10

Always give thanks for all things to God the Father in the name of our Lord Jesus Christ. **Ephesians 5:20**

Be grateful for the special people in your life, the people who love you, and who care for you. They are precious gifts from God, so make sure you treat them with respect, care, and appreciation. You'll never know how much they mean to you until the day they're no longer beside you. God always places people in our lives for a reason, sometimes it's for a short period of time, other times it is for longer. Regardless of how long God keeps someone in your life, always enjoy every minute of time you have with them and try to make the best of the time you have together with someone.

LET'S PRAY: Dear Heavenly Father, thank you for the people you have placed in my life. I know that every single person is in my life to serve a purpose. Lord, I will always treat every human being with respect, appreciation, and love. I know that you will place people in my life to serve a purpose and for a reason. Lord God, I am grateful. I come to You with a thankful heart. I ask You to bless me with a generous and kind heart that I may bless others around me with what You have blessed me with. May I never be selfish with what You have blessed me with, rather, may I share it with Your love. Lord, May I be quick to help those who are in need, that You may help me when I'm in need. May I never hold back in helping others. In the name of Your Son Jesus Christ, we pray, Amen.

JUNE 11

The resolution to the problems you face with others should not always have to result in you being the only person taking action. However, some people will refuse to work toward resolving problems by taking action. This is where God can help when you face issues with others who are unwilling to take action. In these type of situations, you must pray for these people and rely on God to give you the strength to take the high road. You must take the high when you face difficult situations in life. It's not always easy to do the right thing, but at the end of the day, it will be well worth it. Taking the high road will require, dedication and commitment and it will be more work but the lessons you will learn will be well worth the effort.

> Do nothing out of selfish ambition or vain conceit. Rather, in humility value others above yourselves, not looking to your own interests but each of you to the interests of the others. In your relationships with one another, have the same mindset as Christ Jesus. **Philippians 2:3-5**

When you make sacrifices for people, you love it is remarkable in every way, and it shows them how much you truly love them. The sacrifices that Jesus Christ made on the cross for all of us shows us His everlasting love. Making sacrifices is not easy, but it is something that we all must do when we love someone. From Jesus, we learned that putting other people's needs before our own needs is what God wants us to do because it shows that we are selfless and caring. What have you given up or sacrificed for someone you love? Have they shown you appreciation and respect for what you have sacrificed for them? Therefore, we should show respect and appreciation to Jesus for all of the sacrifices He made for us. He died on the cross so that we could be forgiven of our sins and have everlasting life through Him.

LET'S PRAY: Dear Heavenly Father, I ask you to allow me to be selfless and make sacrifices for those who I love. Lord, I want to be able to put the needs of others before my own needs, Lord, please put the goodness in my heart to be able to make these sacrifices daily. I ask for strength, courage, and guidance from you to lead me in a selfless way. Last, I would like to ask that you allow those who I love and respect to show that same amount of love and respect to me. Thank you for this precious day, In the name of Your Son Jesus Christ we pray, Amen.

As a human being I know I am not perfect, I will make mistakes, bad choices and wrong decisions on a daily basis. Thankfully we have an awesome God who loves us unconditionally and forgives us and still gives a chance to start over every single day. Just because you make a mistake, a bad choice or a wrong decision does not give anyone the right to criticize you or give you a hard time about your actions. God will always love you unconditionally, He will forgive you, and He will give you a chance to start over even when others cannot.

> But if you harbor bitter envy and selfish ambition in your hearts, do not boast about it or deny the truth. Such "wisdom" does not come down from heaven but is earthly, unspiritual, demonic. For where you have envy and selfish ambition, there you find disorder and every evil practice.
> **James 3:14-16**

God does not want you to be jealous of others. Instead, God wants you to focus on Him and all that He has placed in your life instead of being jealous. You must realize that jealousy is the art of counting the blessings that God has granted someone else instead of your own. God wants you to be grateful for all the blessings He has placed in your life and all the future blessing that are yet to come. God did not create your life to compete with anyone, and He does not want you to compare your journey with everyone else's. God has specifically created Your journey for you to be traveled with enjoyment and fulfillment, not be in competition with anyone else. Jealousy will only hinder your journey and lead to negative and hurtful thoughts. When you stay focused on God completely and seek Him wholeheartedly you won't feel the need to be jealous, instead, He will remind you of all the blessings you should be thankful for, and He will show you how to appreciate the journey you are traveling.

LET'S PRAY: Dear Heavenly Father, today, I denounce any jealousy that is within me. Lord, I denounce jealousy today because I know that it's not of You, and not from You. Lord, may I be always satisfied, and never jealous of anyone. Lord, may I never be covetous with my desires. May I never desire to covet what belongs to another. Lord, may all my communications be positive. May all that I say and do be honest and pleasing to You. May all my thoughts be pure. May all my desires be humble and of good. May I never be greedy, envious, or jealous. May I rather be generous, humble, and kind. Lord, today, I make You my Trust, my Refuge, my Stronghold, my Fortress, my Buckler, my Shield, my Provider, my Protector, my Healer, and my Strengthener. Lord, as I turn my face toward the path that leads to You, keep my feet from slipping away from the path of righteousness that I may come to You. In the name of Your Son Jesus Christ, we pray, Amen.

Life is a continuous journey, don't ever stop listening to Jesus, don't ever stop praying to Jesus, and don't ever stop following Jesus. An essential part of your faith is to allow Jesus to direct your path, guide your steps, encourage you in every circumstance, and strengthen you in every situation. No matter what you are facing today, you must keep moving, growing, learning and making progress. No matter how busy your schedule is, you must make time to read your Bible, go to church, pray, spend time with your family, your children, and your friends.

JUNE 16

Trust in the Lord with all your heart and lean not on your own understanding; in all your ways submit to him, and he will make your paths straight. **Proverbs 3:5-6**

Instead of pushing so hard to make your life happen, relax and allow God's plan for your life come to pass so that you can enjoy every moment of it. Instead of trying to control your life when you have no control of it, surrender to God completely and wholeheartedly so that He can reveal His amazing plan for you. Instead of stressing out and worrying as you try to figure out a solution to all your problems, allow God to show you a solution to every problem you face in His perfect timing. When you try to force things to happen in your time you are interfering with the plan that God has established for you according to His will. You must realize that your life will be much more enjoyable and stress-free when you follow God's plan and not your plan.

LET'S PRAY: Dear Heavenly Father, today I give myself to You. I surrender my whole being to You. I want to be used by You for Your honor and Your glory. Lord, I offer my pain, my joy, my lack, my plenty, my inabilities, my abilities, my cry, and my thanks to You. Lord, I ask You to use me for righteous purposes. Use me as You please. Use me to win souls for You. Use me to share Your Word to as many as possible. Use me to bring Your Word, peace, and joy into the hearts of many. Lord, use me as an instrument to fulfill Your purposes and to spread your word and do your work here on earth. Lord, today I cast all my worries, anxieties, and cares upon You because You care. Lord, may I never worry but surrender everything to You because with You I can do everything. May Your Words dwell in my heart as I read the Bible, and may it influence every aspect of my life. Fuel me with Your Word and accomplish great things through me. In the name of Your Son Jesus Christ, we pray, Amen.

People who say mean and hurtful things and people who cause destruction and chaos in your life are being controlled by the devil. You won't ever have to worry about being treated like this by a child of God who is focused on God 100% and living their life for Him every day. But a child of God who is not completely focused on God and living their life for Him every day will often fall prey to the devil's evil schemes. When this happens, the devil will control them and manipulate them resulting in mean and hurtful words and destructive and chaotic actions. It is imperative to pray every day for these type of people and pray hard so that God can purify and soften their heart and remove all the evil from within them.

JUNE 18

That you may walk worthy of the Lord, fully pleasing Him, being fruitful in every good work and increasing in the knowledge of God. **Colossians 1:10 (NKJV)**

Ask yourself today, are you right with God? Are your intentions right by God? Are your actions right by God? Are you living for God? Are you obedient to God? Are you following God's commandments? Are you willing and ready to surrender everything to God and allow His will to take priority in your life? These are questions you should be asking yourself daily. Everyday day that you wake up is another gift that God grants you. Every day that you wake up to see another day should be an incentive to not only thank God but to live right by Him, follow His commandments and allow His will to be done in your life. Don't take the gift of this day for granted. Don't put God on the back burner. Do not allow thoughts into your mind that are not of God and thoughts that are not pleasing to Him. Do not commit actions that are not of God and actions that are not pleasing to God. And do not speak words that are not of God and words that are not pleasing to Him. Make sure He is in the center of thoughts. Make sure He is in the center of words. Make sure He is at the center of your actions. And make sure He is at the center of your day and the center of your life.

LET'S PRAY: Dear Heavenly Father, throughout this day, may everything that I do bring You glory, and only You. May I never do anything for the glory of myself or anybody except You. I want my thanksgiving to be pleasing in Your sight. I want my songs of praise to be acceptable in Your sight. Lord, I seek all of You authentically, with a humble and receptive heart. I seek Your will in all that I do. I seek Your presence by doing what's right at all times. I seek Your comfort by making my actions, words and thoughts glorify You. Lord, I honor You, and I honor Your Name. May I be obedient to You at all times. Give me the grace and strength to always keep Your commandments. I want to lean on Your wisdom, and I want to follow

Your instruction. Lord, I want to increase in wisdom and understanding. Lord, send Your Spirit to me today that it may fill me completely with Your wisdom that I may act wisely, and do things just the way You want me to do. Lord, I invite You to walk with me, teach me, guide me, and counsel me. I invite You to dwell in me as Your Word dwells in my heart. May all that I do be done with You, under Your light, according to Your Will, in a way that pleases You. Lord, give me the grace to keep my heart free from unrighteousness that I may be pure in my words, actions, and thoughts. In the name of Your Son Jesus Christ, we pray, Amen.

Even though you may face many trials for a little while if you remain faithful and trust God you will face very few trials for a long while. You must always remember to remain obedient to God and steadfast with patience while He eliminates your difficulties.

The fear of the Lord is the beginning of wisdom; all those who practice it have a good understanding. His praise endures forever. **Psalm 111:10**

God has the power to turn your wounds and worries into wisdom; you must allow Him to guide you. As a believer, you must accept what has happened and use it as a learning lesson from God so that you can move forward and allow Him to open new doors and new opportunities in your life. God is always working in your life, and He knows everything you've experienced, and He will use tough situations to give you strength and guidance to deal with everything you have yet to experience. Once you allow God to take control of your life and you realize that His plan is the only way, only then will you be set free from difficult circumstances and unpleasant situations.

LET'S PRAY: Dear Heavenly Father, thank you for turning my wounds and worries into wisdom. Thank you for guiding me and allowing me to accept what happens in my life so that I can use it as a learning lesson from you. Lord, I am thankful for all the doors you have opened in my life and the amazing opportunities you have made possible in my life. Lord, I know that you have brought me through every difficult situation and unfathomable circumstance to strengthen me and make me more resilient against attacks from the enemy. Lord, I want you to take full control of my life so that your plan for my life can prevail. In the name of Your Son Jesus Christ, we pray, Amen.

You can show God love by loving people. You can bring glory to God by being kind and caring towards people. You can show God you are thankful for all He has done by respecting people and being honest with people. You can demonstrate to God that you are humble and selfless by putting the needs and necessities of others before your own needs. You can show God you are humble by giving up something you enjoy to someone who is less fortunate than you.

Do not be conformed to this world, but be transformed by the renewal of your mind, that by testing you may discern what is the will of God, what is good and acceptable and perfect. **Romans 12:2**

Allow God to help you to be mindful in tough times. Allow God to keep you calm when things go wrong. You may feel weak but believing in God will keep your spirit strong. There are two kinds of pain: pain that hurts and pain that changes you. When you let God lead your life, and you accept the changes you need to make instead of resisting it, you will find that both kinds of pain will help you grow. Even though change can be difficult if the change you need to make is part of God's plan you need to do it without hesitation. It may not be the change that you necessarily want to make, but rather it is a change that you need to make according to God's plan for your life.

LET'S PRAY: Dear Heavenly Father, I ask you today to give me the strength to be mindful in tough times and calm when things go wrong. I ask that when I feel weak that you will lift me up and keep my spirit strong with your love and grace. Lord, I know the changes that I need to make in my life, but I can't do it on my own. Lord, I need your strength, courage, and guidance to help me make these much-needed changes in my life according to your will. I need you to guide me every single day so that I am living the plan you have for my life. In the name of Your Son Jesus Christ, we pray, Amen.

God has put it on my heart just now to ask you this question. Regardless of your age, regardless of your gender, regardless of your nationality, regardless of how long you have been a Christian, regardless of how often you go to church, and regardless of how often you pray. How much time do you spend each day, each week, each month, and each year focusing on God by doing what He commands according to His will for your life?

I can do all things through Christ who strengthens me.
Philippians 4:13

You must always know in your heart that God's strength is greater than any trouble you will ever face. You must continue to rely on God to remain strong, positive and courageous through every struggle that you experience. Life is not to be endured it is to be lived to the fullest according to God's will for your life. God will place obstacles in your path for a reason, the more obstacles you overcome, the stronger you become. When you rely on God's strength and power He will help you get up when you fall down; as a result, you will be much stronger than someone who has never fallen down or struggled. You will never know how weak you are until relying on God's strength is the only choice you have. Stay focused on God, rely on Him at all times and He will give you will the strength to keep growing spiritually.

LET'S PRAY: Dear Heavenly Father, I come to You today, asking You to bless me with the strength to overcome every obstacle I face, wisdom to make wise decisions, and understanding to do the right things at the right time. Lord, I surrender all my ways to you, direct my path, establish the works of my hands, and make Your strength perfect in my weakness. Lord, transform my lack to plenty, my weakness to strength, my struggling to thriving. Lord, I know that You have prepared greatness ahead of me. I know that You will take me away from this point of struggle to Your dwelling place of blessing. Lord, I come into Your Presence before Your throne of grace with a humble heart asking You to deliver me from my troubles. Lord, I want to thank you for all the amazing things to have done in my life. In the name of Your Son Jesus Christ, we pray, Amen.

Have you ever thought or felt that someone didn't have the skills, knowledge, or capability to do a job or a task? It's not always our responsibility to determine if someone is qualified for a job or if they have the necessary skills and abilities. God equips his children with specific skills, abilities, and capabilities for a reason to do his work in His time according to His will. So today, instead of discrediting someone in your own opinion, look at them and see their skills knowledge or capabilities through God's eyes and allow Him to guide your thoughts and actions towards them.

JUNE 26

Let nothing be done through selfish ambition or conceit, but in lowliness of mind let each esteem others better than himself. Let each of you look out not only for his own interests, but also for the interests of others. **Philippians 2:3-4 (NKJV)**

God expects you to put the needs of others before your own needs. Stop and think about how Jesus put our needs ahead of His own by sacrificing His life for all of us so that we could be saved through Him. Instead of going through this day thinking about what you want or what you need, think about what those who are less fortunate. Think about how good it will feel to help someone out who needs help today. Some people are disabled, mentally and physically ill, and those who are up in age that need help. God will reward you for the deed of helping others, but don't do it just for the reward, do it out of the kindness of your heart. God knows all your intentions, so make sure your actions are of good intentions.

LET'S PRAY: Dear Heavenly Father, may I be selfless in my actions, and not always concerned about myself alone. Give me the zeal to always share unselfishly with others around me. May I share the little I have that I may be blessed more and more each time I let go of something I have to someone who needs it more than I do. Lord, I ask You to bless me with a generous and kind heart that I may bless others around me with what You have blessed me with. May I never be selfish with what You have blessed me with, rather, may I share it with Your love. Lord, may I treat everybody with compassion. May I be quick to help those who are in need, that You may help me when I'm in need. Lord, May I never hold back in helping others. May I see the importance of praying for others just as I pray for myself. May I never forget that there are many people out there who are in need more than I am. May I never be selfish with my thoughts that I do not put others into consideration. In every decision that I make, may I put others first before myself. In the name of Your Son Jesus Christ, we pray, Amen.

If we would make decisions based on what we feel in our heart instead of what we see with our eyes our choices and decisions would be much better and much more pure. So, from this day forward, I ask that you join me in seeking what God is putting in your heart every day and make your decisions based on what God is allowing you to feel in our heart rather than what you see with your eyes in the world we live in today.

JUNE 28

> This service that you perform is not only supplying the needs of the Lord's people but is also overflowing in many expressions of thanks to God. Because of the service by which you have proved yourselves, others will praise God for the obedience that accompanies your confession of the gospel of Christ, and for your generosity in sharing with them and with everyone else. **2 Corinthians 9:12-13**

God wants us to live as loving, caring, compassionate, non-judgmental human beings. He gives us the ability to be understanding, sympathetic and perceptive so that when someone in our life is going through a difficult time, we can comfort them and show them love, adoration, and kindness. No matter if a family member, friend, coworker or neighbor is going through a difficult time, God expects us to step up and help them, care for them, pray for them, and inspire them. Remember in every smile there is beauty. In every heart there is love. In every mind there is wisdom. In every human being, there is a soul; there is life, there is worth, all these precious gifts come from God. The next time you see someone who is hurting or struggling look beyond the surface of what is causing them to hurt or struggle and do what God expects all of us to do, show them love, compassion, and understanding.

LET'S PRAY: Dear Heavenly Father, thank you for loving me and giving me the ability to be loving, caring, compassionate, and non-judgmental towards others. Lord, I feel blessed to be able to inspire others and comfort them when they are down. Lord, You are full of love, mercy, grace, and compassion. I know that it is not by my efforts what I feel in my heart, it is only through You who shows us unconditional love and grace. Lord, I ask that You continue to bless me with Your compassion and Your mercy. Fill me with it and allow me to share it with others who need it much more than I do. In the name of Your Son Jesus Christ, we pray, Amen.

Always believe in what you pray for, if you don't, how do you expect God to know that you trust Him and have 100% faith in Him?

> Dear friends, let us love one another, for love comes from God. Everyone who loves has been born of God and knows God. Whoever does not love does not know God, because God is love. This is how God showed his love among us: He sent his one and only Son into the world that we might live through him. This is love: not that we loved God, but that he loved us and sent his Son as an atoning sacrifice for our sins. **1 John 4:7-10**

God is love, He created it, and He not only shows us His unconditional love He commands us to love unconditionally. God's love empowers you, enables you, and strengthens you; it doesn't weaken you or debilitate you. God's love allows human beings to love others unconditionally through Him, by allowing us to express passion, kindness, and goodwill. When you seek God's love and allow Him to give you strength, guidance, and wisdom, His love will allow you to be able to share your love with someone special. God will allow you to love someone unconditionally only when you seek His love and allow Him to show you His unconditional love.

LET'S PRAY: Dear Heavenly Father, thank You for loving me so much. Thank You for loving me more than I love myself. Thank You for sending Your Son to save mankind from self-destruction. Thank You for without You mankind will never know what true and unconditional love is. Lord, thank You for the gift of life and the gift of salvation. Thank You for giving mankind a chance to inherit Your kingdom. Lord, hold my heart within Yours and enfold it with Your love. Renew my mind, body, and soul with Your love, joy, and strength so that I can love others. In the name of Your Son Jesus Christ, we pray, Amen.

JULY

JULY 1

Sit alone in silence with God for at least ten minutes every day. Use this time to talk to Him, and to think, plan, reflect, and dream. Creative and productive thinking flourish in solitude and silence. In quiet times, you can hear your thoughts, you can reach deep within yourself, and you can focus on mapping out the next logical, productive step in your life. Allow God to be involved in your quiet time and every moment of your life.

In everything you do, put God first, and he will direct you and crown your efforts with success. **Proverbs 3:6**

In order to do right by God, you must make Him your main priority every single day. All of your thoughts and actions throughout the day must be guided and facilitated by God. Any thoughts or actions that are not from God or not of God will result in unjust behavior that will not be pleasing to God. When you allow these types of thoughts and actions to take place, you are inviting the devil into your mind and allowing Him to conduct his evil activities which will place you in situations and circumstances that you will regret. You can see why God must be the main priority in your day and why all your thoughts and actions must be pleasing to Him. You can quickly get yourself into a bind when you choose to make things of this world a priority over God.

LET'S PRAY: Dear Heavenly Father, I want to please You with the words I say, the actions I make, and the very thoughts of my mind. I want to please You with the desires of my heart, the content of my character, and the way I treat people around me. I want my everyday life to be an example of what a true Christian should be like. I want my daily life to glorify You. Lord, I know that I cannot achieve these things without faith. I need an unwavering, non-dwindling, an ever-increasing faith in You. I need no place for doubt in my heart. Lord, I want to please You that You may find joy in listening to my prayers and answering me. Lord, as I come to You today, making the desires of my heart known to You, I ask that You find delight in rewarding me for the diligent work of my hand. Lord, I have chosen to abide by Your laws in the Bible and keep Your commandments and make sure that my words and actions are pleasing to You. In the name of Your Son Jesus Christ, we pray, Amen.

Before you can put your trust in people, you must first put your trust in God. When you keep your mind completely focused on God, your mindset will be positive, and your thoughts will be pure. You must refrain from allowing the devil to take your focus off God. Whenever the evil one tries to be the main focus in your mind and your thoughts, you must call out to God, and the devil will flee.

JULY 4

But if from there you seek the Lord your God, you will find him if you seek him with all your heart and with all your soul. **Deuteronomy 4:29**

In order to accomplish great things, you must not only seek God, but you must follow His commands and allow Him to lead your life according to His plan. You must believe in Him wholeheartedly and know that His way is the only way. When you seek God daily He will allow you to be a courageous and cheerful thinker. A positive motivator, a productive doer and a blessed servant who will always keep Him in the forefront of your mind at all times. Let the spirit of passion and possibility ignite a fire for God so deep within your soul that it will inspire you to do God's work every day. When you spread the word of God to those around you, it will give unbelievers a chance to know God and live in the light of His salvation.

LET'S PRAY: Dear Heavenly Father, I know that I often do not receive because I fail to ask. I know that I usually do not find what I seek for because I do not seek You. I know that I am often surrounded by closed doors because I fail to knock on the gates of heaven in prayer. Lord, today, I ask that You bless me completely. May I find happiness, joy, peace, and progress in Your presence. Open the gates of heaven unto me and pour blessings upon my hands that whatever I touch may be established. Lord, I call on You in prayer that You may answer me. I seek deliverance from all my troubles. I ask that You open my understanding to make wise decisions that will prosper me. In the name of Your Son Jesus Christ, we pray, Amen.

There are two ways of being rich: One is to have all you want and need according to the world, the other is to be satisfied with all you have and need according to God. Accept and appreciate the blessings God has granted you and all you have now, and you'll find more happiness in every moment you live. Joy and happiness come when you don't complain about the inconveniences and troubles you have and are thankful for the difficulties and problems that you don't have. You might need to battle through some difficult days, but you won't face these battles alone because God will be there beside you through them all. And remember, you might need to fight through some difficult days to learn the greatest lessons of your life. But either way, God will always be there for you and He will always be walking right alongside you no matter what you face.

JULY 6

Let no corrupting talk come out of your mouths, but only such as is good for building up, as fits the occasion, that it may give grace to those who hear. **Ephesians 4:29**

When negativity surrounds you, God wants you to remain positive. You will often find yourself in the middle of negative situations and circumstances in life, but God expects you to remain positive regardless of how bad a situation might seem. God wants you to smile when others try to bring you down. God wants you to keep your head up when others try to give you a reason to look down. This will allow you to remain at peace so that you focus on God and allow Him to lead you in the right direction. As you know, all the positive things come from God, and all the negative things come from the devil. You will have a positive attitude when you seek God. You will be able to smile from ear to ear When you seek God. You will be able to keep your head up and see life when you seek God. Don't ever let the devil steal an ounce of your happiness and joy, instead seek God completely at all times.

LET'S PRAY: Dear Heavenly Father, I ask that You bring me along the path of those who are wise and will draw me closer to You. I ask that You bring me in contact with those that will increase my wisdom and my understanding. I ask that You bring me in a company of those who will positively change my life. Lord, bless me, my family, my friends, my loved ones, and everybody that I meet, especially the ones who impacted positively in my life, with long life and prosperity, that we all may live to broadcast Your goodness in our lives. May my relationships, communication, activities, thoughts, and desires be free from negativity, discontentment, covetousness, and jealousy. Lord, may all my relationships draw me closer to You. In the name of Your Son Jesus Christ, we pray, Amen

Are you tithing 10% every week at
your local church? Do you know
why it is important to tithe?

The Bible tells us in Leviticus 27:30: "A
tenth of the produce of the land, whether
grain or fruit, is the Lord's, and is holy."

So often we struggle with giving the full 10% of
our weekly income back to the Lord. Sometimes
we feel as if we don't have enough money to
make it through the week if we tithe the full
10%. This is where a lot of us go wrong by
thinking this way. Tithing should not be an
option if you are a Christian and you dedicate
your life to God and His will. Regardless of what
you're going through you must have faith in God
and that means tithing faithfully every week.

Our mindsets in the flesh make us think in
the negative and that we are going to be short
on money by the end of the week if we tithe.
But if we trust God and if we are faithful, our
mindsets in the spirit will allow us to think

positive and that God will provide. The Old Testament teaches the principle of first fruits (Exodus 23:16; 34:22; Leviticus 2:12-14; 2 Chronicles 31:5). God expects you to give from your best crops, not from the leftovers.

JULY 8

> Do not be yoked together with unbelievers. For what do righteousness and wickedness have in common? Or what fellowship can light have with darkness? What harmony is there between Christ and Belial? Or what does a believer have in common with an unbeliever? **2 Corinthians 6:14-15**

As a Christian, the only way to find true love that is sincere and genuine is through God because He is love. A man must seek God, and He will reveal a woman that loves God more than him. A woman must seek God, and He will reveal a man that loves God more than her. This is the foundation of perfect love because it is facilitated by God Himself. In Hebrews 13:4 God tells us that marriage should be honored by all, and the marriage bed kept pure, for God will judge the adulterer and all the sexually immoral. God commands us to keep the marriage bed pure and not engage in sexual immorality before marriage. In this situation, we must always demonstrate self-control to bear the fruit of the Spirit. Only in this situation will you be able to experience honesty, truth, respect, and appreciation. When you allow God to be the foundation of any relationship two people will become equally yoked in God's love. God's love is eternal, God's love is unconditional, and God's love is omnipotent. You won't ever find love that is greater than God's love. And there is no greater relationship than one that is established by God and overflowing with His love.

LET'S PRAY: Dear Heavenly Father, you have displayed the best example of love and charity. You have loved us in the most genuine and sincere way – never boasting and never expecting anything in return. Let your unconditional love shine upon us and direct us in building the right relationships with others. Help us Lord to be Good-natured children of God. Lord, I cannot thank You enough for such a wonderful display of love. Lord, I am grateful that nothing in this world will ever separate me from the amazing love. In the name of Your Son Jesus Christ, we pray, Amen.

Take your focus off everyone and everything in this world and focus only on God so that you can see, hear, and feel His purpose and will for your life.

JULY 10

As you come to him, the living Stone—rejected by man but chosen by God and precious to him. **1 Peter 2:4**

God uses rejection to protect you from what's not meant to be. It doesn't mean you aren't good enough; it means that God has something better in store for you. It means God wants you to have more time to improve yourself, to grow, to be stronger spiritually and to be completely ready for what He has planned for you. When you are strong spiritually you will allow God to lead and guide every aspect of your life. The person who didn't call back after a date, the potential job that didn't pan out, or the business loan rejection letter are all signs that God has something better in store for your life. You must rely completely on God to give you the patience to wait for His plans and His timing. God has established great plans for your life, but you must allow Him to reveal the plans He has for you in His time. This means that you need to be patient and have faith that He has plans for that that are far beyond your expectations.

LET'S PRAY: Dear Heavenly Father, I want to thank You for finding delight in blessing me and using rejection to protect me. Lord, I want to thank You for the many amazing plans that You have for me. Lord, bless me with the strength, grace, and knowledge to accomplish your will, and as You do, keep me in Your land of provision and protection. Lord, I want to be found worthy to enter Your kingdom on the last day. Lord, I ask You to send Your Spirit to me today to teach me, guide me, and protect me. Lord, my plans are worthless without Your Will. I know that many are my plans, but it is Yours for me that will prevail. I know that without Your grace, all my plans amount to nothing. Lord, I admit that I am weak, and I have You, and You're a strong God. I admit that I can do nothing without You, and I have You, and You're the God of all flesh, and there is nothing too hard for You. In the name of Your Son Jesus Christ, we pray, Amen.

Being a wealthy, caring, and giving person is a mindset. Be sure you understand this. Give more to others, want less for yourself, and appreciate everything you have.

JULY 12

So God created mankind in his own image, in the image of God he created them; male and female he created them.
Genesis 1:27

God made you in His image. God made you to love. God made you to feel. God made you to strive. God made you to enjoy life. God placed you in this world for a reason, so put your heart into what you believe in and let God guide you and lead the way. If you choose to avoid God and His plan for your life, one thing's for certain; you will make it to the end of your days, feeling empty and unfulfilled. Don't waste a single day of your life; each day is a gift from God so make sure you make the most of it. When you allow God to lead your life and you do exactly what He is commanding you to do your life will be amazing and fulfilling. So today show some love, express how you feel, continue to strive and enjoy the life God has given you.

LET'S PRAY: Dear Heavenly Father, I am grateful for the gift of life You have blessed me with. I am grateful for all the things You have blessed me with. Lord, in the morning, I shall wake up to a beautiful day You have made and give thanks to You for letting me see another day. I shall offer a prayer of thanksgiving to You blessing Your Name for giving me the gift of life. At midday, I will come to You, asking You to bless me with the strength to move on, wisdom to make wise decisions, and understanding to do the right things at the right time. Lord, at night, before I go to bed, I shall come to You asking You to watch over me while I sleep, protect me from the devil, and keep me dwelling in Your comfort. In the name of Your Son Jesus Christ, we pray, Amen.

Part of trusting God's plan is trusting in His timing. He may not come when "you" want Him, But He will be there right on time when you need Him.

JULY 14

You make known to me the path of life; you will fill me with joy in your presence, with eternal pleasures at your right hand. **Psalm 16:11**

Your life is a courageous journey that was created by God. You cannot become who you want to be by continuing to do exactly what you've been doing. You will become who God created you to be by seeking Him daily and following His plan for your life according to His will. You must listen to your inner voice when God is whispering to you, and what He is guiding you to do, not the jumbled opinions of everyone else. God wants you to do what you know in your heart is right for you. God has created your path, and He will guide you down it, but it's your path and yours alone. Other people might be able to walk your path with you, but nobody can walk your path for you. God wants you to appreciate every single day of your life. There will be days when God will make things good to give you happiness. There will be days when God will make things difficult to give you experience. There will be days when God will allow you to struggle enough to teach you lessons. But you must always remember that everything that God places in the path of your journey is to help you not to hinder you.

LET'S PRAY: Dear Heavenly Father, Your Word is a lamp to my feet, guiding me in my journey along the path of righteousness. Lord, I ask that You aid me in this journey called life to do what's right. I ask that You send Your Holy Spirit to help me and guide me to do what's right at all times. Lord, May I live above sin, and stay so, that You may fulfill Your many wonderful promises to me. Lord, I ask You to stay with me every second of the way, guiding my path, and blessing me with divine inheritance. Lord, I have dedicated my life to follow You; and I will never turn back. I will always worship You in truth and spirit, and do everything to bring glory to Your name. Lord, may I set my heart on serving you by doing Your work to fulfill my purpose in this life. In the name of Your Son Jesus Christ, we pray, Amen.

Right now it may seem as if God isn't going to answer your prayer. It looks like God won't come through for you. But I dare you to keep walking by faith and not by sight. Don't let what you see in the natural stop you from believing in God in the supernatural. Stay focused on God, keep believing in God, keep trusting in God, and keep praying to God and He will do amazing things in your life.

Then I acknowledged my sin to you and did not cover up my iniquity. I said, "I will confess my transgressions to the Lord." And you forgave the guilt of my sin. Therefore let all the faithful pray to you while you may be found; surely the rising of the mighty waters will not reach them.
Psalm 32:5-6 (NIV)

It is not uncommon for someone who has fallen deeply into sin to face difficult trials and tribulations. Being disobedient to God, not following His commands, and allowing thoughts, words, and actions that are not pleasing to Him will only result in great struggles. When you put God on the back burner of your life, you are refusing to accept what He has already established for your life. When you don't have God in the forefront of your thoughts, and you refuse to acknowledge the need for His existence in your life, you are hanging yourself out to dry. The Good news is that God will always be there to rescue you in desperate times of need. But you must remember all he has done for you the next time you feel the need to put Him on the back burner and all the trouble you will face by not seeking Him and relying on Him every day of your life.

LET'S PRAY: Dear Heavenly Father, I confess my sins to You today. I ask for Your mercy upon me. Forgive me and hear my humble prayers. Receive my supplications, and shine Your mighty light of blessing upon me. Lord, give me the strength and the grace I may need to keep Your commandments. Lord, I know that I am a weary sinner. I know that I fail You daily and I fall short of Your expectation and Glory daily. I know that I am not always faithful, but I want to thank You for Your grace upon me. Lord, bless me with the strength and grace to be faithful. May I be worthy of Your acceptance. Through Your mercy and Grace may I be worthy of being blessed by You. Lord Jesus, I know that You came to this world not to condemn sinners but to save them from sin and clothe them with the garment of righteousness. Lord, today, I ask for Your forgiveness. In whatever way I have fallen short of Your glory, forgive me. Give me Your righteousness that every other thing may be added unto me. In the name of Your Son Jesus Christ, we pray, Amen.

The only way we can ever possibly get
what we want is by first allowing God to
give us what we need. If it's His will, then
it will be given to you in His time.

Therefore, I urge you, brothers and sisters, by the mercies of God, to present your bodies as a living sacrifice, holy and acceptable to God, which is your spiritual worship. Do not be conformed to this world, but be transformed by the renewal of your mind, that by testing you may discern what is the will of God, what is good and acceptable and perfect. **Romans 12:1-2**

Let things in your life be less than perfect and accept everything just the way it is. Enjoy your life and smile every chance you get, not because your life has been easy, perfect, or exactly as you had anticipated, but because you choose to be happy and grateful for all the good things God has done in your life. You must accept the fact that life is not perfect, that people are not perfect, and that you are not perfect. Only God is perfect, and His way is perfect, His word is flawless, and His promises prove to be true. You must always remember that things of this world will not reward perfection, but God will reward you for good deeds done and constant obedience in Him. It's ok to be imperfect in this imperfect world because God is perfect all the time and His plan for your life has been perfectly created.

LET'S PRAY: Dear Heavenly Father, I am grateful for the gift of life You have blessed me with. I am grateful for all the things You have blessed me with. Lord Jesus, You are the Way, the Truth, and the Life, and because of You, I will never be lost in this imperfect world. Lord, I offer my body to You as a living sacrifice, holy and pleasing to You. I worship You and acknowledge that you are perfect. Lord, bless me with the strength and grace to be faithful. May I be worthy of Your acceptance. Lord, thank You for not letting any good deed go unrewarded. This brings me comfort that I have a reward for all the good deeds I have done, and all the good things I will do in the future. May I never be reluctant to do good. May I never expect my reward from any man. May I always look up to You for my reward. May I always realize that You are the One who created me to do good things and that You who created me will reward me. In the name of Your Son Jesus Christ, we pray, Amen.

When you make God your #1 priority He will put amazing people in your life and He will do amazing things for you, but you must trust him 100%. You must believe that he is the almighty Redeemer and He can do the impossible. Are you struggling with things in life? Have you had a bunch of misfortunes? Have things seem to be going downhill in your relationship or marriage? Have you been struggling financially? If so do you have God #1 in your life? Do you spend time with Him and let him know you are struggling? When you put God # in your life, you will be amazed at how your life can turn around. A life lived in faith with God is a life well lived.

Be completely humble and gentle; be patient, bearing with one another in love. Make every effort to keep the unity of the Spirit through the bond of peace. **Ephesians 4:2-3**

God created long-term relationships and marriages to be enjoyable and amazing, but they are rarely easy and take a lot of work from both people. God wants you to understand that the hard times or difficult situations that you might face in your relationships happen for a reason, and that good can come out of them. Therefore, God must be at the center of the relationship so that He can facilitate and guide both of you. God can make good things come out of difficult situations so that you can learn and grow from them, but you must allow Him to lead the relationship fully and completely. Finding the willingness to view the challenges as an opportunity to allow God to work in your relationship will give you the energy and strength you need to continue to move forward and grow your relationship according to His plan.

LET'S PRAY: Dear Heavenly Father, today I ask You to come into our relationship, allow both of us to be understanding, caring and kind. Lord, I ask that You will allow both of us to forgive each other for any wrongdoing just like You have forgiven us. Lord, I ask You to lead our relationship and guide both of us to make good choices and decisions every day. Lord, allow us to enjoy every moment of every day that we spend together and appreciate each other wholeheartedly. Lord, allow us to love and respect each other from our heart at all times and in all situations. In Jesus name, we pray, Amen.

JULY 21

Please join me in prayer today for those who are disrespectful, unappreciative, selfish, judgmental, in love with money, worldly possessions and those who are addicted to alcohol and drugs. These people know who they are and God knows who they are and that they are being deceived, manipulated, and controlled by the devil. Pray with me today that these people would find God, seek Him at all times, and follow Him in every way. These people are lost and hopeless and desperately need God in their lives and a lot of prayers. In Jesus name, we pray, Amen.

Do not love sleep, lest you come to poverty; Open your eyes, and you will be satisfied with bread. **Proverbs 20:13 (NKJV)**

God expects you to rise early, and not sleep the day away. This is the day that the Lord has made, you can't accomplish what God expects of you today by sleeping all day and not rising early and going late to rest. At times you will need extended sleep because of certain circumstances that require much of your energy. But there is a big difference between extended sleep occasionally and sleeping most the day on a regular basis. God will always provide you with the strength you need to handle the tasks at hand so that you can make it through this day. But you must seek God and allow His plan for this day to prevail in your life. Scripture tells us that laziness will be the result of sleeping too much. God tells us in Proverbs 6:9-11: "How long will you lie there, you sluggard? When will you get up from your sleep? A little sleep, a little slumber, a little folding of the hands to rest and poverty will come on you like a thief and scarcity like an armed man." The Bible also teaches us that there is a time to sacrifice sleep for greater spiritual good. Jesus rose early to pray on a daily basis and even prayed all night on many occasions, recognizing that sometimes communion with God is more necessary for His children than physical rest. The night before Jesus' crucifixion, for example, He told Peter, James, and John to pray that they would "not enter into temptation." When they fell asleep instead, the Lord rebuked them and said there would be other times for sleep. Their abandonment of Jesus during His arrest and trial was a result of their choice to sleep rather than seek God. It is more important to spend time seeking God then waste time oversleeping, as God will give you appropriate times of rest and He will also give you enough strength even when you feel weak and weary, God will always come through and supply your needs.

LET'S PRAY: Dear Heavenly Father, I ask that you guide me and help me accomplish all that I am expected to do by rising early and going late to rest so that I can make the most of every day I am here on earth. May I never use Your faithfulness and provision as an excuse to be lazy. Lord, may I always realize that laziness is the brother of destruction and that a lazy man will have no bread to eat. I ask that You fill me with the strength to go about my daily work and renew my strength each passing day that I may be able to accomplish everything that You created me to do. Lord, May I be of sound mind, and positive energy. May I have a creative mind, and not a destructive one. May I build with my hand, and not destroy. Lord, bless my mind, body, and soul. In the name of Your Son Jesus Christ, we pray, Amen.

Having trust, hope, and faith in God is when you completely obey His every command even though it seems impossible to you. Nothing is impossible with God.

JULY 24

All praise to God, the Father of our Lord Jesus Christ, who has blessed us with every spiritual blessing in the heavenly realms because we are united with Christ. Even before he made the world, God loved us and chose us in Christ to be holy and without fault in his eyes. **Ephesians 1:3-4**

The life you live is ultimately the life you choose. But the life that you're meant to live is the life that God has planned for you. Most people want the life that is the easiest, living each day putting forth minimal effort and just doing enough to make it by. Living your life by doing as little as you can will not be rewarding and certainly will not be pleasing to God. He wants you to live your life honoring him, being honest with people, respecting people, appreciating people and doing good deeds. He wants you to use your God-given talents and abilities to accomplish great things in life. When you turn your focus to God the creator of the universe and live the life He has planned for you, not only will it be pleasing to Him, but He will reward you in ways you never thought were possible.

LET'S PRAY: Dear Heavenly Father, I want to thank you for the life you have planned for me here on earth and the sacrifices that you made for all of us so that we can have everlasting life in heaven. Lord, I ask today that every choice I make will be guided by you so that I can live a life full of your everlasting love. I ask that you lead me down that life path you have chosen for me so that I can please you in my daily walk. In Jesus name, we pray, Amen.

The most popular form of communication today is prayer. Prayer is the greatest wireless connection that there is or will ever be and it's FREE. No other service provider will never compare to the quality of prayer. It has unlimited minutes, unlimited messages, and guaranteed connection at any location. You will never get disconnected, experience a weak signal, or a dropped call, through prayer you got it all.

JULY 26

The Lord is my rock, my fortress and my deliverer; my God is my rock, in whom I take refuge, my shield and the horn of my salvation, my stronghold. **Psalm 18:2**

God will often allow you to struggle in order to realize that your true strength comes from Him. Until you are broken, weak and vulnerable, you won't know how much you must depend and rely on Him. Pain and heartache don't just show up in your life for no reason. It's a sign that something needs to change, God will often use this pain and heartache to help you grow. For as long as there is faith in God, there is hope; and if there is hope, there is joy in living life according to God's plans.

LET'S PRAY: Dear Heavenly Father, in my time of struggle You are my comforter, and in my time of weakness You are my strength. Lord, I know You will always have me in the palm of Your hand, comforting me, teaching me, leading me, and providing for me. Lord, I know that this is not possible unless I keep Your commandment and please You with all that I do, say, and think. Lord, I want everything that I do to be in agreement with Your will for me. Lord, May I prosper and not suffer, may I grow and not fall. May I have hope. In the name of Your Son Jesus Christ, we pray, Amen.

JULY 27

Has there ever been a time in your life when you realize the path you're currently on is not the path God has chosen for you? Do you feel deep down in your heart that God has better plans in store for you? Have you been feeling that way lately? You might not be on a bad path or doing bad things, but have you been feeling in your heart lately that your current circumstances could be better and more focused on God's will for you? Will it be easy to change your path according to God's will? Of course not, but do feel at this point in your life it is a necessary step? Nothing good comes easy, nothing well worth it will ever be unchallenging, and nothing that God calls you to do to better His kingdom will come without sacrifice. But to show God, you trust Him and that you have faith in Him, you must change your current path to the path God has established for you. We don't grow if we remain in what is comfortable. We grow when we become vulnerable to the unforeseen and uncomfortable circumstances called life. If you trust God and have faith in

Him, you must allow Him to guide you down the correct path according to His will even if it makes you uncomfortable. Do you have enough trust and faith in God that you will do whatever He is calling you to do no matter how challenging it might be or how uncomfortable or vulnerable you must become to do His will?

JULY 28

> Do not conform to the pattern of this world, but be transformed by the renewing of your mind. Then you will be able to test and approve what God's will is—his good, pleasing and perfect will. **Romans 12:2**

Life is too short not to live it the way God intended. Every morning when you wake up, you must realize that each new day is a gift from God and a chance to allow Him to transform your life. Every great accomplishment starts when you allow God to work on the inside and mold you into who He meant for you to be. When God speaks to you, and He commands you to do something, and you say, "I will" instead of "What if" you will unlock the most amazing blessings from God. He does not expect you to be perfect and do everything right all the time, but He does expect us to be obedient and do what he commands at all times.

LET'S PRAY: Dear Heavenly Father, God of provision, God of miracles, God of courage, and my God of hope. I ask You to transform my life and fill me with all Your joy, peace, and love until I overflow with Your blessing. Lord, I want to overflow with Your love that it may enter into the hearts of all those around me. I want to overflow with Your blessings that I may bless all those around me. Lord, I not only want my life to be filled with Your Holy Spirit. I want to overflow with the gifts of Your Holy Spirit. I want to be overwhelmed with the joy and peace that comes with believing in You. May my life abound completely in Your hope day by day through the power of Your Holy Spirit that rests upon my heart. In Jesus name, we pray, Amen.

I think all of us men, women, and
children need to be reminded of this:

In life, it's not about who has the best phone,
nicest car, or the biggest house. It's about living
your life according to your means and what you
can afford. If God wants you to have something,
He will provide a way for you to afford it. If
not, don't be upset, angry, or discouraged,
instead be humble and thankful for what you
do have. And always remember it's better to
give to someone who is in need than it is to
receive. The most important things in life are
priceless and can't be bought with money like
faith, time, love, hope, health, and family.

But God has chosen the foolish things of the world to put to shame the wise, and God has chosen the weak things of the world to put to shame the things which are mighty; and the base things of the world and the things which are despised God has chosen, and the things which are not, to bring to nothing the things that are. **1 Corinthians 1:27-28 (NKJV)**

Life is full of choices. God will give you plenty of opportunities to make good choices and decisions. But God can't make your choices for you; He can only inspire you and guide your thoughts according to His plan for your life. It's up to you if you decide to follow His plan or your plan. But remember, you will face difficult times when you make poor choices and decisions and when you do not follow God's plan. The good news is that God is always near you, and He will always forgive you and give you an opportunity to make things right. But you must seek God and ask Him for forgiveness for your actions, and you must be true and sincere. God will forgive you immediately after you seek Him and ask for forgiveness. When your actions prove your faithfulness to God He will know that you are true and sincere your words and deeds.

LET'S PRAY: Dear Heavenly Father, help me to know what Your will is for me in everything that I do. Lord, may I be at peace with everybody around me. May I make the right choices at all times, and the right decisions in everything that I do that my life may please and glorify You. Make me realize that I can do everything through You who strengthens me. Bless me with kindness, patience, gentleness, righteousness, and selflessness. Lord, help me make wise decisions especially when my decisions directly or indirectly affect the lives of others. Lord, today, I come before Your throne of grace asking for forgiveness for all my sins. Lord, I am deeply sorry for all the wrongs I have done, and all the rights I had the opportunity to do but failed to do them. Lord, I draw near to You with a sincere heart in full assurance of faith, knowing that You will draw near to me too. Lord, I come with an unclean heart, and I need You to cleanse me from all my sins and guilt. Lord, set my heart free from the guilt that I may move forward to the bright future You have prepared for me. Lord, wash away my sins with the blood of Your Son my Savior Jesus Christ that I may be completely free from the shackles of sin. In the name of Your Son Jesus Christ, we pray, Amen.

Live your life in this very moment, don't worry about what will happen an hour from now, a day from now, a week from now, or even a month from now. Don't worry about what might occur in the future or what circumstances or situation you might face good or bad. Enjoy every moment of your life in the now, not in the past or the future. You can't change the past, and only God knows the future. God knows the plans for your life, every minute and every single detail and He wants you to enjoy every single moment of life that you are given. Stay focused on God at all times, and He will keep your mind focused on this very moment so that you can enjoy it.

AUGUST

> I will give him the key to the house of David—the highest position in the royal court. When he opens doors, no one will be able to close them; when he closes doors, no one will be able to open them. **Isaiah 22:22 (NLT)**

God opens and closes doors based on His plan and what He wills for your life. We often look at a door that God closes as a bad or negative thing because we are only thinking about what is best for us according to our plan and not what is best for us according to God's plan. God will often open a door for a short period of time and then close it only to teach us something that we need to know. He does this so that we can learn from it and allow us to be prepared for the next door He will open. You can be assured that when God closes a door not only is there a reason for it but you can be certain that He will open another door that will lead you to a better place with more opportunity for growth, experience, knowledge, and capability. You must rely on your faith to understand that God knows what He is doing at all times. In the moment you might be asking yourself why is this happening? You might say to yourself; this was the perfect opportunity for me, why is God changing it now? God knows what's best for you; He knows what you need and when you need it. And He knows what will ultimately be best for you in the long run. You must rely on your faith and allow God to take control so that He can guide you down the path that will lead to the right door of opportunity for your life.

LET'S PRAY: Dear Heavenly Father, I know that You open and close doors based on Your plan and Your will for my life. Lord, I know that I often do not receive because I fail to ask. I know that I usually do not find what I seek for because I do not seek Your face. I know that I am often surrounded by closed doors because I fail to knock on the gates of heaven in prayer. Lord, make me realize today that when You close a door, it means that You are opening another door with more opportunity for growth, experience, knowledge, and capability. Lord, I know that You are currently working in my favor. Even when doors are opening and closing, I know that You are using each opportunity to put everything in their proper place. I do not want to be going in the wrong direction in life. I do not want to be where I should not. I want to be on the right path, which is the path of righteousness. I know that You deliver, bless, and protect the righteous. Lord, as I wait for You to manifest Your mighty will in my life, I will praise You in the hallway as I wait for You to open the right door of opportunity that will bless my life greatly. In the name of Your Son Jesus Christ, we pray, Amen.

Today and every day you need to have an attitude of gratitude, and you will experience peace, joy, and gratefulness.

AUGUST 3

> If you walk in My statutes and keep My commandments, and perform them, then I will give you rain in its season, the land shall yield its produce, and the trees of the field shall yield their fruit. **Leviticus 26:3-4 (NKJV)**

Live completely for God. Strive to keep His commands every day. Make sure your actions reflect obedience, glory, and praise to Him. When you follow God's commands, and your actions align in obedience to His word, you will bring Glory to His Holy Name. Every morning when you wake up you have two choices, you can follow God's plan or follow your plan for the day. If you choose to follow God's plan, you can be assured that your day will be filled with positive, delightful, and joyful moments. But if you choose to follow your plan, be prepared to run into problems which will lead to difficult trials and tribulations without God's help or guidance. In order to receive God's blessing, strength, guidance, and direction you must seek Him daily and live your life for Him and according to His plan, not yours. And in order to live your life completely for God, you must follow His commands, be obedient to His word, and bring Glory to His name. You must make these three things a priority in your everyday life in order to receive grace and salvation from God.

LET'S PRAY: Dear Heavenly Father, You are a just God. You give all that You have promised, and I want to thank You for Your goodness to me. Lord, not one word from You fails. All Your good promises made are always fulfilled. I ask You to be with me today. Never leave or forsake me, Father. I turn my heart to You, asking You to guide me that I may walk in all Your ways and keep all Your commandments. I commit my heart and my ways to You. As I endeavor to live by Your Words and obey Your commandments at all times, may Your beauty come upon me, and place You first in everything that I do. Lord, I want to walk along the path of righteousness and bliss, and not the path of worldliness and agony. Lord, I want my life to be in harmony with Your Word. I never want to be found wanting. I want to keep Your commandments at all times, especially when confronted by temptations. Lord, bless me with the strength to resist any form of temptation and when it's too much, create a way for me to escape. Lord, I commit all my ways, and days into Your Holy Care, use me for Your purpose and bless me exceedingly. In the name of Your Son Jesus Christ, we pray, Amen.

AUGUST 4

Nobody on this planet is perfect. Your integrity, dignity, and morality will show your Godliness.

Your words, thoughts, actions, and character are not to be judged by man but judged by God for the good works you do to glorify His name.

AUGUST 5

Repent therefore and be converted, that your sins may be blotted out, so that times of refreshing may come from the presence of the Lord, and that He may send Jesus Christ, who was preached to you before, whom heaven must receive until the times of restoration of all things, which God has spoken by the mouth of all His holy prophets since the world began. **Acts 3:19-21 (NKJV)**

The end times are near. Are you right with God? Are you ready to meet your creator? Are you prepared for your final home in heaven with God? These are questions we should all be asking ourselves today. Though Christ warned that no one but the Father knows the exact day and hour of His return, Scripture provides us with a vast amount of signs that illustrate the time is drawing near. Here are just some of the many signs in Scripture.

False Bible teachers of our day will have many followers, they will lead false doctrines of the Christian faith, they will be hungry for money and fancy material items, and they will be smooth and sly talkers. They will come as a wolf in sheep's clothing. They will appear to lead people to Christ, but the true motives in their heart will lead people away from Christ (2 Peter 2:1-3). It will be evident that people will fall into the ways of the world as there will be an increase in those who exercise homosexuality in the end days (2 Timothy 3:3). There will be a lack of food and resources. There will be a fatal epidemic of diseases. There will be many Earthquakes at all ends of the earth (Matthew 24:7). Anxiety and stress will saturate those who allow it to overtake them (2 Timothy 3:1). People will be disobedient to God and fail to live by the Ten Commandments as a moral code and as a result, people will steal, lie, commit adultery, and even kill. (Matthew 24:12). Nations will rise against nations and kingdoms against kingdoms (Matthew 24:6). There will be denying God's power in the way of a cold religious system that will be led by evildoers (2 Timothy 3:5). In the end times, the institution of marriage will be defiled, disobeyed and even forsaken by many (1 Timothy 4:3). In the Bible, we read that in the end time there will be false prophets, counterfeit ways of believing, and a wide array of deception across the land. These evildoers will lead many to sin, deception and wicked ways. So, ask yourself, are you right with God and are you ready for the return of His Son, Jesus Christ?

LET'S PRAY: Lord Jesus, I look forward to Your second coming because I know that You will be able to take all of those who are righteous to where they belong, their permanent home for all of eternity. I long to see Your glorious coming with the Father. Lord, I continually wait for that blessed hope and faithful day when the righteous will be free of the temptations of the devil. Lord, nobody knows when that day may be but only the Father. May I always do what's right, keeping Your commandments, and loving You and everybody. Lord, may I be found worthy to enter the kingdom of heaven on that fateful day of glory. I know that You will reveal salvation, glory, and perfection on the last time when You come again to earth to take the righteous to Your kingdom. Lord, may I be ready for that fateful day. May I not be found wanting or lacking. May I be found worthy to enter Your kingdom along with all those who did what was right while on earth. Lord, forgive me my sins, and cleanse me of all unrighteousness, and fill me with Your Spirit that I may have the grace to live a sin-free life. In the name of Your Son Jesus Christ, we pray, Amen.

Defensive actions show the denial of admitting the truth. There is no denying the truth in any situation you face; the truth will reveal actions of denial. The truth will always set you free; denial will always hold you captive which will lead to defensive and guilty actions. Jesus Christ is the way the truth and the life.

AUGUST 7

> A final word: Be strong in the Lord and in his mighty power. Put on all of God's armor so that you will be able to stand firm against all strategies of the devil. For we are not fighting against flesh-and-blood enemies, but against evil rulers and authorities of the unseen world, against mighty powers in this dark world, and against evil spirits in the heavenly places. **Ephesians 6:10-12 (NLT)**

Don't ever feel defeated. Don't allow the words, actions, or opinions of others make you feel like you're less than important or that you don't have an important and significant purpose. The one and only opinion that truly matters is God's opinion. When you allow other people to make you feel defeated, you are not completely focusing on God; you must allow Him to control your thoughts and saturate your heart and mind with His Word. God made you to serve a specific purpose, and He has great plans for your life. He will use you in various ways to do His work and to serve the most important purpose of all, His purpose. Your life is a direct result of God's existence and proof that He is our Creator and Heavenly Father. God's grace upon all of creation is a result of His unconditional love, unlimited humbleness, and His infinite dedication to His Children. So, the next time someone tries to make you feel defeated, unimportant, or insignificant remember who your Creator is.

LET'S PRAY: Dear Heavenly Father, my Creator and the Creator of everything seen and unseen. Lord, I want to thank You for bringing me into this world. Lord, You have a purpose for creating everyone, and I ask that You, please, reveal mine to me. Lord, bless me with the strength to defeat the enemy even when they gather in large numbers. Lord, bless me with the wisdom to treat those who hate me with love and pray for those who persecute me. Lord, I ask You to send Your Spirit upon me that I may live in power and not weakness. Lord Jesus, You died that I may live, I dedicate the rest of life to living in a way that pleases and glorifies You.

Lord, I know that where my treasure is, there will my heart be. Lord, I ask that You keep my heart in Your Word, and my treasure will be in Your Kingdom. Lord, I set my love on things in Heaven, and not things on earth for earthly things are vanity, and heavenly things are eternal. I focus on You Lord for You are my refuge and strength. Lord, I want to thank You for the many amazing plans that You have for me. I know that You have wonderful plans to prosper me and protect me. In the name of Your Son Jesus Christ, we pray, Amen.

In order to have a healthy relationship with God, you need to trust Him, respect Him, appreciate Him, communicate with Him, and understand Him. The best way to understand God is to read His written word in the Bible as often as you can.

> For God did not call us to be impure, but to live a holy life. Therefore, anyone who rejects this instruction does not reject a human being but God, the very God who gives you his Holy Spirit. **1 Thessalonians 4:7-8 (NIV)**

Live by the standards of God, not by the standards of this world. As a Christian, the Bible is your daily life manual by which you are to utilize and apply God's word as the means of discerning the truth by God's standard. Living your life for God is a choice, and those of us who call ourselves a Christian have no other choice than to live for God every day and follow his commands. In order to be a Christian, you must be a follower and a believer of the "anointed one" Jesus Christ. God tells us in 1 John 2:1-2: "My little children, these things I write to you, so that you may not sin. And if anyone sins, we have an Advocate with the Father, Jesus Christ the righteous." God's standard of holiness for His Children is not to sin. 1 John 2:6 reads like this: "He who says he abides in Him ought himself also to walk just as He walked." The world has standards, and we are settled on them. You can be just as settled on God's word when it comes to the standard that you should be living. You must drop our former opinions, theories, and traditions and simply read the bible and let God saturate your hearts with His holiness. The world is filled with people who tell you that it is impossible to live above sin. If someone who never heard a preacher preach the word of God and never made contact with religious people got saved and started to read the Bible, they would read about holiness, holy living, and life above sin. They would learn about God and His standards and allow Him to remove the standards of this broken world.

LET'S PRAY: Dear Heavenly Father, I know that You do not judge a man by the works of the law but by his faith in You. I know that Your standards are infinitely above the standards of men. I know that Your ways are infinitely above the ways of man and beyond the comprehension of even the wisest of all men. Lord, I know that my understanding is foolishness in Your sight. Lord, I ask You to make me more like You. Strengthen my faith in You. I believe in You completely. I believe that You are the Son of God, the Messiah, the only way to the Heavenly Father, and my good Shepherd that provides for me. I know that it is uneasy to walk after the Spirit, because the devil and his minions are constantly roaming the earth, seeking those who endeavor to do what's right and try to make them stray away from the path of righteousness. Lord, I ask for the strength and wisdom needed to resist and rebuke the wiles of the devil. Lord, in You there is no condemnation, so I ask that You raise a standard against the enemy when they attack and condemn any tongue that rises against me. Lord, I am sorry for coming short of Your glory. I am sorry for falling short of Your standard. Lord, forgive me my sins and bless me with a brand-new heart filled with Your love, peace, and joy. In the name of Your Son Jesus Christ, we pray, Amen.

Today, be mindful of your words and your actions and think about the positive or negative outcomes of what you say or what you do before you say it or before you do it. God is always watching, and one day you'll have to answer for all your words and all your actions.

Daily Guidance from God

> How do you know what your life will be like tomorrow? Your life is like the morning fog, it's here a little while, then it's gone. **James 4:14 (NLT)**

In what ways would you live your life if you were told that you only had a very short time to live? How would you spend the rest of your days? What would you do differently than what you are doing now? Would you appreciate your life more and everyone in it? And most importantly, would you give your life to God and live the remaining days of your life for Him? There is a simple answer to all of these questions. You should be living your life as if you only had a month to live every single day. As a human being, there is no way of knowing when your last day on this earth will be only God knows the exact date and time. It could be today; it could be tomorrow, it could be two weeks from now or two years from now. Only God knows when your life will end because He knows the exact number of your days. My point is that you should not take a single day for granted. Your life is precious, the time you have here on earth is limited, and your days are numbered, so make the most of it. You need to live every single day like it is the last day of your life. You need to live your life for God so that you can be assured that you will spend eternity in heaven with Him. Make the most of this day by appreciating every moment of what this day has to offer. Thank God for the gift of this day and the opportunity to enjoy and experience every aspect of this day.

LET'S PRAY: Dear Heavenly Father, I am grateful for the gift of life You have blessed me with. I am thankful for all that You have created. May I never take a single day of my life for granted because I know there is a purpose for every day that I am on this earth. Lord, in the morning, may I never forget to give thanks to You for waking me up and letting me see another beautiful day. In midday, I will come to You, asking You to guide me throughout the day and bless me with the strength to move on through the day, wisdom to make wise choices and decisions, and understanding to do the right things at the right time. Lord, at night, before I go to bed, I shall come to You asking You to watch over me while I sleep, protect me from the roaming minions of the devil, and keep me dwelling in Your comfort. Heavenly Father, the Alpha and the Omega, I ask You to speak Your Word over me this day. I ask You to breathe life into me this day. Add to me all the good things of life that I lack, and remove from me all forms of unrighteousness that are taking root within my heart. Enfold my heart with Your love, and make it Yours. In the name of Your Son Jesus Christ, we pray, Amen.

Here on Earth, you have the choice to live the way you want to live your life. You have the choice to either live your life according to God's plan or according to your plan. But what matters is where you go when you move on from this place. What is important is the way you live here on Earth because that will determine where you go after you pass on. There are only two places to go either heaven or hell, remember the choice is yours.

But now the righteousness of God apart from the law is revealed, being witnessed by the Law and the Prophets, even the righteousness of God, through faith in Jesus Christ, to all and on all who believe. For there is no difference; for all have sinned and fall short of the glory of God, being justified freely by His grace through the redemption that is in Christ Jesus. **Romans 3:21-24 (NKJV)**

Are you right with God? You must first understand what is wrong in your life and why You need God in your life before you can get "right" with God. The answer is continual, repeated sin, living for things that are not of God and refusing to follow His commands. Are you living your life for God or are you living your life for things of this world? Are you putting God's will first or are you putting your own will first? Are you doing what is pleasing to God or are you doing what is pleasing to you? Are your thoughts, words, and actions from God or are they from things of this world? These are the five essential questions that you need to ask yourself. But the most important question that you need to ask yourself right this very moment is, are you truly right with God? And you need to ask yourself this question before it is too late. Because if you are not right with God, you need to get right with Him now or you may forfeit your chance to make it to heaven when Jesus returns. Do you want to give up the opportunity to experience true salvation in heaven for all of eternity with God?

LET'S PRAY: Dear Heavenly Father, I want to make things right with You. I come to You today, asking for forgiveness. With total sincerity, I ask for forgiveness, promising to turn away from my sinful ways. Lord, may sin and every form of unrighteousness be a thing of the old. May they pass away, and may Your righteousness be my priority from now on. Give me the strength to refrain from my sins and live a sin-free life. Lord, take pleasure in me and in all that I do. Look upon me with mercy and bless me in every aspect of my life. Restore and renew my sinful heart and look beyond my iniquities. Prosper me, heal me, comfort me, redeem me, crown my every effort, satisfy my every desire and forgive me of my sinful ways. Your love for me was perfect on the cross; where You died for a sinner like myself. Lord, remove any form of punishment in my life as a result of my sin. Forgive me of all my transgressions and give me the strength to refrain from any sin, that I may enjoy the benefits of righteousness by dedicating and living my life for You and to fulfill your purpose for me. In the name of Your Son Jesus Christ, we pray, Amen.

God did not put you on this earth to do mediocre or average works and deeds. God put you on this earth to serve an important purpose, accomplish great things, and to do His extraordinary work according to His will.

AUGUST 15

Put on the full armor of God, so that you can take your stand against the devil's schemes. **Ephesians 6:11 (NIV)**

Don't allow the devil to deceive you. Do not allow the devil to dictate your thoughts words or actions. Do not allow the devil to deny your God-given right to walk by faith in our Lord and Savior Jesus Christ. By focusing on God, you are shutting the door of evil deception and suffocating the devious and disappointing acts of the devil. By being obedient to God, you are showing the devil who your faithful redeemer and provider is. And by seeking God and following His commands, you are proving that the devil is a liar, a deceiver, a coward and he is weak. Every time you do what is right and pleasing to God, you are making the devil angry because you are not allowing him to control your thoughts, words, or actions and that brings Glory to God's Holy name.

LET'S PRAY: Dear Heavenly Father, may I never forget that evil thoughts will corrupt my good mind. May I never be deceived by the devil to engage in evil actions. May all my thoughts and actions be free from evil, immorality, and covetousness. May all my thoughts and actions bring glory to You. Lord, anything that will corrupt my good mind and attitude, I ask that You destroy it today. I want to grow holier in my thoughts, words, actions, and attitude. Lord, I ask that You give me the wisdom to identify the truth when I see it, hear it, and read it. May the lies of the devil never dwell in me. May I rely on the Holy Bible for the truth and not vain doctrines of men. Lord, may I never be tricked or deceived into believing what's false. Give me the wisdom to identify one when the devil is trying to sneak in. May I bring glory to Your name in all that I do, think, and say. In the name of Your Son Jesus Christ, we pray, Amen.

There is a simple solution to every problem you face. Give it to God, and He will handle it.

Behold what manner of love the Father has bestowed on us, that we should be called children of God! Therefore the world does not know us, because it did not know Him. **1 John 3:1 (NKJV)**

Spend time with God today. You can never read too much of God's word, you can never do too much of God's work, and you can never be in God's presence too much. In fact, the more you do to Glorify God, and the more time you spend with Him, the closer you will become with Him. You can't have a close, personal, and meaningful relationship with God if you only make time for Him when it is convenient for you according to your schedule. God must come first in your daily life over all other things. The main priority in your life must always be God. You must spend time with Him on a daily basis in order to have a good relationship with Him. God's children have always come first, and He expects to be first in your life too. God has proven over and over that we are His main priority, He has shown this through His unconditional love that is unfailing, undeserved, and unilateral. God is love. Few people understand what true unconditional love is, they can't comprehend the unconditional love of God. One of the most important examples of God's unconditional love for us was the sacrifice of His only begotten Son Jesus Christ who died on the cross for our sins.

LET'S PRAY: Dear Heavenly Father, I need to spend time with You today. I need to be as close to You as possible. I need to be closest to You because from You I find comfort and provision. Lord, I draw near to You today that You may draw near to me and I may hear You without any distraction, and You may hear me too when I come to You in prayer. May I delight in talking to You, rather than trying to figure out things by myself. May I always be reminded that You're always there for me, and You never want me to do a thing alone because with You there is nothing I can't accomplish. Lord, from this moment on, I promise never to try figuring things out myself. In the past, I have made terrible decisions that cost me a lot, and I do not want that anymore. I want to make wiser decisions that will benefit me and all those I love. Lord, I invite You to walk with me, teach me, guide me, and counsel me. I invite You to dwell in me as Your Word dwells in my heart. Lord, may all that I do be done with You, under Your light, according to Your Will, in a way that pleases You. Lord, thank You for loving me so much. Thank You for loving me more than I love myself. I trust completely in You. I trust entirely in Your love. I know that nothing, no one, and no power can separate me from Your love, and I thank You for such amazing unconditional love. Lord, Thank You for without You mankind will never know what true and unconditional love is. Lord, thank You for the gift of salvation. Thank You for giving mankind a chance to inherit Your kingdom. In the name of Your Son Jesus Christ, we pray, Amen.

At any given time, God gives you the freedom to choose what you think, what you say, and what you do. You can choose to think positive thoughts, speak positive words, and engage in good deeds and actions that are pleasing to God. Or you can choose to think negative thoughts, speak negative words, and engage in negative deeds and actions that are not pleasing to God. Either way, it's your choice but always remember that your mind is a Battlefield, every word you say, and every action you do comes from what you think. Your mind is where the devil will try to get you to fall for his evil schemes. So, when you are thinking about things make sure you are seeking God first so that your thoughts, words, and actions will be pure and pleasing to God.

> For I am not ashamed of the gospel, because it is the power of God that brings salvation to everyone who believes: first to the Jew, then to the Gentile. **Romans 1:16 (NIV)**

Choose salvation over sin. Being a sinner won't stop you from getting into heaven. But refusing to be saved by accepting God and His Son Jesus Christ into your heart as your personal Lord and Savior will. Salvation is deliverance from sin and its consequences including danger or suffering. Being saved by grace is to be delivered and protected by God. When we think of the word "saved" it reminds us of being victorious through God in this life, being healthy through God in this life, and being preserved by God in this life. God has rescued us through the death of His Son, Jesus Christ on the cross and because of His resurrection we can receive salvation. How can you receive salvation? First, before you can be saved and accepted into the kingdom of God through His Son Jesus Christ, you must admit that you are a sinner, ask for forgiveness of your sins, and accept Jesus Christ as your personal Lord and Savior of your life. Second, you must hear and understand the gospel, the good news of Jesus's death and resurrection. Third, you must believe in God and fully trust in His plan for your life. You must understand that the only way to seek God is through His Son Jesus Christ. This means that you must repent which will initiate a significant change with the motives within your heart. It will also initiate a change in your heart about what it means to sin and how it will affect your life with Christ. You will not receive salvation unless you fully understand the importance of the death and resurrection of Jesus Christ.

LET'S PRAY: Dear Heavenly Father, I do not want to be a sinner anymore. I want to be as close to You as possible. I want to be closest to You because from You I find comfort and provision. Lord, all good and perfect gifts come from Your kingdom, and I see no point why I should try to do everything myself when I have a super powerful Helper willing to help me when I'm strong and when I'm weak. Lord, I want to thank You for

Your undying love for the world. I want to thank You for loving me even while I was a sinner. I want to thank You for laying down Your life that I may be reconciled with the Father and be blessed with eternal life, and be free from death. Lord, today, I stand; still, I worship You, I acknowledge that You are my God and the source of my salvation. Today, I seek You completely. I put You before everything and everyone. I confess today that You are my God, my light, and my salvation. Lord, as I decide to put You first in everything that I do, may I come first in everything that I do. In the name of Your Son Jesus Christ, we pray, Amen.

Scripture is a reminder of the truth and wisdom of God's Word in the face of Satan's lies.

AUGUST 21

> And let the peace of God rule in your hearts, to which also you were called in one body; and be thankful. Let the word of Christ dwell in you richly in all wisdom, teaching and admonishing one another in psalms and hymns and spiritual songs, singing with grace in your hearts to the Lord. And whatever you do in word or deed, do all in the name of the Lord Jesus, giving thanks to God the Father through Him. **Colossians 3:15-17 (NKJV)**

Do good works in God's eyes. Speak good words in God's Presence. No matter what you do or say, make sure that your words and actions are pleasing to God. So many times, you say and do things that you know are not pleasing to God and act like it is not a big deal and you act like is it not important to please God. You think that you can continue to commit these sins without any regard, concern or punishment from God. Stop and think for a minute, if you prayed to God for a good break or an opportunity that you have been waiting for, or more importantly, healing of your child who is very sick with cancer. How would you feel if God had the same attitude as you and said that answering your prayer is not important or a big deal? God would not do that to His children because He is a loving and forgiving God and He only wants the best for all of us. God knows that you are going to make mistakes, He knows that you are going to sin, He knows that you are going to make bad choices and decisions. God also knows that He has equipped you with a loving heart that is always filled with love and compassion. God knows that He fills your mind with positive thoughts daily. God knows that he has created your mouth to speak kind and polite words. The next time you feel the need to speak or act in a way that is not pleasing to God, stop and think about how you would feel if God acted and treated you that way.

LET'S PRAY: Dear Heavenly Father, I want to be kind, humble, polite, cheerful, grateful, and righteous. I want to please You in any way possible, and in every way. Lord, I know that You reward the kindness of every man. I know that You reward the good works of every man. Lord, I want to be kind with my words and my actions too. I want to find more delight in giving than receiving. May I never be cruel, arrogant, selfish, proud, and ungrateful. Remind me every day that cruelty destroys. May I never pay evil for evil, but find the wisdom to repay good for evil. Lord, I ask You to cleanse my heart, so that it will be a kinder, wiser, and more-prayerful heart. Reveal to me the words, thoughts, and actions that are not pleasing to You. Lord, put Your peace and love in my heart. May Your love keep me from making foolish decisions, utterances, and actions. May Your peace keep me safe from harm and keep me dwelling in Your land of grace, now and forever. In the name of Your Son Jesus Christ, we pray, Amen.

The actions of an honest, sincere, and respectable brother or sister in Christ will only add positivity to your life that will lift you up closer to God not add negativity that will pull you away from God.

AUGUST 23

> Therefore submit to God. Resist the devil and he will flee from you. Draw near to God and He will draw near to you. Cleanse your hands, you sinners; and purify your hearts, you double-minded. Lament and mourn and weep! Let your laughter be turned to mourning and your joy to gloom. Humble yourselves in the sight of the Lord, and He will lift you up. **James 4:7-10 (NKJV)**

Submit yourself to God instead of being competitive in your faith with those around you. It's not important how many bible verses you can quote, how good you are at biblical prophecy, how long you have been saved or even how often you go to church. What is important is that you understand the teachings of the Bible and apply it to your daily walk with God as well as share it with others around you. You can inspire your family, friends, neighbors, and coworkers by simply showing your true humbleness in your actions. You need to take "spiritual competition" out of your relationship with other believers and add "spiritual fellowship." God is not concerned with who is better at certain things or more talented or more devoted to pleasing God. He already knows the talents and gifts that you have been granted. The Bible tells us in Philippians 2:3-4: "Do nothing from rivalry or conceit but in humility count others more significant than yourselves. Let each of you look not only to his interests but also to the interests of others." Your walk in faith is not a competition; it's about submitting yourself to God and surrendering your life to Him. Living your life for God is about following His plan for your life and bringing glory to His name by doing what is right and pleasing to Him. The best way you can achieve this is by being honest, humble, kind and caring when interacting with others.

LET'S PRAY: Dear Heavenly Father, direct my path for I submit my life to You. I acknowledge You in all I do; I acknowledge the fact that I can do nothing without You. Lord, speak to me for I, Your humble servant will listen to You. I want to meditate on You throughout the day in whatever I do. I want You to reveal things to me. I choose to stand still, and hear what You command for that is what I will do. I know You are God, and I submit myself fully to Your will. Lord, I want to live a life with purpose. I want to have a purpose-driven life. I want to have a life that is driven by Your Spirit. I do not want to live a purposeless and meaningless life. I want to live a life that will impact positively on all those around me. I want my words to be blessings to people and not curse's. I want my words to motivate people and not demotivate them. I want my words to heal and not destroy. I want my words to encourage and not discourage. Lord, I want to speak with kindness and be polite to everyone that I meet regardless of their social class. I want to be as humble as Jesus Christ was while He was here on earth. I want to be a better person that I may inherit Your kingdom and all blessings that come along with it. Lord, as I endeavor to achieve this, send Your Spirit to help me achieve this that I may become a new creation in You. In the name of Your Son Jesus Christ, we pray, Amen.

AUGUST 24

Positive words lead to positive actions, and negative words lead the negative actions.

People can speak positive words when they are facing negative situations. It's called having a positive attitude while facing negative situations in your life. But when people speak negative words when they are facing negative situations shows they have a negative attitude. And having a negative attitude while facing negative situations in your life will not help the situation.

I keep my eyes always on the Lord. With him at my right hand, I will not be shaken. **Psalm 16:8 (NIV)**

Keep your eyes on God. Keep your mind on God. Allow your thoughts to be guided by God. Allow your words to be directed by God. He will guide your life in the right direction, and He will lead you down the right path according to His will. The moment you take your eyes off of God and switch your focus from God to things of this world, your life will go into a tailspin, and you will face difficult situations and circumstances. You will not be able to recover from the tailspin without God's help. Once you refocus your thoughts and place your eyes back on God, He will take the difficult situations and circumstances and turn them into blessings and opportunities. So often you learn the hard way that God is the answer and the only true way to live your life. When you veer off the path that God has established for your life, you find yourself running back to God when you have fallen so deep into the muck of this world that you are unable to pull yourself out without God's help. You need God every moment of your life whether you realize it or not. We are human, we make mistakes, we fall off the beaten path, but God is perfect, and His plan for your life is perfect, and only he can fix what the mistakes you have made.

LET'S PRAY: Dear Heavenly Father, I know that I am of You. I know that I belong to You. I know that You hold my future. I know that my life and my heart is in Your Hands. Lord, the world is chaotic, wicked, and selfish, and I do need Your peace to fill my heart and keep my mind sound, and my eyes focused on Your righteousness. Lord, I need Your guidance. I want everything that I do to be in accordance to Your Will for me, and I want my whole being to be found pleasing in Your sight. Lord, bless me with the strength, grace, and knowledge to accomplish this, and as You do, keep me in Your land of provision and protection. Lord, I invite You to guide me and counsel me. I invite You to dwell in me as Your Word dwells in my heart. May all that I do be done with You, under Your light, according to Your Will, in a way that pleases You. Lord, You are the Way, the Truth, and the Life, and I don't want to be lost in this world. I do not want to be where I should not. I want to be on the right path, which is the path of righteousness. Lord, I ask that You help me in my journey along the path of righteousness. This is a lifetime journey, and I ask You to stay with me every second of the way. Lord, guide my path and bless me with my divine inheritance. In the name of Your Son Jesus Christ, we pray, Amen.

Genuine faith leads to authentic thoughts, words, and actions which will result in powerful, positive, and truthful outcomes.

So that you may live a life worthy of the Lord and please him in every way: bearing fruit in every good work, growing in the knowledge of God. **Colossians 1:10 (NIV)**

Live completely for God. You can't love God with one half of your heart, while you like things of this world with the other half of your heart. When it comes to God, there is no such thing as halfway faith or a part-time Christian. You must believe in God 100% of the time, you must walk in faith 100% of the time, and you must be a Christian 100% of the time in order to experience the full power and blessing of God. Just as you can't allow God to only rule half of your life while you allow the devil to rule the other half of your life. Our almighty God does not work like that; you must allow Him to saturate 100% of your heart and soul at all times. Every fiber of your being must be completely dedicated to Him and His word. God did not sacrifice half of His Son's life on the cross for our sins, and He does not give us half of the salvation He promised. God sacrificed His Son's entire being, His flesh, blood, heart, soul, body, and mind. God made this ultimate sacrifice so that we could be forgiven of our all our sins and have eternal life in heaven through His Son, Jesus Christ.

LET'S PRAY: Dear Heavenly Father, today I promise to live the remaining days of my life completely and wholeheartedly for You. I believe in You completely, I will walk in faith completely, and I have dedicated my life to be a Christian. Lord, I invite You to saturate every fiber of my being with Your Love and fill my entire heart, mind, and soul with Your Spirit, Your Strength, Your wisdom, and Your guidance. Lord, I ask you to rule my life with Your righteousness and your resolve. Thank You for the gift of salvation and reconciliation You gave us through Your Son our Savior Jesus Christ. Thank You for sending Your Son Jesus Christ into the world that all sinners may be saved. Lord, thank You for showing us how You want all humans to be by giving us an example of Jesus. I believe in You, and in what You are able to accomplish. I believe that You are God of all flesh, and there is nothing that is impossible for You. In the name of Your Son Jesus Christ, we pray, Amen.

God will lead you to your passion, and you know it because you will be able to feel it deep in the recesses of your heart. And once God reveals your passion and you are at a place where your passion is overflowing in your heart you need to not only become it, but you need to let it become a part of you. And when you finally let go and allow God to breathe life into your God-given passion amazing things will happen to you, and for you as a result of following God's commands and allowing Him to take control of your life. At times things won't always work out as you have planned. But know that everything will work out according to God's plan for your life. When God gives you something to be passionate about, and this passion fills your heart and brings glory to God, it will never be a waste of time. My passion is to inspire people with the words I write and to bring as many people as possible who are lost to the Lord. My other passion is to create a place that people can come to receive prayer, feel revived, and renewed. I have done that with the prayer group that I founded.

AUGUST 29

Put on the whole armor of God, that you may be able to stand against the wiles of the devil. **Ephesians 6:11 (NKJV)**

Do not deal with the devil. Do not allow his deception into your mind. Do not allow him to corrupt your thoughts. Do not allow him to dictate your actions. The devil is on a 24-hour mission to destroy all works of God. The devil is working overtime to force his evil ways into the minds of those who believe in God. The devil never takes a break, he never rests, and he is always trying to creep into your mind. The devil will not only torment you and taunt you; he will provoke you and cause stress and tension in all areas of your life. In this world, the devil is the popular choice of those who refuse to believe in God and His existence. These people go about their days living in sin and committing deceiving, dishonest, and deceptive acts in an effort to bring corruption to as many people as possible. The devil never attacks his minions and evildoers who are already under his evil spell. He attacks good honest Christians who are sincere and dedicated to living their life for God and spreading His words to those who need it. If you are doing good things for the Glory of God, there is a good chance you are being attacked several times a day by the devil. Do not let the devil win, even when you allow yourself to get frustrated or upset you are allowing the devil to win and that is satisfying to him. The best defense against all evil acts of the devil is the almighty armor of God. You must seek God and seek him truthfully, honestly and wholeheartedly, and He will protect you against every attack of the devil.

LET'S PRAY: Dear Heavenly Father, I know that prayer is the armor against the wiles and wrath of the devil. Lord, I know that the devil will try hard to keep me from my blessings. I know that the devil will continuously try to put thoughts of doubt within me when I pray. I ask that You send forth Your Spirit to fill me completely and leave no space for any foul spirit of the devil. May I never forget that the devil will continuously try to plant ungratefulness in the hearts of humans to prevent them from giving thanks to You for the things You have blessed them with. Lord, may I never take Your mercy and grace for granted. May I never take Your mercy and grace as a license to sin. I do not want to be controlled by the devil. I want to be guided by You, and I want to be Yours. Lord, thank You for sending Jesus to reconcile us. May the devil never steal Your gift of salvation and eternal life away from me. Bless me with the strength to resist the devil that He may flee from me, and I may live above sin. In the name of Your Son Jesus Christ, we pray, Amen.

The strength of your faith and your trust in God will not be tested when your life is going smooth. The strength of your faith and your trust in God will be tested while you are facing adversities and difficult situations. You will feel the power of God's strength the most when you are feeling down, weak, and defeated. In life, you can't control what happens, but you can control what you see, what you think, and how you react to every adversity and difficult situation in your life.

AUGUST 31

This is the day the Lord has made. We will rejoice and be glad in it. **Psalm 118:24 (NLT)**

So often you see God taking your family and friends home to rest in heaven without having a chance to say goodbye. You repeatedly take life for granted without even realizing how amazing this life is and how much you should appreciate every single day. God wants you to understand that every day He grants you in this life is a special blessing and the time He gives you on this earth is a precious gift that you must spend wisely. Every day when you wake up, you need to not only thank God for the gift of another day you need to be thankful and appreciate all the people in your life who received the gift of another day with you. Instead of worrying and stressing about things that won't even matter tomorrow because they are pointless, enjoy this day that God has made and appreciate the fact that you are still alive and able to experience all of God's great creations. Your days here on earth are numbered, and God knows the plan for your life, and He knows exactly when your last day will come. So, enjoy every aspect of this day and appreciate everything you experience and every person you spend time with today because you might not have the gift of waking up to another day tomorrow.

LET'S PRAY: Dear Heavenly Father, I promise that I will appreciate every day that You grant me and I will show You how grateful I am for the gift of each day by spending my time wisely and bringing glory to You in everything I do. Lord, every day when I wake up the first thing I will do is thank You for the gift of a new day. Lord, thank you for all the amazing people you have placed in my life, I know there is a reason for every person that You place in my life. Lord, I know that You bring your children home with you for a reason in Your time and according to Your marvelous plan. Lord, when You bring people home, it may be unexpected to us, but it is never unexpected to You because You know when it's time to bring Your children home. Lord, I know that I often take people in my life for granted, so I ask You today to give me strength and courage to make sure I spend time with those who matter most. Lord, when I woke up this morning, I did not know what was in store for this day, but you knew everything that would take place today because this is a day that You have made. In Jesus name, we pray, Amen.

SEPTEMBER

I don't know about you, but on the weekends I like to sleep in a little but not sleep my whole day away. When I wake up the first thing I do is thank God for the gift of this day. Then I think what does God have planned for me to do today? I want to do the things that God wants me to do today according to His will and not what I want to do according to my own will. Each day is a gift from God, don't waste it or abuse it on meaningless things and never take each day you are given for granted.

> But if Christ is in you, then even though your body is subject to death because of sin, the Spirit gives life because of righteousness. And if the Spirit of him who raised Jesus from the dead is living in you, he who raised Christ from the dead will also give life to your mortal bodies because of his Spirit who lives in you. **Romans 8:10-11 (NIV)**

The resurrection of Jesus was just as important to your salvation as His death was. There are a lot of Christians who do not realize the importance of this. You must give thanks to Jesus Christ for sacrificing His life for you every day. Your salvation is not just something that Jesus paid for with His life on your behalf. It is a gift that Jesus has given to you by means of union with Him. The Bible tells us in 1 Peter 3:21-22: "There is also an antitype which now saves us-baptism (not the removal of the filth of the flesh, but the answer of a good conscience toward God), through the resurrection of Jesus Christ, who has gone into heaven and is at the right hand of God, angels and authorities and powers having been made subject to Him." We are forgiven through His death of Jesus because, through our union with Him, we died on the cross with Him. And we receive the gift of eternal life because we were also raised in new life through His resurrection. The work that Jesus did by rising from the dead on the third day ensured that we would have a new spiritual life when we come to faith through Jesus Christ. His resurrection also assured that when we enter eternity, we will receive our own resurrected and glorified bodies, just like the eternally resurrected and glorified body of Jesus Christ.

LET'S PRAY: Dear Heavenly Father, today I give You all the glory for everything that I am and will be. Thank You for Your great and abundant mercy through which You have given me a new birth into a living hope through the resurrection of Your Son my Savior Jesus Christ from the dead. Lord, bring me into an inheritance that can never perish, spoil, fade, or be stolen. Keep my inheritance in heaven for me. When my life here on earth is over, may I be reunited with You and be called 'great' in heaven because I did not only keep Your commandments, but I also taught others to do the same. Lord, through faith, I ask You to shield me by Your mighty power of protection. Thank You for sending Your Son to save mankind from self-destruction. Without You, mankind will never know what true and unconditional love is. Lord, thank You for the gift of salvation. Thank You for giving mankind a chance to inherit Your kingdom. I want to make it to heaven after my time here on earth is over. I ask You to bless me with the strength to continue doing what's right. Bless me with the grace to never draw away from You. As I endeavor to do what's right at all times, I ask You to make Your strength perfect in my weakness that I may do everything I set my mind to through You who blesses Your children with undying strength. In the name of Your Son Jesus Christ, we pray, Amen.

SEPTEMBER 3

God will place the heaviest burdens on those who He knows can carry its weight and He will give His toughest battles to those who are His strongest soldiers. God will never send you into a battle without equipping you with the proper resources needed to handle the battle.

The God of my strength, in whom I will trust; My shield and the horn of my salvation, My stronghold and my refuge; My Savior, You save me from violence. I will call upon the Lord, who is worthy to be praised; So shall I be saved from my enemies. **2 Samuel 22:3-4 (NKJV)**

God will protect you from vicious acts of the devil when you seek Him wholeheartedly. Don't let the devil deceive you by clouding your mind with negative and immoral thoughts. When you allow this to happen, the devil will try to fill your mind with thoughts of corruption to block any help from God. Your mind is a battleground, and there will be many battles fought there. The devil will continuously try to invade your mind and eventually he will try to take it over completely. But when you seek God and allow Him to fight your battles, He will consume every thought in your mind, and He will be in the forefront of your conscience. When you have God on your side you are not fighting these battles alone; you have the almighty, all-powerful and omnipotent God backing your every move. The devil has no chance against God because He is supreme, invincible, unstoppable. His divine power, strength, and wisdom are unlimited, unrestricted, and immeasurable. God will always protect you because he wants only the best for His children because His love is infinite and unconditional.

LET'S PRAY: Dear Heavenly Father, I need Your help. I am poor in strength, wisdom, and understanding. I need You right now. I need Your deliverance in my life. Lord, save me from the deception of the devil, protect me from the wrath of the enemy, keep me safe from violent people. Even though I walk through the valley of the shadow of death, I fear not because You are with me. Place the blood of Your Son Jesus Christ over the door of my house that the enemy may never penetrate. When the enemy tries to attack to my house, may he see the blood of my Savior and walk away because we are covered by Your protective and comforting presence, and there is nothing that can ever harm us. Lord, may Your power go with me wherever I go and protect me from the plans and attacks of the devil, and may Your presence remain with me and watch over me at all times. Lord, I ask You to deliver me from all forms of evil. I am not afraid because I know You walk with me and You will protect me. Even when danger surrounds me, it will never come near me. In the name of Your Son Jesus Christ, we pray, Amen.

Strength is what keeps you holding on.
Faith is what keeps you moving along.
But hope is what keeps you alive when
everything seems to be going wrong.

SEPTEMBER 6

The hope of the righteous brings joy, but the expectation of the wicked will perish. **Proverbs 10:28 (ESV)**

You should never try to live up to the expectations of others, regardless of what they say or how they act. You should strive to live up to the expectations of God and God only. He will never expect you to do more than what He already knows you are capable of. You were put on this earth to bring Glory to God and to please Him in everything you do, not to please everyone else. Once you are able to understand this mindset, you will be able to live your life without worrying if what you are doing is good enough for everyone else. When you focus your mind on pleasing God, the expectations of everyone else won't even be in your thoughts. God is your creator, your provider, and your protector. God is the only one who controls your life, and therefore His expectations are the only ones you should be trying to live up to.

LET'S PRAY: Dear Heavenly Father, I come to you today in prayer asking You to keep my mind, and my thoughts completely focused on You. Lord, I know that Your expectations are the only expectations that I need to live by. Lord, I want to bring Glory to You and please You in everything I say and everything I do. Lord, I ask you today to help realize that what others expect of me is not only pointless; it is also insignificant compared to Your expectations of me. Lord, I know that I can live a stress-free and worry-free life if stay focused on You at all times. Lord, you are not only my Heavenly Father you are also my creator, my provider, and my protector. Lord, I know that You are in complete control of my life and that You will never expect me to do more than what You already know I am capable of. In the name of Your Son Jesus Christ, we pray, Amen.

"Lord, open my eyes that I may see the Truth and open my ears to hear the Truth. Open my heart to receive it by faith. Renew my mind to keep it hopeful."

SEPTEMBER 8

Do not love sleep, lest you come to poverty; Open your eyes, and you will be satisfied with bread. **Proverbs 20:13 (NKJV)**

Make the most of this day. You can accomplish all of what God expects of you by rising early and going late to rest. There are times when it is appropriate to have extended sleep patterns based on our work life and circumstances that we face such as sickness and grief. But if you sleep too much when you are not facing these types of circumstances, it will reflect a lack of faith and trust in the Lord. As some people will often sleep and for extended periods of time to avoid the difficulties in life when they are depressed, stressed, or worried. God will always give you the strength you need to make it through the day, but you must seek Him wholeheartedly. If you are allowing God to lead your life according to His plan, there will be nothing that can keep you from succeeding in whatever you do. Scripture also associates laziness because of too much sleep. God tells us in Proverbs 6:9-11: "How long will you lie there, you sluggard? When will you get up from your sleep? A little sleep, a little slumber, a little folding of the hands to rest and poverty will come on you like a thief and scarcity like an armed man." The bible also tells us that sacrificing sleep in order to make a difference spiritually for the good of others is an acceptable practice. On many occasions, Jesus would be up early in order to pray, and He often stayed up and prayed all night long. This allowed Him to recognize that it is more important and necessary to be in communion with God rather than having physical rest. Jesus had specifically told John, James, and Peter, to pray that they would not fall into any temptation the night before His crucifixion. But the Lord had rebuked each one of them and told them that He would give them an opportunity to sleep another time once they had all fallen asleep. But as a result of their choice to sleep rather than to seek the will of God, it resulted in their abandonment of Jesus during His arrest and trial. It is much more important to spend time seeking God than to waste time oversleeping, as God will give you appropriate times of rest.

LET'S PRAY: Dear Heavenly Father, I ask that you guide me and help me accomplish all that I am expected to do by rising early and going late to rest so that I can make the most of every day I am here on earth. May I never use Your faithfulness and provision as an excuse to be lazy. Lord, may I always realize that laziness is the brother of destruction and that a lazy man will have no bread to eat. I ask that You fill me with the strength to go about my daily work and renew my strength each passing day that I may be able to accomplish everything that You created me to do. Lord, May I be of sound mind, and positive energy. May I have a creative mind, and not a destructive one. May I build with my hand, and not destroy. Lord, bless my mind, body, and soul. In the name of Your Son Jesus Christ, we pray, Amen.

Dear God, please allow my children, family,
friends, co-workers, and neighbors feel
Your presence through Your love, hope,
peace, and joy. Give them an opportunity
to have faith when all seems hopeless!

My dear brothers and sisters, take note of this: Everyone should be quick to listen, slow to speak and slow to become angry. **James 1:19 (NIV)**

Find patience in God. Be quick to listen and quick to forgive. Be slow to speak and slow to become angry. Understand this, when you become quickly angered, you are allowing the devil to fill your soul with fear and rage instead of allowing God to fill your heart and mind with peace. Getting angry doesn't solve anything in God's eyes, it only allows the devil to feel fulfilled and satisfied because of your ungodly acts. God tells us in Proverbs 14:29: "Whoever is patient and slow to anger shows great understanding, but whoever has a quick temper magnifies his foolishness." When you feel yourself becoming angry, stop immediately and take a few moments to seek God. He will guide your thoughts, control your words, and direct your actions. You will be at peace by allowing yourself to be guided by God, instead of being frustrated by being deceived by the devil. Your day will be pleasant, joyful and fulfilling when you remain positive, peaceful, and patient in God.

LET'S PRAY: Dear Heavenly Father, I ask You to replace my heart with a cleaner, kinder, wiser, and more-prayerful heart. I ask that you renew my spirit daily and allow my thoughts, words, and actions to be good so that all that I say and do is right and pleasing to You. Reveal to me where my words, thoughts, or actions are not pleasing in Your sight. I want to be slow-to-anger, and quick-to-forgive. Help me achieve this. Give me the strength to let go of any anger or grief within me. May anger, discontentment, confusion, and evil thoughts never take root in my heart. Lord, help me change my character when needed. I long to be a person after Your loving and merciful heart. Strengthen me to be the person You created me to be, and may I always speak and listen to You in prayer because in Your hands rests the best solution to any problem. Lord, I ask that you forgive me for the times I've failed to bring You glory with my words, actions or thoughts. In the name of Your Son Jesus Christ, we pray, Amen.

If you have time to commit sin and commit acts that are not pleasing to God, it's a sign that you are not focused on Him at all times and that you are not seeking Him enough. This should be a reminder and an opportunity for you to change your ways and a reason for you to start seeking God wholeheartedly.

SEPTEMBER 12

For this is the love of God, that we keep His commandments. And His commandments are not burdensome. **1 John 5:3 (NKJV)**

Obey God's commandments at all times. When you are not obedient to God by following His commandments, all things that God does not tolerate become tolerated in your mind. "Do your own thing" becomes the motto, and instead of obeying God, you are going about your life on your terms. And so nothing can be labeled as "sinful." No act is right or wrong. As a result, there is no need for God to forgive you. God calls you to obey the commands He has given you according to His written Word. He also reminds us that when we fail to keep His commandments, and when we fall to temptation that leads to sin, there is still forgiveness in Christ. Where there is forgiveness available, it follows that your actions, whether in thoughts or deeds, can only be dealt with once you confess and ask God for forgiveness. The act of confession to God and the offer of forgiveness from God go hand in hand with the call to obedience. We are offered the "test" of obedience daily as the basis of having the assurance of knowing God. Those who know God are faithful and obedient to all of His commands.

LET'S PRAY: Dear Heavenly Father, I honor You and I honor Your Name. May I be obedient to You at all times. Give me the grace and strength to always keep Your commandments. Lord, help me make wise decisions especially when my decisions directly or indirectly affect the lives of others. If there is any foul spirit trying to lead me to acts of disobedience, I ask that You destroy any structure of the devil within me, and drive any foul spirit away from me. Lord, as I obey Your commandments, bring all the desires of my heart into fulfillment. May I never stop being pure in all I say and hear and do. May I be always honest and truthful in all things I say and do. May I always be pure in mind and heart, and in all, I think and desire each day. Lord, I live by faith in You, because You love me and gave Your life for me. From this moment I promise to live for You. Give me the strength to stay faithful to You, and keep all Your commandments that I may bring You glory with all that I do. May Your peace come into my heart, fill it until it overflows, rule in it, and influence everything that I do. In the name of Your Son Jesus Christ, we pray, Amen.

The devil is Devious, Disobedient, Dangerous, Delusional, Desperate, Dishonest, Deceitful, Doomed in Darkness, in Denial and Defeated. The devil is a Dictator, a Deceptor, a Deceiver, a Destroyer, a Debauchery, and a Disgrace.

SEPTEMBER 14

The Lord is my rock and my fortress and my deliverer; My God, my strength, in whom I will trust; My shield and the horn of my salvation, my stronghold. **Psalm 18:2 (NKJV)**

Thank God for this day. When you first woke up this morning did you take time to thank God for the gift of this beautiful day? Or did you go about your normal daily routines and start your day without even acknowledging the gift that God has given you? The foundation of your day must begin by thanking God in three ways. First, by thanking him for bringing you through the night safely and watching over you while you were sleeping. Second, by thanking Him for waking you up to the gift of this beautiful day. Third, by asking Him to guide and direct your path through this day. It is essential and necessary that God is the foundation of your life and the foundation of this day. You can be assured that He will not only guide and direct your path, but He will also keep you safe from tragedy and protect you from all evil acts of the devil. When you take your mind off yourself, the difficulties, and the circumstances that you face today, and put your focus on God, He will allow you to enjoy everything this day has to offer.

LET'S PRAY: Dear Heavenly Father, I promise to make you the foundation of my life today and every day. Thank You for bringing me through the night safely and watching over me while I was sleeping. Lord, thank You for waking me up to the gift of this beautiful day, thank you for allowing me to experience everything this day has to offer. Lord, I ask to guide and direct my path through this day, keep me safe from tragedy and protect me from all evil acts of the devil. Lord, in You, I take refuge. You are my foundation. You are my faithful Creator. You are my light and my salvation. You are my refuge and my dwelling place. You are my provider. You are my ultimate healer. You are my redeemer. You are my hope.

You are my strength in my time of weakness. You are my shield and my protector. You are my comforter. You are my Savior, my Messiah. You are my inheritance and my ultimate Source of blessing. In the name of Your Son Jesus Christ, we pray, Amen.

If there is anything or anyone in your
life that causes you to become weak and
stumble by falling into the devil's negative
and evil schemes, you must remove
them from your life immediately.

Every good gift and every perfect gift is from above, and comes down from the Father of lights, with whom there is no variation or shadow of turning. **James 1:17 (NKJV)**

Give thanks to God for all the blessings and gifts He has granted you. A blessing is an act of God, and they can come in many ways, shapes, or forms. When God releases his blessings into the lives of Christians, He alone will determine if someone is eligible to receive his blessing since He knows all the needs, thoughts, actions, and hidden motives of all His children. We must remember that a blessing isn't always receiving something good in our life, but it could be the prevention of something bad happening. The Bible gives no firm promises or guarantees as to the timing, form, method or quantity of a blessing. In a general sense, God blesses all His children because He has provided for all of us spiritually. However, in actuality, God only blesses His children who believe in Him and those who are honest and sincere in their faith. When God releases blessing, He takes into consideration of His children who have a clear sense of his grace, salvation, and providence in this world. God speaks through his word in Psalms 41:1: "Blessed is he who considers the poor; The Lord will deliver him in time of trouble." God also tells us in Acts 20:35: "I have shown you in every way, by laboring like this, that you must support the weak. And remember the words of the Lord Jesus, that He said, 'It is more blessed to give than to receive.'" It is in Christ that the Father spiritually blesses man today. Apostle Paul tells us in Ephesians 1:3: "Blessed be the God and Father of our Lord Jesus Christ, who hath blessed us with all spiritual blessings in heavenly places in Christ." As a child of the most high God, you must understand and appreciate the fact that "all spiritual blessings" are in Christ.

LET'S PRAY: Dear Heavenly Father, the Giver of all things good, the Lord that provides, the Lord that never forsakes His people. I know that You are able to do exceedingly abundantly above all that I ask for or think of. I know that there is no limit to the greatness You can unleash in my life. I understand that no eyes have seen, no ears have heard, no mouths have spoken, and no mind has conceived the blessings that await those who trust in You, and wait patiently on You. Lord, today, I ask that You bless me completely. May I find happiness, joy, peace, and progress in Your presence. Open the gates of heaven unto me and pour blessings upon my hands that whatever I touch may be established. Lord, I call on You in prayer that You may answer me. I seek deliverance from all my troubles. I ask that You open my understanding to make wise decisions that will prosper me. Lord, You are the God of all grace, and every good and perfect gift comes from You. I open my hands ready to receive the blessings You are about to bestow upon me. Though I know that You already know my every need, I will always come to You every day, acknowledging that You're God and that You will meet my every need according to Your will and Your riches. In the name of Your Son Jesus Christ, we pray, Amen.

The best part of the devil being in disguise by using people and situations as a way deceive you or weaken you only makes you stronger by allowing you to see the light of God's salvation instead of the darkness of the devil's deception.

SEPTEMBER 18

Stay focused on what's above, not on earthly things,
Colossians 3:2 (VOICE)

Focus on God today, not people of this world. People will upset you, hurt you, disrespect you, take advantage of you, and ignore you, but God never will. These types of people are being guided by the devil, and they are on a mission to commit evil acts against you. God is a faithful God; He is a God of love and compassion, He will protect you and cover you with His righteousness at all times. Strive to impress God and prove your faithfulness to him by your actions and remember only God's opinion matters. Don't worry about what others say about you or think about you, focus on God and His plan for your life. There will always be someone who has something to say about you or the way you go about your life. It is important you realize that your life is a result of God's creation and that you are a child of the most high God. You were placed on this earth to fulfill His purpose in order to please Him and bring Glory to His name.

LET'S PRAY: Dear Heavenly Father, the world is chaotic, people are wicked, selfish, and I need Your peace to fill my heart and keep my mind and my eyes completely focused on You. Teach, instruct, counsel, and guide me every day, and in everything. Help me to keep my eyes, and my mind focused on Your Word. I want to live a life that is focused on You, and a life that has You in its center. Lord, I want to live a life driven and directed by Your Holy Spirit. I want to live the life that You created me to live. I want to be an overcomer, a great achiever, and a victor. Lord, I find comfort in your presence, I stand upon Your word and promises today. Protect me against the attacks of the evil one, deter every plan of the wicked towards my life, abolish the efforts of the devil in my life and strengthen me to withstand every attack of the wicked. Be my Protector, my Shield, and my Sword. Keep me free from harm. I ask to walk in Your light. May I seek to bring glory to Your Name with all that I do. I seek to glorify You with my whole being. In the name of Your Son Jesus Christ, we pray, Amen.

Nothing good will ever come out of ungodly, negative, and lustful thoughts that are the result the devil using someone as a way to deceive you so that he can creep into your mind in an attempt to corrupt it with thoughts that are not of God.

SEPTEMBER 20

Seek the Lord while He may be found, Call upon Him while He is near. **Isaiah 55:6 (NKJV)**

You must seek God when you face difficult, complicated, or frustrating situations. There is nothing in this world that is too difficult for God. After all, He is the creator of Heaven and earth and everything in between. In order to receive help from God, you must not only seek Him, but you also need to believe in Him and trust His will. There will be times in your life where it seems like everything is going wrong, things are not going as "you" planned or as you wanted or thought they should go. When things seem to be going all wrong in your life you need to stop what you're doing, stop thinking how things should be going and seek God so he can show you the plan He has established for your life. When you seek God and follow His plan for your life, you will start to notice that everything that was difficult and everything that caused you trouble is no longer even a problem at all. When you follow God's plan and allow him to guide you down the right path, everything in your life will go much smoother, and your life will be much more fulfilling and enjoyable. God has placed you here on this earth for a reason and to serve a purpose, and you will not be fulfilling your purpose when you don't follow God's plan for your life.

LET'S PRAY: Dear Heavenly Father, my strength comes from You. I will make an effort every single day to seek You as long as I live. I will continually come to You in prayer when I face difficult situations. I will constantly reference You in all that I do. I will seek You even when all hope seems to be lost for You never leave nor abandon Your children. Lord, I know Your plans for me are that of prosperity and not of harm, that of hope and a great future. I call upon You today in prayer asking You that You may listen to my humble cry. I seek You today and every day with all my heart. Lord, even though I cannot see where You are taking me, I trust You, and I will follow Your lead because I know that Your plan for me is to do good works to Glorify Your name. Lord, I will take up my cross and follow You. I will leave behind any worldly pleasures. May all my pleasure come from doing Your will. Guide me in times of difficulty, direct me in times of struggle, bless me in times of lack, and heal me in times of weakness. In the name of Your Son Jesus Christ, we pray, Amen.

Because narrow is the gate and difficult is the way which leads to life, and there are few who find it. Matthew 7:14-16 (NKJV)

God gives all His children the opportunity to go to heaven after this life but not all His children make it to heaven. Even though we all have the opportunity to go to heaven it is up to us to prove we are worthy of God's grace, salvation, and His unconditional love. We must show God by our actions that we are living our life for Him every single day of our lives. We must consistently show God that we are doing His working and living our lives to fulfill our purpose in this life and on this earth according to His will. Your actions here on earth will determine If you get into heaven or not on judgment day, so be aware of your actions and how you are living your life.

> I will ruin these haughty and wicked people who ignore My words, who follow their own stubborn hearts, who run after other gods, who bow down to lifeless idols. They will end up like this rotten undergarment in your hands—completely worthless! **Jeremiah 13:10 (VOICE)**

God is very angry, about the current state of our world and the direction it is going. God is very unpleased about the number of unbelievers in this world who not only refuse to acknowledge Him as their creator; they refuse to acknowledge that He even exists. This has resulted in many unbelievers living their life day by day not even realizing how they got here, why they are here or even taking a second to thank God for the gift of life. They struggle day by day and make one bad decision after another. The choices they make are dictated by the devil, and as a result, their actions are saturated with greed, anger, temptation, and self-pride. These very same unbelievers refuse to take time to talk to God or seek Him for help, but they will be the first to wonder why their daily life is a constant struggle. These are the people who need God, and they need your help to preach the Good news about God's Word to them. God is also not pleased with the way His young children are being raised. They are not being taught about God and the importance of His word in their daily lives. Their hearts and minds are not being instilled with all the fundamental morals, values, ethics, standards, and life principles that come with a proper Christian upbringing. God tells us in Proverbs 22:6: "Train up a child in the way he should go, and when he is old he will not depart from it." We must start teaching our children the truth about God and the right lessons in life according to His word. To God, His children are His children forever, regardless of their age and regardless if they believe in Him or not.

LET'S PRAY: Dear Heavenly Father, may I never enjoy the company of unbelievers. Instead, may I be the light through which they are led to You. May I never stay away from them, instead, may I teach them to keep

Your commandments just as I do. Lord, may I never forget that there is a reward of greatness in the kingdom of heaven for all those who do so. May I never forget that it is my divine responsibility to go into the world and preach the gospel; converting as many as possible, and winning souls for You. Lord, when I am in the midst of unbelievers, may I never leave without sharing Your love with them. Give me the strength, wisdom, and understanding to speak Your blessing upon them. Lord, may I be the light, leading them to You that You may lead them to the Father. While on earth, You didn't stay away from unbelievers. Instead, You shared the message of righteousness with them. Lord, may I be more like You, and bring Your light to their darkness. Lord, when people who don't know you ask me what's the reason of my hope, may I be ready and bold to tell them that my help comes from You, the Maker of Heaven and earth. In the name of Your Son Jesus Christ, we pray, Amen.

Showing someone you love with respect and appreciation is done by actions not by words. Jesus taught us His unconditional love by sacrificing His life on the cross for all of us. Jesus paid the ultimate price for us so there is no reason why someone who loves you can't show you respect and appreciation with their actions. And if someone is consistently unable to show you respect and appreciation with their actions but only in words, you need to re-evaluate your relationship with them. God wants only the best for you, and he promises the best for you. But ultimately it is up to you to decide if you are going to settle for mediocre or the greatness that God has promised. Stop and ask yourself right now, I am living according to what God has promised or am I living a mediocre life. If you are not living according to God's promises, you must take a stand and step out in faith right now today. Even though God has made you specific promises, He can not and will not force you to live according to those promises.

Only you can step up and step out on faith and live out those promises. Don't ever settle for any less than what God has promised you and you will love a happy, joy-filled, peaceful life.

SEPTEMBER 24

This is the day the Lord has made; We will rejoice and be glad in it. **Psalm 118:24 (NKJV)**

Today is a gift from God. Just like every other day that God has given you, today is a new chapter in the book of your life. Today is a fresh start, a clean slate, a chance to start over and do things right in God's eyes. Today is another chance to correct the mistakes you made yesterday, an opportunity to right all the wrongs you made yesterday, and a chance to replace all the bad decisions of yesterday with good choices today. God wants you to make the most of this day, He wants you to enjoy this day, and He wants you to appreciate all of this day. No matter what you do today, no matter what you say today, and no matter how you act today, make sure that it is pleasing to God and that it brings glory to His Name. All your days here on earth a predetermined and numbered by God. He knows exactly how many days you will live, and He knows the purpose of each and everyone one of your days. So today, do what is pleasing to God in every respect, and He will guide and direct the path of your day so that you will be able to enjoy every single moment of this glorious day.

LET'S PRAY: Dear Heavenly Father, I begin this day by praising You for the gift of life, sound health, and a sound mind. All good and perfect gifts come from Your kingdom; I am thankful for the gift of this day, I am grateful for the gift of this life. Lord, You are the Giver of happiness to those who fear You. I humbly ask for Your strength and guidance this day. Replace my problems with Your joy, and my troubles with Your peace. I am not afraid of the works of the devil because You are with me, and You protect me. As I go about my daily activities, I ask that You help me accomplish what needs to be done according to Your will. Today, I ask you to give me the opportunity to correct the mistakes I made yesterday. I ask you to give me the opportunity to right all the wrongs I made yesterday. I ask you to give me the opportunity to replace all the bad decisions of yesterday with good choices today. Lord, I will strive today to make sure all my actions, all my words, and every choice and decision I make are pleasing to You and bring Glory to Your Name. I ask You to guide my path this day and direct me according to the journey You have established for my life according to Your will. In the name of Your Son Jesus Christ, we pray, Amen.

Make this most of this day by allowing God to guide and direct your thoughts, words, and actions throughout this day. Show God how thankful you are for the gift of this day by your actions. You must put the needs of other people before your own needs on a daily basis. Do what God is leading you to do today even if it makes you uncomfortable or you don't feel like doing it. The reward for stepping out in faith and doing what God is commanding you to do is worth it. If you step up and do what God is commanding you to do today not only will it bring glory to God but it will make you feel good.

Together, we are his house, built on the foundation of the apostles and the prophets. And the cornerstone is Christ Jesus himself. We are carefully joined together in him, becoming a holy temple for the Lord. Through him you Gentiles are also being made part of this dwelling where God lives by his Spirit. **Ephesians 2:20-22 (NLT)**

The church is God's house. The church is where we come to worship God, and the church is where we join in fellowship with other believers under God's authority. The church is an essential part of being a devoted Christian. In the Apostle's Creed (200 A.D.) it states - "I believe in the holy church; this statement emphasizes the importance of participating in the church." God wants you to know that attending church is an integral part of being a Christian. To some Christians, God is their Heavenly Father, Jesus is their Lord, and the Holy Spirit is their advocate, but they want to avoid attending church on a regular basis. There is a reason God wants His children to visit His house often. The church is not only a place to worship God and fellowship with other believers, but it is also a sacred place where you can get cleansed, revived, renewed, restored and refreshed in God's presence and His Word. God tells us in Hebrews 10:24-25: "Let us think of ways to motivate one another to acts of love and good works. And let us not neglect our meeting together, as some people do, but encourage one another, especially now that the day of his return is drawing near." It is very pleasing to God when His children are gathered in His house to worship in His presence and fellowship with other believers. As a community, as a city, as a state, as a country, we must unite as one world. We must unite as one body in Christ to restore the church and revive God's word in our daily lives and in the lives of those who are lost.

LET'S PRAY: Dear Heavenly Father, today I ask You to put Your peace into my heart and fill my household with Your peace too. I ask You to diffuse Your peace throughout my neighborhood, my church, and my nation. Uproot any source of unrest, disagreement, hatred, grudges, and envy from around me. I pray for this today that I may have peace of mind to do that which I ought to do every day. Lord, as I endeavor to attend church and meet active like-minded Christians, bring us together in Your love. As we share Your Word, open our understanding that we may get the deepest meanings of what You are speaking to us about. As we come together in prayer, declaring progress, healing, and protection over our lives may it be done for us all by the Father in heaven who created us all, and through Whom all good things come. Lord, I do not want to be a lukewarm or part-time Christian that only observes Your commandments on Sundays or at the church, I want to be a full-time, wholehearted Christian. Lord, may I realize that the church is everywhere I go. May I realize that I am the church, and Your church is a heart that is open to Your love. Lord, forgive me for the times I served You only on special occasions. In the name of Your Son Jesus Christ, we pray, Amen.

Are you right with God? Are your words, thoughts, and actions pleasing to God? If you're not right with God and your words, thoughts, and actions are not pleasing to God are you willing to surrender everything to Him? Are you willing to unselfishly give all your problems to God? All your bad habits, addictions, all your lies, and all your mistakes? Are you willing to give it all to Him and ask for forgiveness so that you can be right with God?

SEPTEMBER 28

Go out and make disciples in all the nations. Ceremonially wash them through baptism in the name of the triune God: Father, Son, and Holy Spirit. Then disciple them. Form them in the practices and postures that I have taught you, and show them how to follow the commands I have laid down for you. And I will be with you, day after day, to the end of the age. **Matthew 28:19-20 (VOICE)**

God uses his servants to bring hope to the hopeless. Today He may give you an opportunity to fill someone's heart with hope. When the opportunity is presented, You must be ready and willing to step up to the plate and do what God has commanded. Without your help today, a precious child of God who has lost their hope may never have the opportunity to find hope again before it's too late. God has all His faithful servants out on missions every single day. If you are a true Christian, then you are a servant of God, and as a servant of God, He expects you to spread the Good News of His written word to those who are lost and need to find hope. God tells us in Mark 16:15: "Go out into the world and share the good news with all of creation." God is very clear in His Word that He wants all of His faithful servants to go out into the world and spread His written Word to everyone. As a Christian, it is your duty to reach as many people as possible who are lost by sharing the word of God with them. When you share the word of God with the hopeless you are not only filling their hearts with hope, you are pleasing God and bringing Glory to His Holy name.

LET'S PRAY: Dear Heavenly Father, today, I ask You to use me as Your faithful servant to spread Your Word to those who are hopeless. You are the source of all righteousness. You never forsake Your children, and You never leave us to go begging. You are the great Provider. All those who put their hope in You completely, You always provide for them. You never put to shame those who love and trust in You completely. Lord, stay with me even when the world rejects me. Uplift me even when the world writes me off. Give me the strength, courage, and wisdom to spread Your word to those who need You in their lives. When I meet unbelievers who are lost, may I be focused on helping them find You. May I be focused on winning their lost souls for You. When I speak to unbelievers, speak through me. May I enjoy the fellowship of righteousness and not the fellowship of unrighteousness. May I do all that I do under Your light and not under darkness. May I embrace Your light because all my act is without immorality. I pray for all the lost souls that are either too proud to acknowledge You or too ignorant to realize that You are the Messiah and the only true Way to the Father. Lord, I ask You to show Your love to them in an extraordinary and non-ignorable way. I want You to bring Your presence upon them and show Your wonders to me in a way that is undoubted. Lord, show them beyond any doubt that You are the Alpha and the Omega, the Beginning and the End, the King of kings, and the Lord of lords. Lord, may they realize that You have died on the cross that they may be saved and have life in abundance. In the name of Your Son Jesus Christ, we pray, Amen.

It's ok to rely and depend on your loved ones to a certain degree but don't rely and depend on them too much because one day they will no longer be here. It is important always to remember that you must rely and depend on God because He will always be here for you until the day He delivers you from your temporary home here on earth to your permanent home in heaven.

Instead, You direct me on the path that leads to a beautiful life. As I walk with You, the pleasures are never-ending, and I know true joy and contentment. **Psalm 16:11 (VOICE)**

Faith is a choice. God is your creator, your heavenly Father, and your sovereign Redeemer. It's your choice if you decide to follow God and His plan according to His will. Your life is full of choices, and the choices you decide to make today will affect your life tomorrow and forevermore. If you choose to follow God and His plan, you will receive His mercy, grace, blessings and the ultimate gift of eternal life in heaven. But the choice is yours to make, no one on this earth can make this choice for you. God can guide you, give you courage, and strengthen you, but He cannot make this crucial choice for you. God tells us in Matthew 7:13-14: "Enter by the narrow gate; for wide is the gate and broad is the way that leads to destruction, and there are many who go in by it. Because narrow is the gate and difficult is the way which leads to life, and there are few who find it." This verse gives you two important choices, the narrow gate or the wide gate. God tells you to enter the "narrow gate" for it leads to life because it is the path less traveled. The wide gate leads to destruction because many people choose this path because it is easy. In God's eyes, the path that is easy is not the best path because it takes minimal effort and most people choose this path. But the path that is difficult takes much more effort, and a few select people will choose this path. What path are you going to choose the easy most popular path or the more difficult path that is less popular? The choice is yours to make.

LET'S PRAY: Dear Heavenly Father, I come to You in prayer, asking you to guide my thoughts and actions so that I make the right choices according to your will. According to the power that works in me, direct my path so that I may do the right things at the right time, be at the right place at the right time, and make the right choices and decisions at the right time. Lord, guide me at all times to do what's right, that I may not destroy the good plans and future You have for me. Even though I may walk through the valley of the shadow of death from making bad choices, I fear no evil because I know that You are with me at all times. You are my light when I walk through darkness. You are my guide, leading me along the path through the narrow gate which leads to abundant life. Lord, thank You for the reward of eternal life in heaven. I know that I may receive salvation for believing in You, walking in faith, following your commands, and choosing the path less traveled. In the name of Your Son Jesus Christ, we pray, Amen.

OCTOBER

When you choose to seek the ways of the world instead of seeking God you will lose faith, your hope will diminish, and Joy will seem non-existent in your life. In order to experience joy, you must have faith in God and give Him a chance to restore your hope by providing what you need instead of giving you what you desire.

But without faith it is impossible to please Him, for he who comes to God must believe that He is, and that He is a rewarder of those who diligently seek Him. **Hebrews 11:6 (NKJV)**

Today, God wants you to walk in faith instead of just talking in faith. What I mean by this is that when you walk in faith, your actions will be pleasing to God, and it will prove to Him that you have faith in Him and His word. But when you only talk in faith, your words alone will not prove to God that you are faithful. There is no point of "talking the talk in faith" if you're not going to follow it up by "walking the walk in faith," it is simply a waste of time, and you will not accomplish anything. Having faith is not easy, it takes hard work, it takes dedication, it takes commitment. Talking in faith won't get you very far at all, but walking in faith every day is what will get you salvation and grace from God. Faith in words without action is meaningless to God. An excellent example of Faith in words without action is when you tell God you're going to do what He has commanded you to do, but you end up not being obedient and doing what He has commanded. Anyone can say they are a Christian and that they have faith, but God will redeem only those who walk in their true faith. Faith in your words will not save you, the only thing that will save you is faith in your actions, walking in your faith, proving to God consistently on a daily basis that you have faith in Him and His will for your life.

LET'S PRAY: Dear Heavenly Father, today, I come to you in prayer, asking You to strengthen me and guide me so that I may walk in faith instead of talking in faith. I want my actions to be pleasing to You; I want to prove to You by my actions that I trust You and I have complete faith in You. I want to show you that I will work hard to walk in faith, I will be dedicated and committed to walking in my faith every day. I want every single day of my life to be an example of how a true Christian should live. I want every day of my life to glorify You. Lord, I know that I cannot achieve these things without walking in faith. I look up to You Lord, for You are the Author and Finisher of my faith. May I never make talking in faith a priority over walking in faith because talking in faith will accomplish nothing, but walking in faith every day will allow me to receive salvation and grace from You. Lord, I ask that You strengthen, grow, and solidify my faith in Your Word so that I may receive Your blessing upon me, and receive it in abundance. In the name of Your Son Jesus Christ, we pray, Amen.

If you truly want to please God and receive
His blessings you must remove negative
people who refuse to live their life for
God and block the light of His salvation
by living for the ways of the world.

OCTOBER 4

Be still in the presence of the Lord, and wait patiently for him to act. Don't worry about evil people who prosper or fret about their wicked schemes. Stop being angry! Turn from your rage! Do not lose your temper—it only leads to harm. For the wicked will be destroyed, but those who trust in the Lord will possess the land. **Psalm 37:7-9 (NLT)**

God is sovereign, and He wants you to remain calm when you face difficult, frustrating and challenging situations. Don't allow the devil to use these types of situations to get you easily worked up into a vicious rage. When you allow the devil to control you, he will make your mind race, and he will force you to do things you don't mean to do, and he will force you to say things you don't mean to say. The words you say when you're angry are evil words of the devil; they are never nice words, they are words that will hurt the people who are important to you, once you say them you can't take them back. Human anger is the result of allowing the evil one to creep into your mind and control your thoughts instead of seeking God to saturate your mind with positive thoughts that will comfort you and keep you calm. God's word is the truth, and His word will never fail you. When you live by God's word on a daily basis, you will become very resistant to the evil acts of the devil. Being able to comprehend God's word and obey His command is not always easy, it will often require you to remove yourself from situations that are not of God. In James 1:21 God tells us: "So walk out on your corrupt liaison with smut and deprived living, and humbly welcome the word of truth that will blossom like the seed of salvation planted in your souls." If you fail to do what God requires, it's as if you forget His word as soon as you hear it. One minute you're obeying God and doing what He commands, and the next you're allowing your thoughts and actions to overpower God's commands. When you open your eyes to God, it is possible to take in the beautiful, and perfect truth found in His law of liberty and live by it. If you allow God to lead you down the path He has chosen, and do what God has commanded; you will avoid the many distractions of this world and the evil acts of the devil.

LET'S PRAY: Dear Heavenly Father, today, I denounce any spirit of anger within me because I know that anger is not of You, and not from You. I know that You give to Your people a spirit of love, harmony, and peace. I know that anger is a sin, and today, I resist it and all its various forms. Lord, may I never give full vent to my anger and regret saying awful words that I do not mean. May I never during an argument, quarrel or disagreement say hurtful words to those that I love, especially those who are important to me. May I never repay evil for evil, instead may I always find the wisdom to repay good for evil. Lord, may I never be quick-tempered. Grant me the understanding to know why. May I refrain from using words that will hurt people. Instead, may my words bring blessings upon those who hear it, no matter the circumstance. In this life, I know that there will be trials, tribulations, troubles, and temptations, but I know that You want me to stay calm, smile, rejoice, and know that You are a sovereign God, and You have overcome the world. Lord, I ask You to bless me with peace of mind, fill me with the fruit of the Holy Spirit. Teach me how to live in the Spirit. Remove any form of anger within me. I want You to empty me of myself and fill me with the Holy Spirit that I may have its fruit and live a life worthy of You. May I never do anything out of anger but out of Your abundant love. Lord, may Your Word never depart from my lips, and may Your commandment never depart from my heart. I want to obey You and Your law with all my heart. Give me the strength to do this without backsliding. Guide me. Add peace to me, my family, my household, my friends, and those I care so for. Add peace to all those who keep Your commandments for it is a promise You made to us all. May Your peace flow through me like a river with a divine source. In the name of Your Son Jesus Christ, we pray, Amen.

If you love God in your heart 100% if you seek God 100% if you focus on God 100% all the time and everywhere the devil will flee away from you.

OCTOBER 6

> For God so loved the world that He gave His only begotten Son, that whoever believes in Him should not perish but have everlasting life. **John 3:16 (NKJV)**

God sacrificed His only begotten Son for all of us. His Son Jesus Christ paid the ultimate price by sacrificing His life and being crucified on the cross for all of us. Stop and think for a minute, what God and His Son have done so that you could be forgiven of all your sin and have eternal life in heaven. God tells us in Isaiah 53:5: "But He was wounded for our transgressions, He was bruised for our iniquities; The chastisement for our peace was upon Him, And by His stripes, we are healed." Jesus endured excruciating pain, He was bruised and beaten, and He gave His life so that you could be healed for your sins and wrongdoing. Far too often you take things for granted on a daily basis; you don't appreciate the precious gift God has given you. Your actions are often very displeasing to God, you complain about the way your life is going, or you're not happy with what you have or don't have. Whether you believe it or not, everything you have is because God has given it to you. And everything that you don't have is because God has not given unto you for one reason or another. Only God knows what you need when you need it, and why you need it. Instead of complaining about your life, start being thankful for the life God has given you. Your life is a gift, and every day that you wake up is a gift. Start doing the things that bring Glory to God, start showing God appreciation for all He has done, and start acting in a way that is pleasing to God. The Gift that God has given you today could be taken away just as easily tomorrow. Remember to show appreciation for all that God has done when you are given the opportunity to wake up to see another day tomorrow. Today, as you're reading these words, they could be the last words you ever read, today could be your very last day here on earth, it is all up to God and His plan for your life.

LET'S PRAY: Dear Heavenly Father, thank You for sacrificing your only begotten Son and thank you, Jesus, for paying a debt that You did not owe. Thank You for praying the price of my sin. I am forever thankful for Your awesome description of love. Thank You for blessing me with the gift of salvation. Thank You for paying the price for me, and making salvation a free gift to all that walk upright. You paid the price for my salvation in full. Because of You, my salvation is free. You took the humiliation, the beating, the mockery, the suffering, the pain, and finally died amongst thieves. Thank You, Jesus, for such wonderful love You displayed on the cross. Today, I offer myself completely to do Your will. Heal me, and raise me from the captivity of sin to the freedom of truth. Lord, thank You for reconciling God and mankind. Thank You for restoring the great love the Father has for us. Now, there is nothing that can separate us from His love. Because of Your sacrifice, I have inherited everlasting life for free. Lord, Your death on the cross is the greatest display of love ever known to mankind. You put our salvation first and laid Your life down so that we may have life in abundance. As You rose from the dead, I rise with You. Shine Your light upon me, and dispel anything in me that doesn't bring You glory. In the name of Your Son Jesus Christ, we pray, Amen.

Resisting from the acts of the devil in
the flesh will allow you to remain strong
in the fullness of God in the spirit.

Resistance in the flesh = strength in the spirit.

OCTOBER 8

Through whom also we have access by faith into this grace in which we stand, and rejoice in hope of the glory of God. And not only that, but we also glory in tribulations, knowing that tribulation produces perseverance; and perseverance, character; and character, hope. Now hope does not disappoint, because the love of God has been poured out in our hearts by the Holy Spirit who was given to us. **Romans 5:2-5 (NKJV)**

You will always find hope in God and His Word when you face difficult situations in your life. When you have hope in God, you will never be shaken or have a fear of what might happen. It means that you will be at peace and remain calm, even though the most difficult storms in life because you know God will handle all your troubles. God tells us in Romans 8:24-25: "for we have been saved in this hope and for this future. But hope does not involve what we already have or see. For who goes around hoping for what he already has? But if we wait expectantly for things we have never seen, then we hope with true perseverance and eager anticipation." Having hope means being patient, relying on your faith, and trusting God and what He has promised. In God's written word, He has made many promises to His children. In each of these promises, God tells us that when He says He will do something, that means He will do it. When He says He (will not) do something or give you something, you can be assured that it won't be done, given unto you, or come to pass.

LET'S PRAY: Dear Heavenly Father, I know that You have prepared for me a future filled with hope. I ask You to fill me with all Your joy, peace and love that comes with believing in You. You are my light, shining Your beam of grace upon me and leading me where I need to go. You are the light that continually shines through the darkest storm and You always restore my hope in You. Lord, I ask You to strengthen my faith and trust in You, increase my hope in You, and allow me to remain patient at all times. I trust Your promise that You have great plans for me, and You delight in giving me a future and a hope. Please forgive me for the times that I lean on other people or things to meet my needs. Lord, forgive me of the times I placed my hope on other things or people and not You. From this day forward, I will place my trust and hope in Your Word. Without You I can do nothing, without You I am nothing, without You I am incomplete, but with You, I am whole again. You are all that I need because You are everything, and everything is You. May I always lean on Your understanding, wisdom, knowledge, and strength. In the name of Your Son Jesus Christ, we pray, Amen.

You must refuse to let people affect you who consistently follow the ways of this world and think they are always right and know everything. Never allow these types of people try to make you feel like you are inadequate or that your opinions or suggestions don't matter. The sad truth is people who follow the ways of this world and think they are always right and know everything know nothing about God or who He is. These are the type of people who need God in their lives before it is too late. So stand strong in God's strength, wisdom, guidance, and power when you face people who only know the ways of the world. When you face difficult situations with these types of difficult people, it is the perfect opportunity to take a negative situation and turn it into a positive situation by talking to them about God and what He can do for them.

OCTOBER 10

Therefore do not worry about tomorrow, for tomorrow will worry about its own things. Sufficient for the day is its own trouble. **Matthew 6:34 (NKJV)**

Live your life one day, one hour, and one minute at a time. God does not want your mind to be consumed by thoughts that will cause you to overthink and worry about the future because you can't control it. Instead, He wants your mind to be completely focused on Him so that He can fill your mind with positive thoughts. God does not want you to be anxious about what might happen one minute from now, one hour from now, or even tomorrow. God already knows what will take place in the future according to His plan for your life. God wants you to slow down and relax so that you can experience and enjoy every moment of your life here on earth.

LET'S PRAY: Dear Heavenly Father, from this moment on, I will never be anxious about anything in my life. I know that worrying never solves anything but keeps a man busy doing nothing and achieving nothing. From now on, I will come to You for everything that I need. May I never forget that worrying never adds a single moment to my life but removes. Lord, I trust Your promise that You have great and good plans for me, and You delight in giving me a future and a hope. Bless me with confidence to not look into the future because I have nothing to worry about because You are already there. I do not worry about what tomorrow may bring because I am certain that You will take care of my today and my tomorrow just as You have taken care of my past. I know that You care for me and that is why I cast all my worries, cares, and anxieties on You because I know that You will help me get through every day. Lord, take control of my life. In Your hands, I commit all my ways, direct my path, establish the works of my hands, and make Your strength perfect in my weakness. In the name of Your Son Jesus Christ, we pray, Amen.

When you seek God wholeheartedly, obey His every command, and live your life according to His will and His purpose He will make it very easy for you to see who truly belongs in your life and who doesn't. The words of someone who does not belong in your life according to God's plan will allow you to hear the truth, but the actions of someone who does belong in your life according to God's plan will allow you to see the truth. Don't ever avoid the signs from God because you are too afraid to take a step of faith because you are allowing your fears to hold you back. Instead, take that leap of faith so that you can live a joyful and peaceful life according to God's plan in order to fulfill His purpose for you.

> So in Christ Jesus you are all children of God through faith, for all of you who were baptized into Christ have clothed yourselves with Christ. There is neither Jew nor Gentile, neither slave nor free, nor is there male and female, for you are all one in Christ Jesus. **Galatians 3:26-28 (NIV)**

You're a child of God, and you're an integral part of His amazing creation. All of God's children are perfect in His eyes and His spirit, but not in the flesh. As a child of God, you will make mistakes, bad choices, and bad decisions because you are human. You are God's child and His creation, but not all His children are Christians who believe that God is their creator and heavenly Father. God's children who don't believe in Him are very lost, and they need your help to find God so they can accept His Son Jesus Christ into their heart. Once they accept Jesus Christ and make Him their personal Lord and Savior, they will be saved, and they will receive the gift of eternal life in heaven. As a child of God and a Christian, you can glorify God's name by spreading the word of God and reaching out to everyone you can to share the Good news of God with them.

LET'S PRAY: Dear Heavenly Father, thank you for creating me and giving me the gift of being Your child. I was in Your care before I was born. You know me better than anyone. I ask that You set forth Your Spirit to dwell in me and comfort me now and forever. Lord, those who don't know You are just an arm of the flesh that is capable of doing nothing. As Your children who trust in You and believe in you, we know that You will help us accomplish everything, and fight our battles for us. Lord, thank You for making me a victor over the enemy. Thank You for commanding Your army of angels to fight the battle against the enemy, and thank You for winning for me. Lord, without You, I will be a victim of the wicked ones, but because of You, I am now a victor. Lord, as Your child, I want to spend this moment glorifying Your Holy Name. I want to sing songs of praise. I want to worship You. I have come to bless Your Name for all the great things You have done for all Your children around the world. I want to thank You for Your faithfulness. I want to show appreciation for all the things You have blessed me with. In the name of Your Son Jesus Christ, we pray, Amen.

REMEMBERING GOD'S WILL
DURING PRAYER

We all need to remember that when we pray if it is God's will the prayer will be answered in His time. If the prayer is not God's will, the prayer may not be answered to our satisfaction but only to God's satisfaction, and we must not get upset about it. We must always remember that no matter how much we pray, how long we pray, or how many people are praying that the prayer will be answered to God's satisfaction, and in His time not ours.

OCTOBER 14

I will instruct you and teach you in the way you should go; I will counsel you with my eye upon you. **Psalm 32:8 (ESV)**

Always seek God before you speak so that He can saturate your mind with positive thoughts. Do not speak or act without consulting with God. He is your counsel, your Redeemer and the ultimate judge of your thoughts, words, and actions. God can protect you from the vicious results of allowing the devil to control your mind and your thoughts. You must seek God wholeheartedly so that He can consume all of your thoughts and direct your words and actions. Every time you feel the need to speak or act in a negative way you must stop and realize that the devil is trying to dictate your words and actions. The hardest part of directing the ways of the devil will be to flip your mind from negative thoughts to positive thoughts like a light switch. Your mind is the battlefield for your thoughts where many battles will take place on a daily basis. You must seek God in these battles of good versus evil in order to allow Him to take over all your battles with the devil. Once you allow God to rule the battlefield in your mind, the devil will not even stand a chance.

LET'S PRAY: Dear Heavenly Father, I want to please You with the words I say, the actions I make, and every thought in my mind. Reveal to me where my words, thoughts, or actions are not pleasing in Your sight. I want to be slow-to-anger, and quick-to-forgive. Give me the strength to let go of any anger, grief, and negative thoughts within me. May lust, greed, envy, anger, and evil thoughts from the devil never take root in my heart. I want to seek You in all that I do. I want all my actions, words, and thoughts to glorify You, and be done out of Your love that rules in my heart. I want to make wiser decisions that will benefit me and all those I love. I invite You to walk with me, teach me, guide me, and counsel me. I invite You to dwell in me as Your Word dwells in my heart. Increase my wisdom and my understanding. May I always rely on You for everything and put You first in everything. Lord, teach, instruct, counsel, and guide me every day, and in everything. Help me to keep my eyes, and my mind focused on Your Word. Lord, we know that You are the only Way, the only Truth, and the only Life. You give me life because all power belongs to You. You are the Mighty Healer, the Great Physician, the Just Lord, the Holy and True Redeemer. I ask that You give me the wisdom to speak right. May the words I speak be pleasing in Your sight. May my thoughts be pure, and may my actions be blessings upon all my brother and sisters. In the name of Your Son Jesus Christ, we pray, Amen.

Are you ready to make some important changes in your life today by living every day in complete obedience to God by doing exactly what He commands according to His plan in order to fulfill His purpose for your life?

OCTOBER 16

Put on the whole armor of God, that you may be able to stand against the wiles of the devil. For we do not wrestle against flesh and blood, but against principalities, against powers, against the rulers of the darkness of this age, against spiritual hosts of wickedness in the heavenly places. **Ephesians 6:11-12 (NKJV)**

God wants to protect you from all the vicious ways that the devil will try to sneak in and steal your joy. The devil has a large amount of evil tricks and tools that he will use in an attempt to take your focus off God. He will try to make you vulnerable in order to fall into his foolish schemes. The devil is very ruthless and fierce, he will continue to attack you several times a day and will refuse to back off until you call out to God for help. God tells us in James 4:7: "Therefore submit to God. Resist the devil, and he will flee from you." Some of the main tools the devil will use to get you to turn from God are lust, jealousy, anxiety, stress, worry, greed, and anger. You must remain completely focused on God in order to overcome these attacks from the devil. You won't be able to defeat the devil on your power, your plan or with your persistence. You need to be persistent in God's power, strength, guidance, and His written word. Once you are able to focus your mind completely on God and allow him to control your thoughts and your actions you will be able to deflect every single attack from the devil with ease.

LET'S PRAY: Dear Heavenly Father, I need Your help. I need You right now. Lord, I come to you today in prayer asking You to save me from the deception of the devil, protect me from the wrath of the enemy, and keep me safe from violent people. Lord, I do not want to be controlled by the devil. I want to guided by You, and I want to follow your plan for my life. Lord, thank You for sending Jesus to reconcile us. May the devil never steal Your gift of salvation and eternal life away from me. Bless me with the strength to resist the devil that He may flee from me, and may I live above sin. Lord, I know that the devil will continually try to keep me from my blessings. I know that the devil will continuously try to erect tents of doubts within me that I may have doubts when I pray. Lord, I ask that You send forth Your Spirit to fill me completely and leave no space for any foul spirit of the devil. Lord, may I never forget that the devil is always trying to plant ungratefulness in the hearts of your children to prevent them from giving thanks to You for the things You have blessed them with. May I resist the foul spirit of ungratefulness by constant prayers. Lord, I know that prayer is powerful and necessary to fight against the wiles and wrath of the devil. Lord, may I never forget that the devil is continually roaming the earth seeking to disrupt the lives of Your children. Lord, may my prayers keep me safe from the snare of the devil, keep me dwelling in Your land of provision, and heal me completely in mind, body, and soul. In the name of Your Son Jesus Christ, we pray, Amen.

Don't ever settle for less than what you deserve according to God's standards. Don't ever feel obligated to live your life according to the opinion of someone who follows the ways of the world instead of God's ways. And don't ever allow someone who follows the ways of the world make you feel unappreciated, inadequate, incompetent, unimportant, or incapable.

For by Him all things were created that are in heaven and that are on earth, visible and invisible, whether thrones or dominions or principalities or powers. All things were created through Him and for Him. **Colossians 1:16 (NKJV)**

Only in God's beautiful creation will you find vast amounts of fresh air, sunshine, beautiful blue skies and abundant amounts of freshwater in the many lakes, rivers, and streams here on earth. God did not place you on this earth for you to live your life with constant trouble, tragedy or tribulations. God has placed you on this earth so that you can enjoy everything he has created, appreciate everything he has given you, and most importantly to serve His purpose by doing His work. God does not want you to take a single moment or experience for granted. Instead, He wants you to appreciate everything in your life because everything you have in your life is a blessing from Him. Today, God wants you to stop and think about everything that you have, everything that you should be thankful for and everything that you have taken for granted in the past 30 days. For everything you have taken for granted, God expects you to call out to Him right now and apologize. God does not want you to apologize with your words; He wants your actions to show how thankful you are for every gift and every blessing that you have been lucky enough to experience and enjoy. Your life here on earth is short, enjoy it and appreciate it every moment of every day.

LET'S PRAY: Dear Heavenly Father, You are the creator of the Universe, and both heaven and earth, both seen and unseen. You are the God of all flesh, the Lord of all grace, the Light of the world. You are the Sustainer of all Your children, the everlasting Redeemer, and the Healer of all lands. Lord, all things that exist came into existence through You. Lord, I know that all things are for Your glory, and this includes me. Lord, may I realize that a life without You is just a number of wasted years. May I realize that a life that is not focused on You is a life without a purpose. Lord, as I endeavor to bring You glory with everything that concerns me, may I be found worthy to share in Your glory. Lord, You are the giver of every good and perfect gift. You hold absolute power over everything and everyone, and all those who love You and keep Your commandment, You bless us beyond measure. Lord, hear my voice today. Hear my cry, and deliver me from my troubles, tragedies, and tribulations. Lord, I give You thanks for the gift of life. I give you thanks for allowing me to experience all the beauty that You have created. Lord, I give You thanks for finding me worthy to see another beautiful day that You have created. In the name of Your Son Jesus Christ, we pray, Amen.

A true Christian does not claim to live their life for God part-time or when they feel like it. A true Christian does not follow the ways of the world Monday through Saturday and then claim to be a Christian and follow God in church on Sunday. A true Christian does not choose when they are going to be a Christian, where they are going to be a Christian or what they are going to follow according to God's commands and standards. A true Christian shows their intentions by their actions not by their words. A true Christian demonstrates their commitment to God through their works and deeds. And a true Christian will live their life completely for God every single day no matter what. So if you claim to be a true Christian, you better be able to show God that you are committed to living your life for Him every day and for His purpose in every way.

> If My people who are called by My name will humble themselves, and pray and seek My face, and turn from their wicked ways, then I will hear from heaven, and will forgive their sin and heal their land. **2 Chronicles 7:14 (NKJV)**

God needs you to pray to get His Word back into our schools. He needs you to pray so that His young children can express their religious beliefs without offending anyone at school. He needs you to pray so that His Word can be spread everywhere, with everyone at any time. God needs you to pray so that every school in your community can partner with a local church to engage His young children with local Gospel leaders. God needs you to pray for our entire nation and all our leaders, public officials and every member of our government. God is not happy with what is going on in our nation and our world. There has never been a time that God needs all His faithful children to pray and pray often for a nation and a world that is crumbling on a daily basis. Too many people have ignored the written Word of God for far too long, and it must not continue any longer. The Word of God must be instilled in the hearts and minds of God's young children and all the way up to our highest elected officials. Change must take place, and we must resolve all the issues of our world today but it can't and won't happen without God.

LET'S PRAY: Dear Heavenly Father, I come to You today in prayer, not for myself, but for our nation. I ask You to make changes in the leadership of our government. I am not asking that You change the government itself, but I am asking that You change the conscience of our elected officials. Lord, I ask you to correct the conscience of our elected officials and increase their fear for You, so they may make Godly decisions that are right according to Your will, not for their selfishness, but for the betterment of our nation. Lord, may I never forget that prayer is powerful, effective and necessary in the life of every Christian. Lord, may I never forget to pray for the leaders of our nation on a daily basis with my family at home, with colleagues at work, with fellow students at school, and with brothers and sisters at church. Lord, as we come together in agreement in prayer, may we receive all the blessings we ask for. Lord, may You forgive us of all our sin in order to help our nation and heal our land. In the name of Your Son Jesus Christ, we pray, Amen.

OCTOBER 21

Praying, reading your bible, and going to church are three of the most import aspects of communicating with God and maintaining a good strong relationship with Him.

OCTOBER 22

> And He said to them, "Go into all the world and preach the gospel to every creature. He who believes and is baptized will be saved; but he who does not believe will be condemned. **Mark 16:15-16 (NKJV)**

God wants you to stand up and proclaim His Word everywhere and to everyone. God needs all His faithful children to share the Good News of His written Word in this corrupted world. When you share the Word of God, you will be planting the seed of greatness in those who need to seek God. Everywhere you go, God will provide an opportunity for you to share His Word. God will often direct you, guide you, or place you in situations so that you can spread His word to someone who desperately needs to hear it. God places you in more situations than you even realize in order to reach out to someone that needs the help of the Holy Spirit. God will often test you by placing you in a situation where he wants you to share His word to see if you will follow His commands. When you prove to God that you will faithfully follow His commands he will grant you with blessings. As you prove your faith to Him, He will continue to place you in more difficult situations to do His work where you are needed.

LET'S PRAY: Dear Heavenly Father, I ask that You give me the strength to face the challenges of this day. I ask that You give me grace to stand up and proclaim Your Word to everyone you put in my path today and everywhere You lead me. Lord, I want to share the Good News with everyone. I want to tell them about Your love for them all. I want to make them aware that they have the keys to heaven and authority over the devil if they accept You as their personal Lord and Savior. Lord, I want to tell everyone that with You nothing is impossible and without You they can do nothing. Lord, I want to tell them that Your strength is made perfect in their weakness and that You give rest to those who are heavy laden. Lord, I believe in the gospel for it is good news that makes known Your love for us all. I take heed to Your Word for they are the promises made to those who walk along the path of righteousness, and will be fulfilled in our lives. Lord, I want to pray for all those who haven't accepted You as their Lord and personal Savior. I want to pray for all those who haven't realized that You are the only True way to God the Father. Today I want to pray for those who don't know you and as a result they are lost in this world. Lord, send them someone that will share Your good news with them. May they have the gentle accepting hearts of babies and the wisdom of Solomon, and may they accept You completely. In the name of Your Son Jesus Christ we pray, Amen.

A careful, obedient, persistent study of God's Word will educate you far beyond any degree you can ever earn at any college or university. You can go to college to get a lot of head knowledge, but it will never compare to the knowledge and wisdom God's Word will put in your heart.

OCTOBER 24

So God created man in His own image; in the image of
God He created him; male and female He created them.
Genesis 1:27 (NKJV)

When God created you, He made every detail about you uniquely one of
a kind according to His plan for you. God predefined your gender, skin
color, height, eye color, hair color, and every other detail about you before
you were placed in your mother's womb. God already knew what you
would look like when you grew older. He knew what your career would
be. He knew where you would live. He knew who you would marry. And
He knew how many children you would have. God knew every gift and
talent He gave you, and He knew your strengths and weaknesses. He knew
all these details the very moment when He Created you. There is nothing
about you that God does not know. He knows every detail about you and
your life because He created you and He planned your journey in this life
according to His will. To God, you are His perfect masterpiece because
you were created in His image. God tells us in Matthew 5:48: "You,
therefore, must be perfect, as your heavenly Father is perfect." God does
not look at you the same way humans look at you. When God looks at you
He is only able to see the perfect masterpiece He has created in His image.

LET'S PRAY: Dear Heavenly Father, I am thankful that I am Your
craftsmanship and workmanship. I was created in Christ Jesus for Your
purpose to do good works. Lord, You are the beginning and the ending.
You have created everything that we see and know; You are the heavens and
all the earth. We know that You created every man in Your image to reflect
Your Son, Jesus Christ. Both male and female, and I want to thank You for
it is amazing to know that I look like my awesome Creator. Lord, may I
always be reminded of this honor every day for it is an honor to know that
I am created in the image of the Most High. Lord, may I never forget that
we all are created by You, the One True Living and Merciful Father. Lord,
May I be able to see myself just the way You see me; through Your eyes.

Lord, bless me with the strength to accomplish all that You created me to accomplish. Lord, I want to live a life driven and directed by Your Holy Spirit. I want to live the life that You created me to live. Lord, I want to be an overcomer, a great achiever, and a victor. Lord, today, I want to Glorify Your name here on earth by doing everything You have created me to do even to the very last detail. I know that I was created for a purpose. Lord, I ask that You reveal to me what my mission here on earth is. I ask that You bless me with the wisdom, skills, and resources necessary to accomplish my mission on earth. In the name of Your Son Jesus Christ, we pray, Amen.

All forms of sin come directly from the devil. There are several ways that sin affects our daily lives and most of the time we don't even really stop to even think about it. Sin makes us fall short of our destiny and our purpose according to God. Sin deceives us from the truth of God's words and His promises to us. Sin makes us weak that's why we need God's strength. Sin makes us vulnerable, that's why we need God's protection. Sin keeps us from seeing God's blessings. Sin keeps us from hearing God and where He is directing us and guiding us. Sin prevents us from seeing the light of God's salvation. Sin corrupts our mind, and it affects our mindset so that we will think negative thoughts instead of positive thoughts.

Therefore go and make disciples of all nations, baptizing them in the name of the Father and of the Son and of the Holy Spirit, and teaching them to obey everything I have commanded you. And surely I am with you always, to the very end of the age." **Matthew 28:19-20 (NIV)**

You bring glory to God, and you please Him when you spread His word to those who don't know Him and to those who need Him. When you share the word of God to both believers and non-believers, you are reaching and inspiring more people than you even realize. There are a lot of people out there who pray to God in times of need even though they don't believe in Him. As Christians, it is our responsibility to teach people the truth about who God is and why we need him in our daily lives. God tells us in Mark 16:15-16: "He said to them, 'Go into all the world and preach the gospel to all creation. Whoever believes and is baptized will be saved, but whoever does not believe will be condemned.' " There has never been a better time than now to go out into the world to spread the word of God. Every person you share the word of God with will be given the opportunity to know Him and serve Him wholeheartedly. They will also be the key to their permanent home in heaven by accepting God's son Jesus Christ into their hearts as their personal Lord and Savior. God wants you to make a difference in the world today by going out and sharing the good news of His word with everyone you see.

LET'S PRAY: Dear Heavenly Father, I want to thank You for Your undying love for the world. Thank You, Lord, for Your never-ending unconditional love, mercy, and grace for mankind. I want to thank You for loving me even while I was a sinner. Lord, I want to thank You for laying down Your life that I may be reconciled with the Father and be blessed with eternal life in heaven. Lord, as long as I live, I will live for You and not myself. As long as I draw breath, I will do so to spread Your Word of truth to all those I meet. Lord, may I realize that those who obey Your commandment and teach others to do the same shall be called 'great' in Your kingdom. Lord, strengthen me and guide me as I spread the gospel with those I come in contact with each day. Lord, thank You for appointing me one of Your prophets. Lord, As I endeavor to spread the gospel wherever I go, guide my tongue, and bless me with the wisdom to speak. Lord, into Your able Hands, I commit myself. Use me as an instrument to propagate Your good news to every corner of the earth. In the name of Your Son Jesus Christ, we pray, Amen.

While some people may choose to focus on the things of this world, it's essential to focus on God. You must have a good balance of God, work, and play. When you put God first, seek Him in every aspect of your life, and keep Him in the forefront of your mind, everything else will flow from there, your thoughts, your words, and your actions. So, with that being said, when you seek God before you think, your thoughts will be good and positive, if you seek God before you speak, your words will be good and positive, and if you seek God before you act, your actions and works will be Good and positive.

And my God will meet all your needs according to the riches of his glory in Christ Jesus. **Philippians 4:19 (NIV)**

You are a child of God, and that makes you the wealthiest person in this world. True wealth is having something that is priceless and can't be bought with money. God's grace, salvation, forgiveness and most importantly, eternal life in heaven cannot be bought, it can only be received. You can receive God's grace, salvation, forgiveness, and eternal life in heaven by accepting His Son Jesus Christ as your personal Lord and Savior. As a child of God, he wants you to know that you are an heir of His estate in heaven and a permanent part of His eternal kingdom. Accepting Jesus Christ as your personal Lord and Savior is free but its benefits are priceless. God expects you to live your life in a way that is not only pleasing to Him but in a way that brings Glory to His Holy name.

LET'S PRAY: Dear Heavenly Father, may I always realize that I am bankrupt without Your love. May I always bear in mind that I am poor if I do not have Your love in me. Lord, fill me with Your love so that I may be wealthy with Your grace, salvation, and blessings. Lord, because of Your abundant love for us all, You sent Your Son Jesus Christ to give us the gift of eternal life in heaven. Lord, dwell in me and fuel me with Your divine strength so that I may do great things according to Your will because I have the Son of God, the Messiah, my Savior, living within me, and using me. Lord, I want to thank You for Your love, mercy, and grace upon me. It's because of Your love for me that I have the gift of eternal life. It's because of Your mercy on me that I am forgiven. In the name of Your Son Jesus Christ, we pray, Amen.

For He made Him who knew no sin to be sin
for us, that we might become the righteousness
of God in Him. 2 Corinthians 5:21 (NKJV)

Do you know what the only unpardonable sin
is? The only unpardonable sin is not accepting
Jesus Christ as your personal Lord and Savior
so that He can forgive you of all your sins before
you pass on from this life into eternity. There are
no other sins in this life that are unpardonable
no matter how bad they are, Jesus will forgive
you of every single sin that you commit but
you to ask Him with sincerity, honesty, and
integrity. You can only ask Him to forgive you
of your sins if you have accepted Him as your
personal Lord and Savior. Jesus Christ died on
the cross for all us so that we could be forgiven
of our sins, the least we can do to show respect
and appreciation for what He sacrificed is to
accept Him as your personal Lord and Savior.

> Immediately after the tribulation of those days the sun will be darkened, and the moon will not give its light; the stars will fall from heaven, and the powers of the heavens will be shaken. **Matthew 24:29 (NKJV)**

Today, God wants you to understand and realize that the end is very near. He wants you to become saved by accepting His Son Jesus Christ into your heart as your personal Lord and savior if you are not saved. God is showing us that the end is near by displaying His power and authority over everything that is happening in the world today. God wants you to make things right with everyone you have wronged. He wants you to be prepared for what is about to happen. God tells us the promise of His spirit In Joel 2:28-32: "Then, after doing all those things, I will pour out my Spirit upon all people. Your sons and daughters will prophesy. Your old men will dream dreams, and your young men will see visions. In those days I will pour out my Spirit even on servants—men and women alike. And I will cause wonders in the heavens and on the earth-blood and fire and columns of smoke. The sun will become dark, and the moon will turn blood red before that great and terrible day of the Lord arrives. But everyone who calls on the name of the Lord will be saved, for some on Mount Zion in Jerusalem will escape, just as the Lord has said. These will be among the survivors whom the Lord has called." I want to point out where it says "But everyone who calls on the name of the Lord will be saved" therefore it is imperative that you accept Jesus Christ into your heart before it is too late. There is no mistake that the end is very near. There is a reason for all the chaos and destruction in our world today; there is a reason for all the earthquakes and hurricanes, there is a reason for all the wildfires. There is a reason for the blood moons. The fourth and final blood moon took place on Monday, September 28, 2015. The end times are very near, the second coming of the Lord is very near, are you saved? Do you call on the name of the Lord? Are you ready?

LET'S PRAY: Dear Heavenly Father, I ask for the blessing of faith. I ask for faith just as a mustard seed that I may be saved restored, renewed, delivered, and blessed with Your peace, love, joy, and abundance. Lord, I look forward to Your second coming because I know that You will be able to take the righteous to where they belong. I long to see Your glorious coming with the Father. Lord, I continually wait for that blessed hope and faithful day when the righteous will be free of the temptations of the devil. Lord, I know that nobody knows when that day may come but only the Father. May I be ready and always doing what's right, keeping Your commandments, and loving You and everybody. Lord, may I be found worthy to enter the kingdom of heaven on that fateful day of glory. Lord, today I want to pray for all those who haven't accepted You today as their Lord and personal Savior. I pray for all the lost souls that are either too proud to acknowledge You or too ignorant to realize that You are the Messiah and the only true Way to the Father. Lord, I ask You to show Your love to them in an extraordinary and non-ignorable way. I want You to bring Your presence upon them and show Your wonders to me in a way that is undoubted. Lord, show them beyond any doubt that You are the Alpha and the Omega, the Beginning and the End, the King of kings, and the Lord of lords. Lord, may they realize that You have died on the cross that they may be saved and have life in abundance. In the name of Your Son Jesus Christ, we pray, Amen.

God wants all His children to live a humble life and show humility to everyone. Humility is not only a mindset it is an attitude that comes from the heart. True humility cannot be seen on the outside; it can only be felt directly from the heart. When you are humble, you are not prideful, selfish or arrogant.

NOVEMBER

NOVEMBER 1

Stay focused on what's above, not on earthly things.
Colossians 3:2 (VOICE)

Focus on God today and allow Him to guide every aspect of your thoughts, actions, and words. Doing this will help make your day more enjoyable, fulfilling and meaningful. Allow God to lead you through this day by seeking Him in every choice and decision you make today. Think positive, act positive, and speak positively in every situation you face and towards every person you see today. Seek God to guide your thoughts before you think, seek God to guide your words before you speak, and seek God to guide your actions before you act. Be kind, caring, understanding and forgiving to others. God is kind, caring, understanding and He has forgiven you of your sins, and He expects you to forgive others. Be thankful and appreciate all of this day. This day is a precious gift from God; He wants you to show appreciation by your actions. Spend quality time talking with God today. God wants you to tell Him what is on your mind so that He can help you. Share the Gospel with someone who needs to hear the word of God today. You can share a bible verse, a devotional, or a picture with someone. Doing this can inspire someone to reach out to God so that He can completely change the outlook of their day. Take time today to read some scriptures from the Bible. Reading the Bible every day will not only inspire your day, but it will also help you understand the importance of God's word. It is also a good practice to actively read a daily devotional as this will help you remain embedded in God's word and His presence.

LET'S PRAY: Dear Heavenly Father, fill me with Your Spirit today so that I may stay focused, dedicated, and persistent at seeking you to guide my thoughts, actions, and words. Lord, I seek you today to direct my path so that I may do the right things at the right time, be at the right place at the right time, and make the right decisions at the right time. Lord, I seek You today to guide my thoughts before I think. Lord, I seek You today to guide my words before I speak. And Lord, I seek You today to guide my actions before I act. Lord, I want to be kind with my words and caring with my actions. Lord, as we share Your Word, open my understanding so that I may grow stronger in faith, and draw closer to You each passing day. Lord, may I be quick to completely forgive those who wrong me so that I may be forgiven by those who I have wronged, even when they haven't asked for forgiveness. Lord, I am very thankful that You have blessed me with the gift of this life and the gift of this day. Lord, I am happy, thankful, and grateful for everything You have done for me. Lord, may I never have a fixed or planned time to pray because I realize that prayer is the only means to communicate with You. Lord, You are the only One I can share my troubles with because I know that You are more than capable of solving them all. Lord, I want to be Your faithful child. I want to be part of Your chosen generation. I want to be part of the generation that will restore righteousness in this world. I want to be part of the generation that will preach the gospel everywhere I go. Lord, thank You for the gift of Your written Word the Holy Bible. As I read the Bible each day, I ask You to open my wisdom and understanding to get the deepest meaning of the messages from Your Word. Lord, thank You for the life you have blessed me with. Thank you for providing a plan for my life according to Your will. And thank you, Lord, for giving me the privilege to communicate with You in prayer. In the name of Your Son Jesus Christ, we pray, Amen.

God wants you to understand the difference
between conviction and condemnation.
When you are condemned, you will feel guilt.
When you are convicted by God, you will
be at peace. Once you have been convicted
by God, He will open your eyes and bring
resolution to the source of your sin.

The righteous cry out, and the Lord hears them; he delivers them from all their troubles. The Lord is close to the brokenhearted and saves those who are crushed in spirit. **Psalm 34:17-18**

God wants you to understand there will be times when troubles enter your life, and you won't be able to do anything to avoid it. You must realize that God has put this difficult situation in your life for a reason. And once you have overcome it, you will fully understand why God put you through this painful situation. You need to focus on God and accept what has happened and keep your head held high. God wants you to stand strong in His grace and know that He will guide your steps through this situation. If you think positive and remain entirely focused on God at all times, you will be able to stay calm and at peace. Today, you must choose to have faith in God and allow Him to lead you through this situation and guide you towards a positive outcome according to His plan.

LET'S PRAY: Dear Heavenly Father, I ask You to bless me with peace. Bless me with courage in the time of persecution, bless me with strength in time of difficulties, bless me with wisdom in time of reproaches, that I may keep moving forward, knowing that there is a reason for my current situation. Lord, I offer my prayer to You, putting my present situation in Your able hands. Lord, I ask You to take the pain, suffering, challenges, difficulties, and troubles away. I no longer want to feel this hurt in my heart. Fill my heart with Your love and completely heal me. Fill it with Your joy, peace, happiness, patience, and understanding that I may grow stronger in faith, and draw closer to You each passing day. Lord, no matter how tough this day is, I will never forget to come to You in prayer, thanking You for blessing me with the gift of life. I will always remember that there is nothing that You cannot handle. Lord, no matter the situation I find myself in, I will always come to You in prayer, giving thanks to You for all that You have given me, and trust in You completely for all that I may need. In the name of Your Son Jesus Christ, we pray, Amen.

You don't ever need to depend on anyone but God. He is all you truly need to be happy because He is the source of all your strength and courage. He grants you the gift of every new day, He gives you every breath that you take, and He guides your every step. You must live your life to serve Him, please Him, and to bring people to know Him. You have been blessed by the grace of God because you must live your life according to His purpose to fulfill His will.

NOVEMBER 5

Seek the Lord while you can find him. Call on him now while he is near. **Isaiah 55:6 (NLT)**

Everyone is struggling with something in one way or another. The only true solution to all your problems is found in one place, God. He tells us in Jeremiah 29:13-14: "Seek Me wholeheartedly, and you will find me. I will be found by you, declares the Lord, and I will bring you back from captivity. I will gather you from all the nations and places where I have banished you, declares the Lord, and I will bring you back to the place from which I carried you into exile." When you are facing difficult situations, or you are struggling with your circumstances, God wants you to seek Him wholeheartedly. When you seek God with all of your heart, He will give you the strength, the courage, and the guidance to find solutions to all your problems. When you call on God, you will find a resolution for all your struggles through Him, in His Word, and in His presence.

LET'S PRAY: Dear Heavenly Father, I come to You today in prayer, seeking Your face that I may find You, and You may bless me. Lord, I have struggled so hard to meet my needs, I have toiled day and night to make ends meet, I have suffered to fulfill all my responsibilities, but it seems like my long and hard hours of work are not paying off. Lord, I know that I need to seek You in difficult times because I know that You have prepared greatness ahead of me. Lord, I know that You will take me away from this point of struggle to Your dwelling place of blessing. Lord, I come before Your throne of grace, and I cry out to You to deliver me from my troubles. Lord, I know that You are more than able to do what I ask for, or I have ever imagined. I ask You today to write my name on the book of life, truth, and blessing according to Your will. In the name of Your Son Jesus Christ, we pray, Amen.

To those who continually choose to put things of the world in front of God on a daily basis, and to those who refuse to take care of your responsibilities. Don't be surprised when you struggle as a result of facing adversities and difficult situations because of "your" choices and decisions. But know that I will be praying for you because I love you and God loves you, and He already knows you need prayer.

For everything, absolutely everything, above and below, visible and invisible, rank after rank after rank of angels - everything got started in him and finds its purpose in him. **Colossians 1:16 (MSG)**

God created you and put you on this earth to serve a purpose. You were born by his purpose, and for his purpose, there is no other reason why you were born but for His purpose. You were placed on this earth to do God's work according to His will for your life. You were in God's thoughts long before God was ever in your thoughts. God knew the purpose for your life long before you were born; He knew your purpose long before your conception. You might think that you know the purpose for your life, but God is your creator, and He created your life for a purpose, and you did not have a say in the matter. You might get to choose your career, your spouse, where you live, or the car you drive, but you do not get to choose your purpose. The purpose that God has created for your life will determine the path and direction of your life. God wants you to understand that without Him, your life will make no sense. God wants you to turn to Him to discover your true purpose in this life. The starting point of your life is God, and God is the source of everything that happens in your life.

LET'S PRAY: Dear Heavenly Father, I want to live my life according to Your Will. Lord, call me according to Your purpose for my life so that all these impossibilities may transform into possibilities. Lord, I look up to You for You are the Author and Finisher of my faith. I put You at the center of my life so that I may live a life with purpose. Lord, uproot any spirit of fear, timidity, fright, and anxiety from me. Plant in me a spirit of confidence, boldness, faith, and courage. Lord, I give You control over my life. Drive me to success. Drive me where You always want me to be. Pick me from where I am and place me where You want me to be. Lord, create a bridge of faith between me and where I need to be, that I may walk by faith from where I am to the place You have prepared for me. Lord, I know that in all things You work for the good of all those who believe in You and have been called according to Your purpose. Lord, I want to live a life with purpose. I want to have a purpose-driven life. I want to have a life that is driven by Your Spirit. In the name of Your Son Jesus Christ, we pray, Amen.

In life, God promises to give you hope and a future, the desires of your heart, and He promises to prosper you and not to harm you. Never settle for anything less than these promises from God. Know your worth and what you deserve according to God's will for your life.

Refrain from anger and turn from wrath; do not fret—it leads only to evil. **Psalms 37:8 (NIV)**

God wants you to know that it is very difficult to be angry when you are grateful. When you are grateful, you will be thankful and appreciate all the blessings that God has granted you. The next time you feel yourself getting angry, stop immediately and seek God so that he can remind you of all the gifts and blessings He has given you. Anger is an action of the devil, and he will use it to control you like a puppet. Once the devil gets you into his trap, it is very difficult to get out. Therefore it is very important for you to seek God so that He can flood your mind with positive thoughts that will stop you from acting out on the devil's evil tricks. To seek God is to receive strength, guidance, courage, and peace.

LET'S PRAY: Dear Heavenly Father, may I never give full vent to my anger and regret saying awful words that I do not mean. May I never during an argument, quarrel or disagreement say hurtful words to those that I love, especially those who hate me. May I never repay evil for evil, instead, may I always find the wisdom to repay good for evil. Lord, may I never be quick-tempered. May I be quick to forgive and slow to become angry. Lord, may Your Spirit replace every hate, anger, disagreement, quarrel, and lack of cooperation, with love. Lord, I want to be extremely slow to anger even when I am pushed to the wall. Lord, may I never do anything out of anger but out of Your abundant love that You fill my heart with. Lord, may I be quick to drop any provoking matter before a dispute breaks out. In the name of Your Son Jesus Christ, we pray, Amen.

To fulfill God's will, we must serve Him by doing His work wholeheartedly and bringing Him glory continuously by pleasing Him with pure and sincere thoughts, and actions.

In the past God overlooked such ignorance, but now he commands all people everywhere to repent. For he has set a day when he will judge the world with justice by the man he has appointed. He has given proof of this to everyone by raising him from the dead." **Acts 17:30-31 (NIV)**

God wants you to repent your sins at all times. Most people think that to repent is to turn from sin. The Bible has much more to say about repentance. The Bible tells us to repent is to change your thoughts and your mind. To truly repent is to seek God wholeheartedly and allow Him to change your negative (evil) thoughts into positive thoughts which will result in changing your negative (evil) actions into positive actions. God tells us in Acts 3:19: "Repent, then, and turn to God, so that your sins may be wiped out, that times of refreshing may come from the Lord." God wants you to understand that you must repent in order to receive salvation. He tells us in Acts 2:38: "Peter replied, "Repent and be baptized, every one of you, in the name of Jesus Christ for the forgiveness of your sins. And you will receive the gift of the Holy Spirit." When you repent and have remorse, you will be forgiven of every sin you have ever committed, and the sins will be gone forever.

LET'S PRAY: Dear Heavenly Father, I come to You in total and sincere repentance asking for forgiveness in every area of my life that failed to give You glory, and grace to live above all sin. Lord, I want to be more like You while You were on earth; righteous, meek, humble, loving, and compassionate. Lord, I want to start today with true repentance of all the wrong things that I've done. I'm sorry for the hidden thoughts of my mind and the deceitful actions that don't bring glory to Your Name. Lord, I ask that You send me Your Holy Spirit to give me better wisdom to understand the deepest meanings of the Scriptures that I may understand it better. Lord, You are my ever-faithful God. You are just and merciful to forgive all those who come to You with a sincere and repented heart. In the name of Your Son Jesus Christ, we pray, Amen.

Your life will be less stressful when you don't purposely put yourself in stressful situations or circumstances. When you take care of your responsibilities and don't neglect what is important, you will prevent yourself from experiencing challenging and stressful situations. This often happens when you refuse to seek God and allow him to guide and direct your thoughts and actions.

No temptation has overtaken you except what is common to mankind. And God is faithful; He will not let you be tempted beyond what you can bear. But when you are tempted, He will also provide a way out so that you can endure it. **1 Corinthians 10:13 (NIV)**

God does not want you to continue living in the situation you are currently living if you are falling to temptation and continually committing the same sins over and over. God has blessed you with the gift of life among many other precious gifts. When He blesses you He expects something in return; He expects your committed promise to follow His will and not to keep committing the same sins. If you continue to sin, your sins will not go unpunished. God tells us in Romans 6:22-23: "But now that you have been set free from sin and have become slaves of God, the benefit you reap leads to holiness, and the result is eternal life. For the wages of sin is death, but the gift of God is eternal life in Christ Jesus our Lord". It might seem that your sins have not affected your blessings, but your sins will catch up with you on God's timetable. There is nothing that you will get by God; He knows when you sin, what the sin is and how often you sin. Remember, God knows all, and He sees all, and He will punish you for every sin that you continue to commit. God will forgive you of your sins, but He will not continue to forgive you for the same sins that you keep committing on a regular basis.

LET'S PRAY: Dear Heavenly Father, I do not want to continue living in sin, I do not want to be a sinner anymore. Lord, I do not want to fall into temptation anymore. Lord, have mercy on me. Forgive me, and wash my sins away. Cleanse me from all unrighteousness that my prayer may not be an abomination to You, but a pleasing solemn request from a humble servant. Lord, as I put You, Your kingdom, and Your righteousness first in everything that I do, hear me when I come to You in prayer and forgive me of my sins. Lord, I come before Your throne of grace asking for forgiveness for all my sins. Lord, I am deeply sorry for all the wrongs I have done, and all the rights I had the opportunity to do but failed to do them. Lord, wash away my sins with the blood of Your Son my Savior Jesus Christ that I may be completely free from the shackles of sin. In the name of Your Son Jesus Christ, we pray, Amen.

It's much easier to allow Satan to consume your mind, control your thoughts, and fall prey to his evil schemes than it is to obey God when your mind is not completely focused on Him. The flesh is weak, but the Spirit is strong when you stay strong in the Spirit you remain strong in the flesh.

My dear brothers and sisters, take note of this: Everyone should be quick to listen, slow to speak and slow to become angry, because human anger does not produce the righteousness that God desires. **James 1:19-20 (NIV)**

God wants you to stop for a moment and think before you act and before you speak. If you stop and seek God before you act on your emotions, He will fill your mind with positive thoughts that will help you handle any situation. From now on when you face difficult situations or difficult people, seek God wholeheartedly for strength, courage, and guidance. He can take the toughest circumstances and turn them around into learning lessons that will help you grow. When you grow from an experience that God has placed in your life, you not only grow in life but in spirit. Whenever you are faced with a difficult situation, always remember what God is trying to teach you as a result of the circumstances you are facing. God will often put you in difficult situations because He wants you to learn and grow so that you will gain wisdom and become stronger.

LET'S PRAY: Dear Heavenly Father, help me to stop and think for a moment so that I can seek you before I act on my emotions. Lord, I ask you to fill my mind with positive thoughts that will help me handle any situation I face. Lord, I know that you often take the toughest circumstances and turn them around into learning lessons that will help me grow. Lord, I want to thank you for always being here for me even when times are hard. Lord, I know that Your plan for my life will not only help me grow it will strengthen me. Lord, thank You for allowing me to seek you in every difficult situation and every challenging circumstance I face. Lord, thank You for always helping me in every. In the name of Your Son Jesus Christ, we pray, Amen.

God wants you to know that just because today might have been a gloomy day does not mean it was a bad day. Everything that happened today took place exactly how it was meant to happen according to God's plan. Your day may have been filled with rain, thunder, lightning and high winds; it may have been filled with roadblocks, difficult people, and tough situations. No matter what made your day seem gloomy, it does not mean tomorrow won't be a brighter day. When you have faith in God, and you live according to His plan you can be assured that tomorrow will be a brighter day.

And he gives grace generously. As the Scriptures say, God opposes the proud but gives grace to the humble. So humble yourselves before God. Resist the devil, and he will flee from you. **James 4:6-7 (NLT)**

God wants all His children to live a humble life and show humility to everyone. Humility is not only a mindset it is an attitude that comes from the heart. True humility cannot be seen on the outside; it can only be felt directly from the heart. When you are humble, you are not prideful, selfish or arrogant. Humility is not something you gain overnight; humility is revealed more and more as you grow in grace, wisdom, and understanding. God not only causes you to be humble, He expects you to be humble. God tells us in 2 Chronicles 7:14: "Then if my people who are called by my name will humble themselves and pray and seek my face and turn from their wicked ways, I will hear from heaven and will forgive their sins and restore their land." Biblically speaking, humility is the opposite of pride, arrogance, and self-importance. God will oppose those who are arrogant, proud, and self-centered, but He has promised to give grace to those who are humble based on the true motives of their heart.

LET'S PRAY: Dear Heavenly Father, I want to live my life with humility and selflessness. Lord, strip me of any form of pride taking root within me. I want to be completely humble. Lord, I know that true humility is exhibiting humbleness towards others by thinking more of others rather than thinking less of yourself. Lord, may I never forget that humility is greatness before Your sight, and You exalt the humble and cut down the proud. Lord, I ask You to bless me with Your Holy Spirit that You may increase my wisdom and knowledge. Lord, send Your Spirit to increase me in wisdom, knowledge, understanding, and humility. Lord, from today, I shall endeavor to treat people with kindness, speak to them with humility, and pray for them without ceasing, that as I do, You will bless me more and more. In the name of Your Son Jesus Christ, we pray, Amen.

There is no denying the fact that a person's priorities will prove what is truly important to them based on their actions. It becomes obvious when the words they say don't match up with their actions. This typically happens when a person makes things of this world a priority instead of making God their main priority.

So be careful how you live. Don't live like fools, but like those who are wise. Make the most of every opportunity in these evil days. Don't act thoughtlessly, but understand what the Lord wants you to do. **Ephesians 5:15-17 (NLT)**

God wants you to create everlasting memories with the people in your life that you love. The memories that you create today are the same memories that you will remember ten years from now. Every moment of your day is precious, every person in your life is precious, and all the people you spend time with are precious. We are all children of God, and He wants us to enjoy the time we spend with one another. God wants all of His children to get along and enjoy time and fellowship with each other. Instead of wasting precious time worrying about things of this world, spend time with family and friends and make it count. You only get one life, one family and one opportunity to make the most of your journey here on earth. God wants you to make sure you make the most of the gift He has given you.

LET'S PRAY: Dear Heavenly Father, I don't want to waste a single moment of the precious time You have given me here on earth. Lord, I want to spend as much time with the people I love as I possibly can. I want to create memories that will help me remember all the precious time I spent with the people who I love the most in my life. Lord, I want to enjoy fellowship with my brother and sisters in Christ. I want to be able to show glory to You by appreciating the time, the experience and all the memories in my life. Lord, I want to thank You for the gift of this life. I want to live a life that is guided, facilitated, and directed by You. In the name of Your Son Jesus Christ, we pray, Amen.

Anybody can say they love God, believe in God, and seek God, but it takes a true, sincere Christian to prove wholeheartedly by their actions that they truly do love God, believe in Him and seek His will every day by doing what He commands. Actions and deeds in faith prove much more to God than words or expressions ever will.

Let us go right into the presence of God with sincere hearts fully trusting him. For our guilty consciences have been sprinkled with Christ's blood to make us clean, and our bodies have been washed with pure water. **Hebrews 10:22 (NLT)**

Condemnation and conviction are two different things. God wants you to understand the difference. When you are condemned, you will feel guilt. When you are convicted by God, you will be at peace. Once you have been convicted by God, He will open your eyes and bring resolution to the source of your sin. When you are convicted by God He will not only give you an opportunity to make things right; He will motivate you and show you How to make things right. God tells us in John 16:8: "And when he [the Holy Spirit] comes, he will convict the world of its sin, and of God's righteousness, and of the coming judgment." Whoever does not believe in Jesus Christ will always be condemned. God tells us in John 3:18: "Whoever believes in him is not condemned, but whoever does not believe stands condemned already because they have not believed in the name of God's one and only Son." It is always better to be convicted by God before, during and after you sin. Being convicted before you sin will make you think about your actions. Being convicted while you sin will make you realize what you are doing is wrong and that you will be punished for your sin. Being convicted after you sin makes you understand that even though you have already committed the sin, it was wrong and you should not commit that sin again. Conviction will not always prevent you from committing a sin, but it will make you think about your actions which will make the sin harder to commit.

LET'S PRAY: Dear Heavenly Father, I ask for a pure conscience that is able to convict me when I do something wrong. I ask for a perfect conscience that is in alignment with Your Word and Your will that I may do what's right at all times. Lord, when I do something wrong unintentionally and unaware, please convict me through my conscience that I may know that I have fallen short of Your glory, and may I ask for forgiveness. Lord God, forgive me and deliver me from condemnation. I ask You to cleanse my heart, cleanse my mind, and cleanse my soul so that I may dwell in Your land of prosperity and provision. Lord, I ask that You deliver me from all condemnation, and lead me along the path of righteousness. Lord, May I never have a conscience that is not capable of convicting me when I do something wrong. Lord, may I never lose my faith in You for anything or anyone. In the name of Your Son Jesus Christ, we pray, Amen.

The only way to be truly happy in your heart, mind, body, and soul regarding any relationship is to make sure that every aspect of the relationship is guided by God. That means every action from both people must be pleasing to God in every way at all times. If one person is following God and their actions are pleasing to God on a consistent basis, but the other person is following the ways of the world the relationship will never work over the long run. When one person in the relationship is following God and doing what He commands, and this other person is following the ways of the world this is the exact definition of being unequally yoked. Being unequally yoked will not only cause problems and differences in the relationship, but it will also cause the relationship to be off balance according to God's will. In this situation, pray for those who are following the ways of the world but do not let their actions affect you or dictate your walk with God. You must distance yourself from these people because when they follow the ways of the world and not God, they have no spiritual fruit to offer you.

Look here, you who say, Today or tomorrow we are going to a certain town and will stay there a year. We will do business there and make a profit. How do you know what your life will be like tomorrow? Your life is like the morning fog—it's here a little while, then it's gone. What you ought to say is, If the Lord wants us to, we will live and do this or that. **James 4:13-15 (NLT)**

God wants you to live your life at this moment right here right now. You must not worry about what will happen in the next hour, tomorrow, or even next week. I know it is easier said than done but God is already there, and He already knows what will happen according to His plans. You have no control of what is already meant to happen according to God's will. There is no reason to worry about the future and create unnecessary stress, God is already there, and He knows what is going to take place. God tells us in Proverbs 3:5: "Trust in the Lord with all your heart, And lean not on your own understanding; Seek his will in all you do, and he will show you which path to take." God wants you to understand that when you worry and stress about what you can't control, you are not only inferring with His plan you are wasting precious time in your life. As God continually tells you, go about your day and live your life at this moment right here right now and do not worry about anything. God wants you to fully enjoy and appreciate everything you experience today.

LET'S PRAY: Dear Heavenly Father, I want to live my life today according to Your will. Lord, I don't want to worry about anything, I want to live in this moment and enjoy all that you have created. Lord, I ask that you guide me from worrying about what tomorrow may bring and allow me to enjoy all this day. Lord, You know the plans You have established for my life, so there is no reason for me to worry or stress. Lord, I give thanks to

You for all You have created in my life, and for all the blessing You have granted me. Lord, I promise to trust in You and seek You in everything I do, and I know You will show me which path to take. In the name of Your Son Jesus Christ, we pray, Amen.

As a Christian, your strength, your courage, your wisdom, and your power comes directly from God because He is present in your life every day. You must let it be known to everyone that His presence is what strengthens you, encourages you, inspires you and what guides your down the path He has established for you according to His will for your life.

NOVEMBER 25

> Jesus answered, "I am the way and the truth and the life. No one comes to the Father except through me. **John 14:6 (NIV)**

If you have not been saved, God wants you to accept His son Jesus Christ into your heart as your Lord and Savior today. Once you have accepted Jesus Christ into your heart, you will not only see your life change you will feel it change from the inside out. From this day forward your life will be changed forever. Your heart will be filled with God's grace. Your mind will be constantly focused on God. Your soul will be renewed with God's salvation. You will love people more, you will appreciate people more, and you will respect people more. Everything from your past that was bad will be wiped away, and you will be renewed in God's kingdom and given a clean slate. One of the many benefits of having God on your side is forgiveness through His Son Jesus Christ. You will be forgiven by Jesus for every sin you have committed and from every unrighteous act. God tells us in 1 John 1:9: "If we confess our sins, He is faithful and righteous to forgive us our sins and to cleanse us from all unrighteousness."

LET'S PRAY: Dear Heavenly Father, thank you for sacrificing Your only Son. Your ultimate sacrifice has given me the opportunity to believe in Your Son Jesus Christ and accept Him as my Lord and Savior so that I will not perish but have eternal life in heaven. Father, I am grateful that my life will be changed forever, and my heart will be filled with Your grace. Father, May I focus on You continually. May I be guided by your strength. May I be renewed with Your salvation. Father, You have wiped away all of my past sins. Father, You have renewed my soul in Your kingdom. Father, you have given me a clean slate because of Your ultimate sacrifice. Father, I am thankful for all of the glorious benefits of being saved by Your Son Jesus Christ. Father, I am thankful for being forgiven of all my sins through Your Son. In the name of Your Son Jesus Christ, we pray, Amen.

When you learn from your mistakes in the flesh, you grow from the opportunities that God has given you in the spirit.

And whatever you do, whether in word or deed, do it all in the name of the Lord Jesus, giving thanks to God the Father through him. **Colossians 3:17 (NIV)**

God wants you to know that you will only be grateful when your mind is focused on Him and in a state of gratitude. Just because you are happy does not mean you are grateful, but when you are grateful, you will always be happy. You can't just say you appreciate God's blessings; you have to show it through your actions in order to prove to God that you are grateful for all He has done for you. You will never take any blessings for granted when you are truly grateful for what God has done. You often forget that the greatest blessing in this life that you should be grateful for is not the air you breathe, but the ability that God has given you to breathe. Without God, you have no air. Without air, you cannot breathe. If you can't breathe, you cannot live. God is the air you need to breathe in order to live.

LET'S PRAY: Dear Heavenly Father, I ask that you allow my heart to always be grateful for all You have done. Lord, I am only happy when I am grateful because happiness is the result of gratitude. Lord, I promise to show my appreciation for all You have done through my actions, not my words. Lord, I will never take any blessings that I am given for granted because I am truly grateful for all you have done in my life. Lord, help me to never forget that the greatest blessing you have given me is the ability to breathe. Lord, May I resist the foul spirit of ungratefulness by constant prayers. Lord, I know that You are always with me, and I am forever grateful for Your faithfulness and love that endures forever. In the name of Your Son Jesus Christ, we pray, Amen.

Face your struggles and difficulties truthfully and honestly using the word of God as your source of strength, courage, and guidance, and He will give you direction and the power to face every problem you encounter.

Always giving thanks to God the Father for everything, in the name of our Lord Jesus Christ. **Ephesians 5:20 (NIV)**

God wants you to realize how precious this day is. God wants you to understand that this day is a gift. God wants you to show Him appreciation and gratefulness for the gift of today. If it were not for God, you would not have woken up this morning to see another day. God is the reason you are able to breathe today because He created the air you breathe. God is the reason you are able to walk about this day and experience everything this day has to offer. God wants you to enjoy this day, and He wants you to be polite, kind, and generous to every person you come into contact with today. You will fully comprehend the true meaning of the gift of this day when you can realize how precious this day is. You will appreciate the importance of this day when you can fully enjoy this day, and you can show God how grateful you are for today by enjoying and appreciating every experience this day has to offer.

LET'S PRAY: Dear Heavenly Father, I want to thank You for the gift of today and the opportunity to experience all the beauty of this day. Lord, I am grateful for the gift of this day and every day that I am given. Lord, I am thankful for every breath of air that You put into my lungs so that I can breathe. Lord, I want to bring Glory to You in everything I do so that I can show appreciation for everything You have done for me. Lord, without You I am nothing, without You I would not be able to breathe a single breath of air, and without You, I would not be able to wake up every morning to enjoy another gift from You. Lord, I promise to be polite, kind, and generous to every person I come into contact with today. Lord, I will fully comprehend the true meaning of the gift I have been given as I experience the reality of how precious this day is. In the name of Your Son Jesus Christ, we pray, Amen.

Do you talk like a believer but act like an unbeliever? Do your words match up with your actions? Are your words and your actions matching up to what God expects and are they pleasing in the sight of God? Stop and ask yourself this important question today wholeheartedly, truthfully, and sincerely! If your talking like a believer but acting like an unbeliever, if your words don't match up with your actions, use this quote as a reminder to stop and think about what you're saying and how you're acting so that you can get right with God. Once you get right with God, your words will match up with your actions, and you will be at peace knowing that God can see that you wholeheartedly, truthfully, and sincerely talk like a believer and act like a believer.

DECEMBER

> Anyone who wants to do the will of God will know whether my teaching is from God or is merely my own. Those who speak for themselves want glory only for themselves, but a person who seeks to honor the one who sent him speaks truth, not lies. **John 7:17-18 (NLT)**

Do you ever ask yourself if you are living your life according to God's will? God wants you to know what His will is for your life, and He wants you to live and follow His will every day of your life. But how do you know if you are living God's will and following His plan for your life? The Bible provides us with all we need to know regarding God's will for our lives. God tells us in Thessalonians 5:16-18: "Be joyful always; pray continually; give thanks in all circumstances, for this is God's will for you in Christ Jesus." God wants you to always be joyful, pray at all times, and give thanks to Him in every circumstance. We can find more statements of God's will in 2 Timothy 3:16-17: "All Scripture is inspired by God and is useful to teach us what is true and to make us realize what is wrong in our lives. It corrects us when we are wrong and teaches us to do what is right. God uses it to prepare and equip his people to do every good work." You can discover God's will for your life through prayer, by trusting His judgment, by Answer When He calls and by following Him closely every day. There are several different ways that God reveals His will; it can often be found in advancements or opportunities that are well in your favor. God's will can also be found in, blessings, relationships, or positive circumstances. Regardless of the way you conceive what God's will is, you must always follow what He tells us in Scripture, that is where you can find the truth of God's will for your life.

LET'S PRAY: Dear Heavenly Father, I promise to seek Your will for my life every day and follow you in closeness and in confidence. Lord, May I never doubt You, but seek Your Will in everything that I do. Lord, may all that I do be done with You, under Your light, according to Your Will, in a way that pleases You. Lord, it is Your Will that I pray everywhere, giving thanks to You, and letting my request known to You. Lord, strengthen my faith in You so that nothing will be able to draw me away from doing Your will. Lord, I want to live my life according to Your will, and You plan for my life. Lord, it is Your Will that I give thanks to You at all times, in every situation, no matter how rough and tough the day may be going. Lord, May my body be used as an instrument to please You and fulfill Your will here on earth. Lord, here I am, send me. May Your Will be done in my life, both now and forever. In the name of Your Son Jesus Christ, we pray, Amen.

What brings happiness and joy to the heart
is not so much a friend's gifts from God but a
friend who is honest, faithful and sincere. A true
friend will be able to display by their actions
that their love comes from God and is for God.

For the Lord is the Spirit, and wherever the Spirit of the Lord is, there is freedom. **2 Corinthians 3:17 (NLT)**

God wants you to know that freedom of religion is your God-given right. No public or government official in this world can tell you otherwise. God is not happy at all about the banning of prayer and other religious activities in our schools and even in some public places. God created this world and everyone in it. Therefore, you are able to express your freedom of religion wherever and whenever you please. Just because someone fails to understand or believe that God does exist and that He created this world does not give them the right to decide where you can or cannot express your religious freedom. God gives all of His children the right to choose or reject Him, so as His child you should have the same right to decide when and where you express your religious freedom. Not only did God create every person who serves in the government of every nation, but God also created the written word in the Bible which outlines the rules according to God's standards. God expects every government official from every nation to uphold His word and his rules.

LET'S PRAY: Dear Heavenly Father, today I thank you for not only creating me in the image of Your son Jesus Christ. I thank you for giving me the gift of this life with the ability to choose You as my Lord and Savior. Lord, help me to stay focused on You at all times and guide me to keep You in the center of my thoughts no matter where I go or what I do. Lord, You tell us in 2 Corinthians 3:17: "For the Lord is the Spirit, and wherever the Spirit of the Lord is, there is freedom." Lord, I am grateful that I have the freedom to express my love and admiration for You wherever I am. Lord, I am thankful that no government official can rule over You and tell me where I can express my religious views and beliefs. Lord, I pray that Your power will reign over any government rule so that prayer and other religious activities will be added back into our schools and public places. In the name of Your Son Jesus Christ, we pray, Amen.

In order to be truly in love, you need to be connected on the inside. What I mean by being connected on the inside is that when two people feel truly connected by God they are not connected by looks, lust or any other physical attribute but connected by God's love, connected by obeying Him, connected by doing what He commands by spreading His word, and connected by pleasing Him. If you are not connected on the inside through God's love, mercy, and grace, it will never be true love. God's love knows no distance, no color, or no national origin. To be truly in love God must be in the center and the main focus because God is love and all love comes from God.

DECEMBER 5

> Now finish the work, so that your eager willingness to do it may be matched by your completion of it, according to your means. **2 Corinthians 8:11 (NIV)**

When God gives you a job or task to do He expects you to fully complete it. He wants you to put your entire heart and soul into everything you do. He does not like when you only put forth half of your effort or when you only do half of the job without completing it. God is a loving God, and He gives you his fullness at all times. He in return expects you to give Him your full self by always putting Him first and by completing His work until it is done. There is nothing about God's kingdom that is mediocre or halfway complete. When God created you, He equipped you with everything you need to do His work according to His will. God created you to be one of a kind, and He took His precious time to make sure you were created exactly how He wanted you to be created according to His standards. God does not want anything you do to be mediocre or halfway done; He wants you to complete everything you start with dignity and grace. The work that you do should not only resemble what you are made of, but it should also resemble who you were made of, Our Lord Jesus Christ.

LET'S PRAY: Dear Heavenly Father, today I promise to complete everything that I start regardless of how difficult it may become. Lord I know that you are a God of fullness and completeness, I want to follow in your footsteps and complete everything I do with dignity and grace. Lord, I am thankful for the way You created me. I am grateful for all that You have equipped me with so that I can complete Your work gracefully and according to Your will. Lord, I seek You wholeheartedly on a daily basis because I need Your strength to complete the work I am doing. Lord, I know that it is impossible to start a task without your supernatural strength and divine guidance. In the name of Your Son Jesus Christ, we pray, Amen.

DECEMBER 6

Obedience to God, following His commands and showing actions that are pleasing to Him is what unlocks blessings and opportunities in our lives.

Deadly Sin #1 "Lust" (Series 1 of 7)

You will have these tassels to look at and so you will remember all the commands of the Lord, that you may obey them and not prostitute yourselves by chasing after the lusts of your own hearts and eyes. **Numbers 15:39 (NIV)**

God does not want any of His children to indulge in any form of lust. It is known that lust is another tool that the devil will try to use to pull you away from following God's commands. When your actions are fulfilled by lust, the devil will not only control you like a puppet; he will trick you into unwholesome situations without revealing the consequences of your lustful actions. God wants you to understand that lust is not only very dangerous and wicked, but lust is also a shameful sin that will not go unpunished. Instead of allowing the devil to consume your mind with lustful thoughts, seek God for strength to help you overcome these evil thoughts the very second that the devil tries to invade your mind. The Bible tells us that God did not call us to be impure but to live a holy life. Therefore, anyone who rejects this instruction does not reject a human being but God, the very God who gives you his Holy Spirit. 1 Thessalonians 4:7-8 (NIV)

LET'S PRAY: Dear Heavenly Father, today I ask for You to cover my entire being with Your strength and guidance and protect me from all evil attacks from the devil. Lord, I ask you to soak every fiber of my being with your grace and salvation. Lord, I do not want to commit shameful sins by falling prey to the lustful tricks that the devil continuously tries to play. Lord, I do not want any lustful thoughts to creep into my mind from the devil. And Lord, I do not want any lustful and selfish desires to consume my mind and contaminate my thoughts. Lord, I will strive to live every day of my life according to your will and by following Your divine commandments. In the name of Your Son Jesus Christ, we pray, Amen.

God has created you and given you the gift of life, the greatest gift of all. You have been given the courage, the strength, the power to accomplish great things. You have been given the knowledge, wisdom, and understanding to know what this life really means and what we are all here for. You have been given the skills and tools to do the work that God has entrusted me to do here on earth. God is your source of light; He is your source of courage, strength, and power. And because of Him, you can and will accomplish great things. Do not settle for anything less than what God has prepared for you and promised you. Never allow anyone to bring you down or try to stop you from fulfilling God's will for your life.

Deadly Sin #2 "Gluttony" (Series 2 of 7)

For I have told you often before, and I say it again with tears in my eyes, that there are many whose conduct shows they are really enemies of the cross of Christ. They are headed for destruction. Their god is their appetite, they brag about shameful things, and they think only about this life here on earth. **Philippians 3:18-20 (NLT)**

God does not want you to overindulge or over-consume any form of food or drink. God does not want you to overindulge yourself in wealth to the point of extravagance or wasteful habits. When your actions are careless and filled with foolishness, and you make obsessive use of God's gifts such as food and drink, He will look at your behavior as an act of heedlessness. Gluttony is a sin that often seems to be overlooked or even ignored by Christians. God has something to say about gluttony as He tells us in Proverbs 23:20-21: Be not among drunkards or among gluttonous eaters of meat, for the drunkard and the glutton will come to poverty, and slumber will clothe them with rags. God wants you to understand that your physical appetite is simply a test of your ability to control yourself within reason. If you are unable to control your appetite, you will most likely be unable to control other habits like lust, greed, and anger. God does not want any of obsessions to control you. He wants you to be able to regulate your appetite and refrain from any addictions such as drinking or drug use.

LET'S PRAY: Dear Heavenly Father, today I seek You for strength to help me resist any form of gluttony. Lord, I ask for Your guidance to help me not to indulge myself in wealth to the point of extravagance. Lord, I need You to help me abstain from being wasteful or careless in regard to the precious resources You have provided for me. Lord, I find comfort in knowing that You will not only help me control my appetite, But You will also help me refrain from all forms of gluttony, lust, greed, and anger. Lord, I find peace in knowing that when I seek Your presence, You will lead me away from any obsessions or addictions that will try to control me. Lord, thank you for being a trusting and obedient God, I am very grateful for all you have done for me. In the name of Your Son Jesus Christ, we pray, Amen.

DECEMBER 10

The name of the Lord is a strong
tower; the righteous man runs into it
and is safe. Proverbs 18:10 (ESV)

Everyone is tempted to make God smaller
than He is. Our brains are limited in how we
understand such an infinite and glorious God.
In prayer, believe the truth that Almighty
God has no equals. Proclaim His glory and
greatness as you run for shelter in prayer today.

DECEMBER 11

Deadly Sin #3 "Greed" (Series 3 of 7)

No one can serve two masters. For you will hate one and love the other; you will be devoted to one and despise the other. You cannot serve both God and money. **Matthew 6:24 (NLT)**

Greed is one of God's biggest dislikes. You cannot serve both God and money, and the worst kind of greed comes directly from money. God tells us in 1 Timothy 6:10: "For the love of money is a root of all kinds of evil. Many people are very eager for money, and it has caused them to wander from their faith, and as a result, they find themselves facing many difficult situations and circumstances. Actions of greed are actions of evil because greed is not of God, it is an act of the devil. Instead of focusing on your money and possessions, God wants you to focus on Him and His sovereign plan for your life. Your life does not consist of the abundance of your possessions of this world; your life consists of the abundance of blessings that God has granted you. God wants you to understand that money itself is not the problem, it is the love of money that is the problem. The love of money is a sin because it not only takes your focus off worshipping God, it will steer you off the path that He has established for you. Instead of focusing on your wealth here on earth, you need to focus on the vast treasures awaiting you in heaven. The most important and valuable treasure that awaits you in heaven is to inherit eternal life with God.

LET'S PRAY: Dear Heavenly Father, I don't ever want to become eager for money, and I don't ever want wonder from my faith in You. Lord, I ask that You keep my actions clear of greed because I know that all actions of greed turn into actions of evil. Lord, I understand that greed is an act of the devil, rather than falling into greed I want to strive to receive Your grace. Lord, I want to focus on Your sovereign plan for my life and the ultimate treasure in heaven instead of things of this world like money and possessions. Lord, I ask that you not only grant me with an abundance of blessings, I ask that you grant me with an abundance of Your salvation and grace. Lord, I promise to live my life in a way that will bring glory to You and not for greed or things of this world. In the name of Your Son Jesus Christ, we pray, Amen.

Unbelievers will act like unbelievers; they act just like you acted before you accepted Jesus Christ into your heart. As Christians, it is our responsibility to reach out to those who are Unbelievers, those who are seeking the ways of the world instead of seeking God. God expects us to spread His word and His will to those in the world who are lost and hopeless. As a Christian God has given you a heart of love, compassion, and caring. God has given you the gifts and tools needed to be the leader and a servant of His word and His work. God wants unbelievers to look up to you; He wants unbelievers to find hope in Him through you. So today be the beacon of hope that God expects you to be to someone who is lost and needs to find hope in God today.

Deadly Sin #4 "Sloth" (Series 4 of 7)

The soul of the sluggard craves and gets nothing, while the soul of the diligent is richly supplied. **Proverbs 13:4 (ESV)**

God does not like when His children commit the act of Sloth or when they are lazy. God did not put you on this earth to be lazy or to become inactive and not follow His plan for your life. Some people are naturally motivated to not only follow God's plan, but they are also driven to get things done and get them done the right way according to God's standards. While other people allow themselves to be less motivated and therefore they let many things in their life lack and fall behind. Even though Sloth or laziness is a lifestyle for people who are less motivated than others, it is a temptation for all of us. The Bible is very clear about how the Lord created the man for work. The bible also tells us that laziness is a sin. God wants you to understand that there is no room for sloth in the life of a Christian and He does not expect you to be lazy. We are motivated by God's grace, and our productiveness and diligence are displayed as a result of love for our Savior Jesus Christ who is our redeemer. As an act of gratefulness, we are expected to not only work hard towards getting things accomplished; we are required to do God's work instead of being lazy and accomplishing nothing.

LET'S PRAY: Dear Heavenly Father, I come to you today in prayer and ask that You never allow me to become lazy or lack energy and motivation. Lord, I ask for your strength to remain motivated and driven to accomplish your work. Lord, I need Your courage to be able to go out into the world and get things done right according to Your standards. Lord, I know that when I seek You and ask for strength and motivation, I will never lack in anything good. Lord, may I be dedicated to my work, and do all that I do with diligence. Lord, May I never forget that those who show diligence to the very end and are never lazy but hard-working, are blessed beyond measure and understanding. In the name of Your Son Jesus Christ, we pray, Amen.

What good is it, my brothers and sisters, if someone claims to have faith but has no deeds? Can such faith save them? Suppose a brother or a sister is without clothes and daily food. If one of you says to them, "Go in peace; keep warm and well fed," but does nothing about their physical needs, what good is it? In the same way, faith by itself, if it is not accompanied by action, is dead. But someone will say, "You have faith; I have deeds." Show me your faith without deeds, and I will show you my faith by my deeds. You believe that there is one God. Good! Even the demons believe that—and shudder. You foolish person, do you want evidence that faith without deeds is useless? James 2:14-20 (NIV)

Saying that you live your life for God, believe in Him and Obey His commands, and showing that you live your life for God, believe in Him and Obey His commands by your actions are two different things. Anyone can say that they live their life for God, believe in Him and Obey His commands, but it takes a dedicated,

sincere, honest and truthful believer to show that they truly live their life for God, believe in Him and Obey His commands 24 hours a day 7 days a week and 365 days a year.

Deadly Sin #5 "Wrath" (Series 5 of 7)

My dear brothers and sisters, take note of this: Everyone should be quick to listen, slow to speak and slow to become angry, because human anger does not produce the righteousness that God desires. **James 1:19-20 (NIV)**

God does not like when His children become angry. Anger is another tool that the devil has in his large arsenal. He will try to use anger not only to get you worked up, but he will also use it in an attempt to take your focus off of God. Anger will not only destroy the good things in your life, but it can also rob you of your joy, and it can affect your health. God wants you to understand that when you get angry, you are allowing the devil to consume your thoughts and actions instead of letting God's strength to saturate your soul. The next time you feel yourself starting to get angry, seek God wholeheartedly so that He can guide your thoughts and actions so that you can remain calm in His presence. God wants you to know that anger is not always considered a sin. The bibles tells us that there is a type of anger which is approved by God. There is a type of anger often called "righteous indignation." God is angry (Psalm 7:11; Mark 3:5), and believers are commanded to be angry (Ephesians 4:26). In the new testament, there are two Greek words, impulse, and wrath; both are interpreted as "anger." One means "passion, energy" and the other means "agitated, boiling." Regardless of the situation, God wants you to hear quickly, speak slowly, and resist all forms of negative anger.

LET'S PRAY: Dear Heavenly Father, I know that I am not pleasing You and bringing glory to You when I become angry. Lord, I ask that You saturate my entire being with Your strength so that the devil will never be able to take my focus off You. Lord, I know that You will protect me from the evil actions of the devil. Lord, I find comfort in knowing that You will always guard me from becoming angry as a result of the vicious methods the devil will use to stir up strife and anger in my life. Lord, I need to remind myself that the devil is constantly trying to sneak in and cause trouble anyway he can. I know that anger is one of the many tools that the devil has in his large arsenal and therefore, I need to remain completely focused on You at all times. Lord, every time I feel myself starting to become angry I promise to seek You wholeheartedly so that You can guide my thoughts and actions so that I can remain calm in Your presence. In the name of Your Son Jesus Christ, we pray, Amen.

There is no denying the truth in any situation you face; the truth will reveal denial. The truth will always set you free; denial will always hold you captive which will lead to guilty actions. Jesus Christ is the way the truth and the life.

Deadly Sin #6 "Envy" (Series 6 of 7)

But if you are bitterly jealous and there is selfish ambition in your heart, don't cover up the truth with boasting and lying. For jealousy and selfishness are not God's kind of wisdom. Such things are earthly, unspiritual, and demonic. For wherever there is jealousy and selfish ambition, there you will find disorder and evil of every kind. **James 3:14-16 (NLT)**

Jealousy and envy are another one of the many tools that the devil will use to control your actions and take your focus off God and sustaining His will. God does not like when you are jealous of your brothers and sisters in Christ. The word "jealous" is often described as a sense of being envious of someone else's gifts and blessings God has granted them instead of appreciating your own. Jealousy that comes from envy is a sin, and it is not how God expects His children to act. When God sees the jealous actions of His children being driven by envy, it is very disappointing to Him, and it shows that you are being controlled by your desires and not guided by God's will. The Bible tells us in 1 Peter 2:1-2 "Therefore, rid yourselves of all malice and all deceit, hypocrisy, envy, and slander of every kind. Like newborn babies crave pure spiritual milk, so that by it you may grow up in your salvation." Jealousy is an indication that you are not grateful for all the gifts that God has given you. God wants you to overcome jealousy today by becoming more like His son Jesus Christ. You can become more like Jesus by reading the Bible often, worshipping regularly, engaging in fellowship with other believers and daily prayer.

LET'S PRAY: Dear Heavenly Father, I come to You today in prayer asking that You to always keep my heart free from envy and jealousy. Lord, I know the devil will use envy as a way to sneak in and steal my focus off of You. Lord, today I ask for Your strength to keep You in the center of my thoughts at all times. Lord, I promise that I will strive to stay focused on You and sustain Your will whenever the devil tries to attack. Lord, I want you to know that I am very grateful for all the gifts and blessings you have granted me. Lord, I always need you to help me from allowing the jealous behavior to take place in my life as a result of envious actions from the devil. Lord, I need You to direct my path so that my actions will show my life is being guided by Your will instead of my desires. In the name of Your Son Jesus Christ, we pray, Amen.

God knows your heart, He knows your thoughts, and He knows your feelings. God knows all the mistakes you have made, He knows all your flaws, He knows your strengths, and He knows your weaknesses. Every day God will forgive you for what you have done wrong, and He will give you a chance to make things right. God should always come first in your life because His opinion is the only one that truly matters. You need to seek God every single day because He is the source of all the amazing gifts, blessings and opportunities in your life.

Deadly Sin #7 "Pride" (Series 7 of 7)

For they brag about their evil desires; they praise the greedy and curse the Lord. The wicked are too proud to seek God. They seem to think that God is dead. Yet they succeed in everything they do. They do not see your punishment awaiting them. They sneer at all their enemies. **Psalms 10:3-5 (NLT)**

God wants you to know that He hates pride that is a result of self-righteousness. Not only is this type of pride a sin, but it also keeps you from seeking God and His grace. The kind of pride that we feel after a job well done is humble pride, and it is much different than self-righteous pride. Self-righteous pride is an evil action that comes directly from the devil. Just like the many other tools that we have mentioned, the devil will use self-righteous pride to trick your mind. Instead of allowing your thoughts and actions to be guided by God the devil will try to get you focused on his evil ways. The Bible tells us in James 4:6 "He gives grace generously. As the Scriptures say, God opposes the proud but gives grace to the humble." God wants you to stop and think about your actions when you feel proud. Ask yourself, are my actions of the devil "self-righteous pride" or are my actions of God "humble pride"? It is imperative that when you show pride, your actions are a result of modesty and humbleness and not self-righteousness.

LET'S PRAY: Dear Heavenly Father, I know that it is very unpleasing to You when my actions of pride are from self-righteousness and not from humbleness. Lord, I ask that You protect me from all self-righteousness through evil acts of the devil. Lord, I want to be granted with Your mercy and grace for being humble. Lord, I need You to be in the center of my thoughts so that the devil will not be able to sneak in and turn my thoughts and actions from good to evil. Lord, I call on You, asking You to bless me with humility. I ask You to strip me completely of all self-righteous pride so that I may become more like the person You want me to be. Lord, please remove any form of pride taking root within me. I want to be completely humble. Lord, may I never forget that humility is greatness before Your sight, and You exalt the humble and cut down the proud. In the name of Your Son Jesus Christ, we pray, Amen.

A Godly friendship that blossoms into a Godly relationship that grows into a marriage between two God-fearing people is a lifelong union that is created by God and can never be broken.

But blessed is the one who trusts in the Lord, whose confidence is in him. They will be like a tree planted by the water that sends out its roots by the stream. It does not fear when heat comes; its leaves are always green. It has no worries in a year of drought and never fails to bear fruit. **Jeremiah 17:7-8 (NIV)**

God wants you to stop worrying about what might or could happen and remain calm because he already has your entire life planned out. Do you often find yourself creating unnecessary stress because you are worried about what if this happens or what if that happens? If you are worried about what might happen in your life, it is a sign that you don't have complete faith in God and you are not allowing His plan to take place in your life. God did not create you and put you in this world to continually worry and stress about the future. God already knows every single detail about your life down to the seconds. God doesn't want you to worry about the future because He is already there. God not only wants you to have faith in Him, But He also wants you to trust the plan that He has created for your life. Start bringing glory to God by living an abundant and joyful life that God created for you instead of living a life full of stress and worry.

LET'S PRAY: Dear Heavenly Father, I ask that You give me the strength to not worry and stress about everything that does not go correctly in my life. Lord, I often find myself stressing and worrying about things in my life that I have no control of and I know that worrying about them will not solve anything. Lord, You are in control of everything and You have a solution to every problem long before it even happens. Lord, today I promise to give it all to You, I want my life to be guided by Your ultimate plan and not by my weary plan. Lord, from this day forward, I promise to bring glory to Your Holy name in every way possible. Lord, I want to show You by my actions, how grateful I am for the abundant and joyful life that You have given me. In the name of Your Son Jesus Christ, we pray, Amen.

DECEMBER 22

When you feel in your heart that someone is not being honest with you do not let it get to you, do not let it stress you out, do not let it worry you, and do not let it steal your joy. Instead, seek God for strength, courage, guidance, and direction to keep your focus on Him and not on the person you feel is being dishonest. God knows all, and He sees all even when people think that anyone is watching, God is always watching. When you seek God in this type of situation you will be at peace, your mindset will be led by God, and your focus will always be completely on Him.

Be alert and of sober mind. Your enemy the devil prowls around like a roaring lion looking for someone to devour.
1 Peter 5:8 (NIV)

God wants you to understand that bars are the devil's playground. Excessive use of alcohol is one of the many tools the devil will try to use to persuade you to do things that are against God's will. The action of a person who is under the influence of excessive alcohol use is essentially being controlled like a puppet by the devil. Instead of allowing yourself to be controlled by the evil one, seek God before falling prey to the devil's evil actions by drinking excessive amounts of alcohol. Nothing good ever comes from a late night of partying at the bar and drinking alcohol it can put you in some very vulnerable and dangerous situations. Regarding alcohol, God commands all Christians to avoid drunkenness. We know that the Bible condemns drunkenness and all the evil effects that it has on you when excessive amounts of alcohol are consumed.

LET'S PRAY: Dear Heavenly Father, I promise to seek You whenever the devil tries to persuade me to do things that are against Your will. Lord, I know that the actions of a person who has consumed too much alcohol are not of You. Lord, I pray that whenever someone has consumed too much alcohol, You will prevent them from driving and potentially hurting others. Lord, people who drink excessive amounts of alcohol on a regular basis, are addicted to this evil tool. Lord, I pray that You will give these people a chance to clean themselves up and the opportunity to know you and seek You on a daily basis. In the name of Your Son Jesus Christ, we pray, Amen.

God wants you to understand there will be times when troubles enter your life, and you won't be able to do anything to avoid it. You must realize that God has put this difficult situation in your life for a reason. And once you have overcome it, you will fully understand why God put you through this painful situation. You need to focus on God and accept what has happened and keep your head held high. God wants you to stand strong in His grace and know that He will guide your steps through this situation. If you think positive and remain completely focused on God at all times, you will be able to stay calm and at peace. Today, you must choose to have faith in God and allow Him to lead you through this situation and guide you towards a positive outcome according to His plan.

What does Christmas mean to you? For those who don't know or understand the true meaning of Christmas or celebrate it for the right reason might find Christmas as a sad and stressful time because they don't have enough money to buy gifts for everyone. When in fact Christmas should be a happy and joyful time for all of God's children because it is the celebration of the birth of Jesus Christ. Christmas is a time of God showing His great love for all of us. Christmas is when all Christians celebrate the birth of God's only begotten Son, Jesus Christ into the world to be born. His birth brought great joy to the world. Shepherds, wise men, and angels all shared in the excitement of knowing about this great event on that cold night in Bethlehem. They all knew this was no ordinary baby.

Luke 2: 4-19 says:

"So Joseph also went up from the town of Nazareth in Galilee to Judea, to Bethlehem the town of David, because he belonged to the house and line of David. He went there to register with Mary, who was pledged to be married to him and was expecting a child. While they were there, the time came for the baby to be born, and she gave birth to her firstborn, a son. She wrapped him in cloths and placed him in a manger, because there was no room for them in the inn.

And there were shepherds living out in the fields nearby, keeping watch over their flocks at night. An angel of the Lord appeared to them, and the glory of the Lord shone around them, and they were terrified. But the angel said to them, "Do not be afraid. I bring you good news of great joy that will be for all the people. Today in the town of David a Savior has been born to you; he is Christ the Lord.

This will be a sign to you: You will find a baby wrapped in cloths and lying in a manger." Suddenly a great company of the heavenly host appeared with the angel, praising God and saying, "Glory to God in the highest, and on earth peace to men on whom his favor rests." When the angels had left them and gone into heaven, the shepherds said to one another, "Let's go to Bethlehem and see this thing that has happened, which the Lord has told us about." So they hurried off and found Mary and Joseph, and the baby, who was lying in the manger. When they had seen him, they spread the word concerning what had been told them about this child, and all who heard it were amazed at what the shepherds said to them. But Mary treasured up all these things and pondered them in her heart."

We all ask ourselves this question, why did Jesus come? Why did God send His only Begotten Son into this harsh and cruel world? The truth is that Jesus was sent to this world to be born so that one day the price could be paid for all our sins. The Bible says that all have sinned. All of us are born with a sinful nature, that is what makes us human. We do things that do not please God. Through the sins of Adam and Eve, we have all inherited that sinful nature. We need to have that removed. The only way is through Jesus Christ. Jesus came so He could die on the cross for all of our sins. If we believe that Jesus died for our sins, we can ask Him to come into our hearts and forgive us. Then, we are clean and made whole. We can know that heaven is a place where we can go when this life is over. If you did not already know, now you know the real reason why we celebrate Christmas.

This is the question I would like to ask you today. Have you ever personally invited the Lord Jesus Christ into your heart to be your Savior? And if you haven't, I have some good news for you. You can invite Him into your heart as your Lord and Savior today, right now.

Repeat after me, Dear God, thank You for loving me, thank You for sending Your Son Jesus Christ as my Lord and Savior at Christmas time in Bethlehem. I receive Him today as my Lord and Savior and I accept Him as the only one who can give me forgiveness of my sins. And if you prayed that prayer, the Bible says that you are a Christian and you have become a part of God's forever family. It is my hope and prayer that you will let someone important know that you have accepted Jesus Christ into your heart as your personal Lord and Savior.

Once you have recited the above statement and accepted Jesus Christ into your heart as your personal Lord and Savior, be sure to post it on Facebook, Twitter, or Instagram!

God wants you to be patient when you find yourself in the middle of a situation that doesn't seem to be going as planned. Instead of getting stressed and worried, seek God and know that He is in control of the situation. Everything will end up going as God intended, you need to remain calm and seek Him for strength and wait on His time. God's plan will always supersede any of our plans. So, the next time you don't think you're going to get paid on time or you don't think that check will be in the mail, seek God fully and really on His timing and not yours.

Therefore if you have any encouragement from being united with Christ, if any comfort from his love, if any common sharing in the Spirit, if any tenderness and compassion, then make my joy complete by being like-minded, having the same love, being one in spirit and of one mind. Do nothing out of selfish ambition or vain conceit. Rather, in humility value others above yourselves, not looking to your own interests but each of you to the interests of the others. **Philippians 2:1-4 (NLT)**

God wants you to step back and take a look at the important people in your life so that you can see how each person plays a significant role in your life. No matter if they're your family, a friend, a co-worker, or a neighbor, God wants you to realize how much you need them in your life. During a normal day or a routine task, you may not realize how much each person contributes to your daily life, but once they are not there, you will notice how much of an integral part they play in your day. God wants you always to be thankful for every person he has placed in your life. He has placed them in your life for a reason and to serve a purpose.

LET'S PRAY: Dear Heavenly Father, thank you for crossing my path with all the wondering and amazing people who have come into my life according to your Will and for Your purpose. Lord, I know that You have placed every person in my life for a reason and to serve a purpose. Lord, I promise always to be thankful for everyone in my life, and I promise to never take them for granted. Lord, I want to not only help my family, my friends, my coworkers, and my neighbors, I want to inspire them and motivate them to be the best they can be according to Your will. Lord, I want my actions and words toward the people in my life to be a blessing. Lord, forgive me for the times that I lean on the people in my life more than leaning on You for the things I need. Lord, I ask that Your blessings will dwell in the hearts of every person that You have placed in my life. In the name of Your Son Jesus Christ, we pray, Amen.

When the destination is certain, the journey becomes worthwhile. The destination is heaven; the journey is living your life in obedience to God by doing what He commands according to His will.

You made all the delicate, inner parts of my body and knit me together in my mother's womb. Thank you for making me so wonderfully complex! Your workmanship is marvelous—how well I know it. You watched me as I was being formed in utter seclusion, as I was woven together in the dark of the womb. You saw me before I was born. Every day of my life was recorded in your book. Every moment was laid out before a single day had passed. **Psalm 139:13-16 (NLT)**

God looks at you a lot differently than you look at yourself, He only looks at what is important and what matters. Instead of looking at all your flaws and imperfections, God wants you to focus on Him so that He can show you everything that is beautiful about yourself because you were made wonderfully and fearfully in His image. If there's something that you don't like about yourself, you need to change the way you see yourself because you are perfect just the way God made you. Even if you don't like the way you look, or how tall you are, or the color of your eyes, you need to be grateful for the life you have been given. God loves you just the way you are, and you need to love yourself for who God created you to be. God wants you to know that if people are unable to love you for the way He created you then they are not a part of the plan for your life.

LET'S PRAY: Dear Heavenly Father, I know that I am created in Your perfect image. Lord, I need to focus on You so that I can see everything that is beautiful about me instead of only looking at my flaws and imperfections. Lord, I am thankful for the way You made me. I am grateful for the life you have given me. Lord, I need you to remind me that You created me in Your perfect image and that nothing will ever change that. Lord, I need to not only focus on You, but I need to focus on what is important and what matters to You. Lord, help me to recognize people who are unable to love me for the way You created me. Lord, I ask that you show me the people who are not a part of Your plan for my life. In the name of Your Son Jesus Christ, we pray, Amen.

So often when we pray we ask God for what we want or need instead of asking for His will to be done in our lives. When we pray to God He will answer our prayers based on His timetable and His will. This also applies When you pray for your family and friends. It's important to understand that when God does not answer your prayer, there is a reason for it, you must keep praying without ceasing and be patient. God knows the plan for all His children and He will only answer prayers based on the plan He has for your life according to His will and His timetable.

DECEMBER 31

Let us then with confidence draw near to the throne of grace, that we may receive mercy and find grace to help in time of need. **Hebrews 4:16 (ESV)**

God wants you to have overflowing confidence in Him even when you feel like you don't have adequate confidence in yourself. Do you often feel like you are trying your best and giving all you have, but you still seem to slip up or fall short? It is during these times that God wants you to seek Him wholeheartedly so that He can be your pillar of strength and give you the confidence you need to remain standing. Even though you might often find yourself slipping up or making mistakes, you must never forget that God is perfect, and His Confidence is vast, and He never slips up and never makes mistakes. It may seem like you're fighting a losing battle when you put your heart and soul into something, and you end up not only falling short, but you miss the mark completely. God wants you to give all your battles to Him. He will not only fight all of your battles for you, But He will also give you the strength and courage you need to continue moving forward and making steady progress.

LET'S PRAY: Dear Heavenly Father, I come to you today in prayer, asking You to overflow my entire being with Your vast confidence. Lord, I often feel that I am doing my very best and putting forth a good effort into everything I do, only to be left feeling like I have fallen short of what is expected of me. Lord, when I am feeling inadequate, I ask that You lift me up and give me strength, courage, and confidence to remain standing. Lord, I need a constant reminder from You that even when I find myself slipping up or making mistakes, I can be assured that You are always perfect, and You make no mistakes. Lord, even when I feel as if I am fighting a losing battle, I know that You will fight all of my battles and You will give me the strength and courage I need to face another day in this journey called life. In the name of Your Son Jesus Christ, we pray, Amen.

NOTES

NOTES

NOTES

NOTES

NOTES